"Successfully including children with autism in general education isn't an accident. Teachers, practitioners, and parents will find practical solutions and important guidelines in this book for making inclusion successful. Dr. de Boer's passion for inclusion of children with ASD is felt throughout the pages of this book."

—*Lynn Koegel, Ph.D., CCC-SLP*, clinical director, Koegel Autism Center, University of California, Santa Barbara

"Finally a book that offers the potential to make inclusion successful for students with autism. This book not only looks at the unique characteristics of ASD, but highlights and addresses the social and behavioral demands of the general education setting for students with autism."

—*Katie Cook, Ph.D.*, early childhood autism specialist, Harmony Early Childhood Center, Olathe, Kansas

"A valuable resource for teachers and administrators working with children with ASD, and a must-read for those aspiring to become teachers. The material is applicable and adaptable for all grade levels and provides the educational cornerstone for the effective teaching of both standard classroom students and students with special needs."

—*Linda A. Hogan*, retired superintendent and New Teacher's Track seminar speaker, Modesto, Calif.

"In this book, de Boer clearly outlines responsible inclusion for students with autism spectrum disorders providing an invaluable guide to an often confusing and overwhelming process. I would highly recommend it as a 'must have' for every special educator's professional library."

—*Kaye Otten, Ph.D.*, behavior and autism specialist, Kansas City, MO

"This book is one of the best I've seen for supporting students with autism in an inclusive environment. A must-have for school teams developing programs for students with autism to be successful. Teachers should keep the checklists and forms in Chapter 7 readily available when preparing for that new student to be in an inclusive classroom."

—*Brooke D. Young*, project coordinator, TEACCH-LEAP Outcome Study, and lecturer, School of Education and Human Development, University of Colorado, Denver

Jossey-Bass Teacher

Jossey-Bass Teacher provides educators with practical knowledge and tools to create a positive and lifelong impact on student learning. We offer classroom-tested and research-based teaching resources for a variety of grade levels and subject areas. Whether you are an aspiring, new, or veteran teacher, we want to help you make every teaching day your best.

From ready-to-use classroom activities to the latest teaching framework, our value-packed books provide insightful, practical, and comprehensive materials on the topics that matter most to K-12 teachers. We hope to become your trusted source for the best ideas from the most experienced and respected experts in the field.

Successful Inclusion for Students with Autism

CREATING A COMPLETE, EFFECTIVE ASD INCLUSION PROGRAM

Sonja R. de Boer

Foreword by Richard Simpson

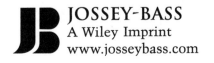

JOSSEY-BASS
A Wiley Imprint
www.josseybass.com

Published by Jossey-Bass
A Wiley Imprint
989 Market Street, San Francisco, CA 94103-1741—www.josseybass.com

Jossey-Bass books and products are available through most bookstores. To contact Jossey-Bass directly call our Customer Care Department within the U.S. at 800-956-7739, outside the U.S. at 317-572-3986, or fax 317-572-4002.

Jossey-Bass also publishes its books in a variety of electronic formats. Some content that appears in print may not be available in electronic books.

Library of Congress Cataloging-in-Publication Data has been applied for.

ISBN: 978-047-023080-0
Printed in the United States of America
FIRST EDITION
PB Printing   10 9 8 7 6 5 4 3 2 1

About This Book

THIS book is a compilation of training materials I have developed during the past fifteen years while working with students with autism spectrum disorders (ASD) and with parents, teachers, paraeducators, and administrators in inclusive education classrooms throughout the United States and parts of Europe. The book has two major purposes. Its primary purpose is to be used as a guide by special educators and school administrators as they create an inclusion program for students with ASD in school districts and at individual school sites. The secondary purpose is to provide information, materials, and some intervention strategies for special educators, general education teachers, and paraeducators to use in the day-to-day process of including students with ASD. The information may also be helpful to other individualized educational planning (IEP) members, that is, parents, speech and language therapists, occupational therapists, and consultants.

The tools and materials used to create and implement a successful inclusion program for students with ASD are included throughout the book, along with explanations of how to employ them, as

✓ Checklists of tasks to perform or components to observe or evaluate

✐ Forms regarding pertinent information

☞ Informational handouts on specific topics

It is hoped that by reading this book and using the tools and materials it provides, the reader will learn about and come to understand the individual components and intricate details as well as the big picture of establishing and maintaining an appropriate and effective inclusion program for students with ASD within a school.

About the Author

SONJA R. de Boer is a Board Certified Behavior Analyst (B.C.B.A.) and obtained her Ph.D. from the University of Kansas in Special Education and Psychology and Research in Education, with an emphasis in autism spectrum disorders (ASD). She also holds both general education and special education teaching credentials.

Dr. de Boer has over 15 years of experience working with students with ASD. She currently operates her own consulting and training business, which specializes in interventions for students with ASD in special and general education classrooms, as well as in the home. De Boer focuses on early intervention for students with ASD; creating applied behavior analysis (ABA) programs for children within homes and classrooms; and inclusive education programs for students with ASD within school districts. Her previous books include *How to Do Discrete Trial Training* (Pro-Ed, 2006) and *Autism Spectrum Disorders: Treatments and Interventions for Children and Youth* (co-authored with Richard L. Simpson et al., Corwin, 2004).

De Boer provides trainings for special and general education teachers, preservice educators, administrators, paraeducators, and parents on early intervention for children with ASD, inclusion of students with ASD in general education classrooms, Discrete Trial Training (DTT), Functional Behavior Assessment (FBA), and Behavior Intervention Plans (BIP). To contact her regarding future trainings, email deboerinclusion@gmail.com.

Contents

Foreword

THE recent attention given to children and youth with autism spectrum disorders (ASD) is remarkable, albeit predictable given the astonishing increase in the prevalence of autism-related disabilities. That ASD is currently more common than Down syndrome, juvenile diabetes, and childhood cancer is a clear reminder of the impact the condition is having on families, schools, and communities. Prominent among the groups that are experiencing the effects of ASD are teachers and other educators who are attempting to successfully and prudently include learners with autism and autism-related conditions in general education classrooms and other inclusion programs.

To be sure, children and youth who carry diagnoses that place them on the autism spectrum are eminently unique and enigmatic. Even when compared to other exceptional students, the behavior and demeanor of individuals with ASD make this group a particularly challenging set. Some learners with ASD have average or above-average cognitive and language abilities; others diagnosed with ASD have significant intellectual and communication deficits. Children and adolescents diagnosed with ASD each bring social skill and social interaction challenges to classrooms, although in highly unique ways. Comorbid conditions such as obsessive-compulsive disorder, seizure disorders, sensory disorders, attention-deficit hyperactivity disorder, and self-injurious behavior further intensify the complexity and challenges associated with effectively educating students with ASD. Classroom personnel and administrators require appropriate guidance and support in order to provide high-quality and effectual educational programs for dealing with these unique elements of ASD in general education classrooms and other inclusive settings.

Successful Inclusion for Students with Autism: Creating a Complete, Effective ASD Inclusion Program is a practical resource for educators and others seeking evidence-based and practical strategies for including students diagnosed with ASD in general education classrooms. It offers a clear and effective road map for guiding educators, school administrators, and others in crafting, implementing, and evaluating appropriate and effective inclusion programs for students with ASD. That it also offers special educators, general educators, related support professionals, paraeducators, and others the practical information and strategies (including ready-to-use and practical forms and other materials) they need to successfully include students with ASD in general education classrooms further adds to its value and appeal.

The foundation of this book is Sonja de Boer's years of practical experience in developing successful inclusion programs for learners with ASD. Recognizing that there is significant debate and that there are often strident differences of opinion related to the inclusion of children and youth with ASD in general education settings, de Boer nevertheless clearly and logically provides historical and philosophical support for the inclusion of students with disabilities, including those with autism-related challenges, in general education classrooms and other normalized settings. Even more important, she artfully, passionately, and skillfully offers practical and scientifically valid tools and strategies that teachers, administrative personnel, and other stakeholders can use to facilitate effective inclusion. Educators have not previously had available such an effective, comprehensive resource guide to assist with inclusion. Thus this book fills a need in an area that has too long been neglected.

For decades there has been a growing trend to include students with disabilities in general education settings. This trend of course includes learners whose exceptionality places them on the so-called autism spectrum. At the same time there have been notable disputes and debates over the appropriateness and means of most effectively facilitating such inclusion. Proponents of full inclusion assert that students with disabilities who are provided appropriate educational experiences and support within general education classrooms benefit both educationally and socially; and that these learners are able to demonstrate superior learning, interaction, communication, and social outcomes when compared to their peers who are placed in segregated settings. In contrast, those who support a continuum of services and placement options for students with disabilities have argued that general education classrooms cannot effectively accommodate all students with special needs and therefore some students require specialized programs and specially trained personnel who are available only in segregated settings. Independent of these debates and of the controversy that surrounds inclusion is the clear reality that children and youth with ASD and other disabilities will continue to receive their education in general education classrooms, and that more and more individuals with special needs will live and work in normalized settings. Additionally, there is undisputed recognition that practical, evidence-based, and reliable information and guidance are the sine qua non for developing effective micro and macro inclusion plans for learners with ASD. Finally, the least restrictive environment clause of the Individuals with Disabilities Education Act makes the general education classroom a rightful placement option for students with disabilities. As a consequence, and without a doubt, there is agreement among parents and professionals that strengthening the capabilities of general education teachers and administrators to effectively meet the needs of learners with disabilities is enormously important. This goal appears to be particularly significant relative to meeting the challenging behavior, social, communication, and learning needs of students with ASD. Unquestionably, in order to pave the way for effective inclusion, educators, administrators, and other stakeholders need high-quality resources and guidance. Without such assets, teachers, related service professionals, administrators, parents, and others are faced with the daunting task of designing and implementing inclusion programs for learners with ASD without the assistance and support of experienced and wise professionals. In *Successful Inclusion for Students with Autism*, de Boer provides the guidance and backing needed for successful inclusion.

Richard L. Simpson
Professor of Special Education
University of Kansas, Lawrence
March 2009

Introduction

The Controversy of Including Students with ASD

The educational placement of students with autism spectrum disorders (ASD) is a topic of vigorous debate and investigation among researchers, educators, and parents.[1] Effectively educating students with ASD requires an understanding of the unique cognitive, social, sensory, and behavioral deficits that characterize this developmental disability. In general, those who are debating agree that these students need individualized and unique instruction in settings that minimize their deficits and maximize their ability to comprehend the instruction provided to them.[2] Subsequently, the traditional techniques that have been used to instruct and manage the inappropriate behavior and reinforce the appropriate behavior of typical students are usually found to be ineffective for students with ASD.[3]

Consequently, it is not surprising that much controversy surrounds the efficacy and appropriateness of placing students with ASD in general education classrooms. Those who are debating do agree that a large percentage of these students should be included in appropriate general education settings that would facilitate these students' overall development and allow them to function within an environment that is as typical as possible.[4] However, it is not universally agreed on that such inclusion is appropriate for *all* students with ASD[5] due to their great diversity of strengths and weaknesses[6] and levels of functioning. This controversy stems largely from the definition of inclusion and whether it is a *philosophy* or a *placement* provided to students with disabilities.[7] The *philosophy* of inclusion centers on the membership and participation of an individual with a disability within a given community, along with the attitudes and perceptions of those who are including the individuals in that community. The *placement* of a student in a specific classroom and the type of inclusion strategies and specific interventions that are used when including the individual stem directly from the philosophy of inclusion held by those who are implementing the inclusion program.

If an individualized educational planning (IEP) team makes the decision to place a student with ASD into a general education classroom, the teaching of *that* specific student within *that* specific environment can be a very complicated process that cannot be implemented successfully by *that* specific general education teacher alone.[8] That specific general education teacher is an active member of the IEP team that develops and implements an appropriate education program for the student.[9] This team generally includes an administrator, other related service providers, the parents, and special education teachers. The team is directed by an inclusion facilitator, who may be the special education teacher and is knowledgeable and trained in ASD and inclusion practices. For this student with ASD to be successful in his inclusive education environment and for each member of the IEP team to function successfully within his or her role, training and support must be implemented. Ideally this includes preservice training as well as ongoing in-service training and support relating to ASD and inclusion techniques. Specifically, training and support are needed in academic methods of instruction, behavioral interventions and ways to facilitate communication, and social interaction skills.[10]

To date, limited training materials, personnel resources, and literature are available for teachers who are including students with any disability, especially students with ASD, into their classrooms. Some literature focuses specifically on social inclusion, that is, on facilitating social interaction between students with ASD and their typical peers.[11] However, few such studies or scholarly articles have addressed models of inclusion and methods for facilitating academic inclusion of these students into the general education classroom.[12]

This lack of knowledge, continual support, and ongoing strategy training on the inclusion of students with ASD greatly affects teachers' attitudes toward teaching these students.[13] The teacher's attitude has long been recognized as the single most important factor in the success or failure of any specific practice, including academic inclusion for those with ASD.[14] Most studies that have looked at perceptions and attitudes toward inclusion have focused on general education teachers who work with students with disabilities. The concept of inclusion was first introduced in the early 1990s when many general education teachers expressed caution due to feelings of inadequacy about working with individuals who have disabilities, although in general they expressed positive attitudes toward the students themselves.[15] However, these attitudes were often accompanied by specific concern about including students with severe disabilities, particularly those with significant intellectual deficits or behavioral disorders.[16] These same teachers also expressed concern about not previously receiving adequate training and support that would enable them to successfully teach students with disabilities in their classrooms.[17]

A review of the current literature (2000–2007) on the inclusion of students with disabilities shows that these attitudes and concerns have continued, even after almost twenty years of inclusion education practice in this country.[18] This review also reveals considerable lack of information about the types of training and support that are currently available specifically to facilitate the inclusion of students with ASD and about the attitudes of teachers toward the inclusion of these students. Indeed, the only published studies on this topic are surveys conducted with general education teachers in Scotland[19] and in England.[20]

As previously stated, children with ASD may display deficits in any or all of the language, communication, social interaction, play, behavior, self-help, motor, and intelligence skills. The combination of these deficits means that ASD falls into the realm of severe disabilities, although its manifestation in a child can range from mild to moderate to severe. Given that there is a scarcity of research, information, training, and support on the inclusion of students with ASD, it is safe to conclude that the amount of training and support provided for special and general education teachers is at best limited. As a result, the attitude of such teachers toward the inclusion of students with ASD is both guarded and fearful.

Purpose of the Book

Given this current level of controversy, the lack of research, and the subsequent lack of training for educators, it has been my work to help educators and administrators develop appropriate inclusion programs that serve and support both educators and students with ASD. I have consequently become passionate about creating appropriate inclusion programs for all students with ASD whose communication, social skills, behavior, and cognition disabilities range from mild to severe. In the book's first chapters I discuss the history of special education in general, and specifically the history of inclusion, services for children with disabilities, and legal issues related to the appropriate education of students with ASD. The book is designed for the reader to gain an understanding of the continuum of options that are available to best place and serve students with ASD and their unique needs.

It is my belief that the least restrictive environment (LRE) clause in the Individuals with Disabilities Education Act gave great power to students with ASD (and to all students with disabilities) to enroll in an appropriate educational program. It is that clause that added the general education classroom to the continuum of placement options available to students with

ASD. Being educated in the LRE is a right that cannot be taken away from any student, and once the student's specific needs are known it must first be considered how his needs can be met in the general education classroom. There is no bias on my part toward the inclusion of any student with ASD in the general education classroom for all, part, or none of his school day. I believe that it is of primary importance that we address each student's needs and that an individualized education program should be developed for him that first considers the general education classroom for his placement. The information, materials, examples, and strategies provided in this book are meant to assist the reader in understanding exactly how to determine if the general education classroom is an appropriate placement, and if it is, how to start inclusion, appropriately increase and decrease inclusion time as needed, and appropriately work with the student in the general education classroom.

This book was written primarily to guide special educators and school administrators in establishing an appropriate and effective inclusion program for students with ASD within the district or individual school. It was also written to provide special educators, general education teachers, and paraeducators with practical information, materials, and strategies for including students with ASD in the general education classroom. Although a wide variety of strategies are included to help teachers and paraeducators work with the individual student, the book cannot provide a comprehensive compilation of all strategies. Many other books have already been written specifically on behavior intervention strategies, communication interventions, social skills interventions, and teaching strategies for working with students with ASD. This book provides guidelines for creating an inclusion program that includes many intervention strategies for all of these areas. The IEP team can utilize the other helpful books mentioned in various chapters of this book as resources for developing detailed intervention strategies.

Many of the structural components of the inclusion program and the strategies discussed for working with students with ASD are applicable to other students with different disabilities. Being aware of this will aid your understanding of the many effective research-based practices (such as involving parents, utilizing applied behavior analysis intervention strategies, and social skills instruction) that are applicable to including a student with any disability in the general education classroom. *The distinction* to be noted, however, is that although many of the inclusion program components and intervention strategies may be applicable to students with other disabilities, *those discussed and described in this book are essential for students with ASD.* For example, one strategy that is discussed involves developing methods for helping students with ASD to transition between activities throughout the school day. Although this strategy may be helpful for some students with specific learning disabilities or Down syndrome, it is unquestionably a crucial and fundamental intervention strategy for all students with ASD.

Overview of the Contents

The chapters in the book are organized into four sections to help the reader divide and chunk the information and inclusion strategies into the overall steps they will follow as they establish an inclusion program. The first section, "Basic Information on Autism Spectrum Disorders and Inclusion," presents the basic characteristics of students with ASD, the history of inclusive education, and the existing legal guidelines for appropriately placing these students. The second section, "Considerations Before Creating an Inclusion Program," discusses what must be accomplished before initiating the inclusion program for a particular student, including determining the student's needs and appropriate services and placements, establishing the overall structure needed to implement the inclusion model in the particular school, and delineating the roles and responsibilities of everyone involved. The chapters in the third section, "Establishment of the Inclusion Program," address the steps to be taken once all of these factors have been considered. These chapters explain how to initiate the inclusion program, facilitate the student's education, implement a behavior management plan, and facilitate social and communication skills within the general education classroom. Finally, the fourth section, "Program Maintenance and Evaluation of Inclusion Program," discusses the methods necessary to evaluate the inclusion program as well as to evaluate the student's progress in the program while developing a successful means of transition to a new classroom during or at the end of each year. It is my desire that as the reader journeys through the successes and trials of working with students with ASD, this book will assist him or her with the inclusion process and to help these special children reach their designed potential.

PART I

Basic Information on Autism Spectrum Disorders and Inclusion

Understanding the Unique Characteristics of Individuals with ASD

CHILDREN with autism spectrum disorders (ASD) are truly unique and special people. ASD, which manifests in children's minds as well as in their bodies, is unlike any other disability; it results in a combination of many disabling conditions, which is why it is such a complex disability. It is difficult initially to understand what ASD is and thus why children who have it behave as they do.

Autism spectrum disorders fall under the American Psychiatric Association (APA) umbrella of pervasive developmental disorder (PDD). This classification consists of the following disorders: autistic disorder (aka autism), pervasive developmental disorder–not otherwise specified (PDD-NOS), Asperger's syndrome, Rett's disorder, and childhood disintegrative disorder. Children who are diagnosed with a pervasive developmental disorder exhibit "severe and pervasive impairments in the developmental areas of reciprocal social interactions skills, communication skills, and/or the presence of stereotyped behavior, interests, and activities."[1]

The three most distinctive and most frequently occurring disabilities that fall under the PDD umbrella and on which this chapter focuses are autistic disorder (from here on referred to as autism), PDD-NOS, and Asperger's syndrome. They are three different disorders with three sets of distinct diagnostic criteria, yet they have similar characteristics. They are all on the autism spectrum and they span a continuum on which all people with ASD fall. The characteristics of ASD are discussed fully in this chapter; the diagnostic criteria for these three specific disabilities are available in the *Diagnostic and Statistical Manual of Mental Disorders, Fourth Edition, Text Revision* (DSM-IV TR).[2]

Each person who is diagnosed with a disorder within the autism spectrum does not necessarily behave or function like another person diagnosed with the same label, and he or she may in some cases appear to be more like a person with a different label on the spectrum. Using the diagnostic criteria within the DSM-IV TR involves determining the quality and quantity of the characteristics that a person currently displays. People who are diagnosed with autism typically display the largest number of characteristics and exhibit the most severe impairments compared to other people diagnosed with other disorders on the spectrum. Those diagnosed with Asperger's syndrome, for example, typically display the least number of characteristics and exhibit the least severe impairments compared to other people on the spectrum. Those diagnosed with PDD-NOS typically fall between autism and Asperger's syndrome because they don't display as many characteristics as someone with autism and yet they display more impairments than those with Asperger's.

Continuum of Autism Spectrum Disorders

As has already been noted, there is a degree of overlap among the PDD disabilities. There are people who are on the border between two labels, and a person may receive one label from one diagnostic professional and another label from another professional. Regardless of the label a person is given on the spectrum of ASD, there are similarities among all of the disorders, and what distinguishes each disorder from the others is the degree to which specific characteristics appear in the person being diagnosed.

The disabilities on the autism spectrum not only share many characteristics among them but also share many characteristics with other disabilities. This fact may be confusing to families of children with ASD and to educators who work with students with ASD because the label *autism*

> ➔ Each person diagnosed with an autism spectrum disorder is unique and displays a combination of characteristics that no other person diagnosed with the same disability displays.

does not appear to be specific enough as a descriptor of this disorder's disabling conditions as might be true of, for example, the label *physical disability*. Instead, the label *autism* essentially denotes the appearance of several disabling conditions within one person, but to varying degrees within each person who receives the diagnosis. In other words, each person diagnosed with an autism spectrum disorder is unique and displays a combination of characteristics that no other person diagnosed with the same disability displays. People typically look for and want to be able to

Exhibit 1.1. Continuum of Autism Spectrum Disorders

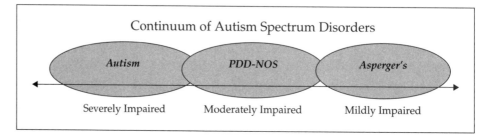

grasp a simple definition of *autism* or *Asperger's syndrome*, but they are confused when the *simple* definition they are given does not help them to understand the disability that a particular child or student displays.

It is therefore imperative to understand that ASD encompasses *multiple* disabling conditions or *multiple* disabilities (although this definition is not to be confused with the Individuals with Disabilities Education Act [IDEA] *multiple disabilities* label). Essentially, people with ASD exhibit to some degree or another characteristics of all the identified disabilities listed in the IDEA: emotional and behavioral disorder, attention deficit disorder, visual impairments, physical impairments, hearing impairments, learning impairments, developmental impairments, and others. For example, a person with ASD often experiences mood swings with many unexplainable and often erratic emotions. He may also engage in numerous inappropriate behaviors (such as noncompliance, aggressiveness, verbal outbursts, or destruction of property), as do children with emotional and behavioral disorders; but because this behavior is not the only disabling condition the student with ASD displays, he or she is not diagnosed with an emotional or behavioral disorder. Some people with ASD behave as if they are deaf and do not respond to sounds that occur next to them or to a person talking to them. Some are mute and use sign language or pictures to communicate. Most individuals with ASD also display many attention deficit characteristics; they are often distracted by sounds or moving objects, have difficulty sitting still, and cannot focus on a given task for any length of time. There are numerous examples of characteristics of IDEA-defined disabilities that would also apply to persons with ASD. Therefore, if a parent or an educator can come to see his or her child or student as possessing multiple disabling conditions that make up the whole of his or her autism, they may begin

> ➜ There are numerous examples of characteristics of IDEA-defined disabilities that would also apply to persons with ASD.

to grasp what autism, PDD-NOS, or Asperger's syndrome means for a particular child or student.

One aspect of ASD that distinguishes it from all other disabilities and further supports the view that ASD encompasses multiple disabilities is that people with ASD display unbalanced patterns within the development of their skills.[3] This imbalance in skill development has resulted in use of the term *splinter skills*.[4] A child may have developed math skills that are several years beyond what is typical for children his or her age, yet the child may still not be able to use the bathroom on his or her own. The term *savant* has also been used to describe people who have a skill or talent in one area, (such as music, math, visual memory, and so on) that surpasses even those who are considered masters in that area, yet they cannot function age-appropriately within all other skill domains.

In order to address the uneven development and multiple disabling conditions that people with ASD display, it is necessary and beneficial to take a closer look at the many possible characteristics of ASD. Looking closely at the multifaceted characteristics of ASD enables parents and educators to understand the developmental pattern and multiple disabilities of a particular child or student. Only then are they able to identify the unique characteristics of that child or student and establish a profile that explains that child's disability.

> ➜ Looking closely at the multifaceted characteristics of ASD enables parents and educators to understand the developmental pattern and multiple disabilities of a particular child or student. Only then are they able to identify the unique characteristics of that child and establish a profile that explains the child's disability.

Typically, a child suspected of having ASD undergoes a formal battery of diagnostic tests and assessments. The results of these tests are then provided and explained in reports to educators and parents in order to help them understand their child's or student's disability. What is often missing from such a report is a simple and comprehensive summary that includes definitions and explanations of the child's autism-like characteristics and discusses how those characteristics result in that child's particular skill abilities and deficits.

The unique characteristics of ASD can be found in the following skill or ability areas:

> ➜ The unique characteristics of ASD can be found in the following skill or ability areas: cognition, learning, social interaction, play, communication, adaptive behavior, behavior, motor, and sensory sensitivities.

- Cognition
- Learning
- Social interaction
- Play
- Communication
- Adaptive behavior
- Behavior characteristics
- Motor skills
- Sensory sensitivities[5]

These characteristics naturally affect each other yet remain distinctive enough to be defined and explained separately. Each of the skill areas consists of a body of abilities and deficits that characterize ASD in general and that can then be used to describe the unique characteristics of a particular student with ASD.

To help parents and educators better understand the characteristics of ASD and then create a profile and appropriate plan of interventions for and placement of their own child or student, a brief but comprehensive overview of each of the nine skill areas is provided here.

Cognitive Abilities

Cognitive ability is one characteristic that distinguishes autism, PDD-NOS, and Asperger's syndrome and holds a significant amount of weight in the diagnostic process. The cognitive abilities and deficits of children with ASD range from severe impairments to gifted abilities. Children who have been labeled autistic often display severe to moderate to average mental deficiencies while those with Asperger's syndrome display average to gifted mental capacities. Those with PDD-NOS typically range from mild or moderate deficits to average cognitive abilities, overlapping on one end with autism and on the other with Asperger's syndrome.

A recent review of the available literature[6] identified three distinct cognitive characteristics that all individuals on the autism spectrum struggle with: metarepresentation, abstract reasoning, and joint attention. Metarepresentation is the "capacity to represent the mental

> ➔ Three distinct cognitive characteristics that all individuals on the autism spectrum struggle with are metarepresentation, abstract reasoning, and joint attention.

states of others."[7] This means that children with ASD struggle with perspective taking (that is, with understanding the thoughts, feelings, and beliefs of others) and with theory-of-mind abilities (that is, with recognizing and interpreting sarcasm, irony, idioms, or pretenses). Abstract reasoning is the "capacity for generating mental representations, thereby permitting the development of novel thoughts and behaviors, hypothetical thinking, and flexible interaction with others in the environment."[8] It enables a child to make meaning out of events and to organize parts into a whole. Children with ASD typically focus on the parts of an event or task or object and fail to see the big picture or to synthesize the different aspects into a whole event. Joint attention, a nonverbal communication skill, is the "capacity to share attention between other individuals and objects."[9] Joint attention is the ability to maintain an ongoing conversation while simultaneously referring to an object, talking about it, and looking at it, while also noting that the other person in the conversation is also looking at and thinking about that object. Children with ASD are typically unable to share their attention with more than one thing or person. Joint attention has been found to be a strong predictor of language development in children with ASD.[10]

Although children with Asperger's syndrome have average to above average cognitive abilities, they often display uneven abilities on formal IQ assessments. They may perform well on item recall, definition of words, factual information, and block design, but perform poorly on comprehension, picture arrangement, problem solving, and coding.[11] Performance scores on other tests administered to children with Asperger's syndrome have demonstrated low abilities in understanding social situations, possessing common sense, interpreting interpersonal situations, and displaying good social judgment.[12]

Thus, the range of cognitive abilities and disabilities of children with ASD extends from severe impairment to giftedness. Many cognitive tests are available for professionals to use to test people with ASD, but

> ➔ The range of cognitive abilities and disabilities of children with ASD extends from severe impairment to giftedness.

cognitive assessment of these students continues to be very difficult. Some tests can be used with children who are nonverbal; the reliability of these tests, however, is often questionable, and until someone can verbally communicate knowledge and reasoning, a true picture of his or her cognitive skills remains elusive. Even when children with ASD do use verbal communication, testing can still be difficult due to their social and behavior deficits. Many children with ASD who are able to complete cognitive assessments may also reveal learning disabilities (such as reading comprehension or auditory processing disabilities) that affect their performance in school.

Learning Abilities

The learning abilities and disabilities of children with ASD are directly related to their cognitive abilities and deficits; therefore children with autism typically have significantly more learning difficulties than children with Asperger's syndrome. Many types of learning difficulties span the ASD continuum; the differences between the specific disorders lie in the degree to which a child's learning is affected. Children with autism struggle significantly with motivation, overselective responding (attending to only a few features or cues within their environment), and generalization (applying knowledge gained about one object or item to other environments and stimuli).[13] They may learn a task using certain materials in one environment but not be able to perform the task with different materials in another environment. Many of these children appear withdrawn and preoccupied and therefore unmotivated to participate in general activities and educational tasks or to explore their environment. It is also not uncommon to find children with autism overgeneralizing (applying one learned concept to all items in that category, for example, all food becomes *apple* because that was the first food label learned). When a child uses the same label for many different objects or activities (for instance, when he calls all animals *dog* because the first animal he learned to identify was a dog, the child is not appropriately attending to or discriminating between different stimuli. Children with autism also do not learn at the same rate as typical children do and often show uneven progress in their academic skill development. If a child also has mental deficiencies, he or she will eventually reach plateaus in the learning of various concepts and tasks.

Many children with autism, PDD-NOS, and Asperger's syndrome perform well on spatial, perceptual, and matching tasks, but auditory processing and abstract reasoning may be quite difficult.[14] They also perform better when picture cues and symbols are added to their learning environment.[15] Some children with ASD have said they think in pictures and not with words, and they have excellent memory and recall skills related to visual processing.[16]

> ➡ Many children with autism, PDD-NOS, and Asperger's syndrome perform well on spatial, perceptual, and matching tasks, but auditory processing and abstract reasoning may be quite difficult.

Children with Asperger's syndrome exhibit learning difficulties in the areas of comprehension, imagination, problem solving, arithmetic calculations, organization, lapse of time, critical thinking, and attention to relevant stimuli (items, activities, or instructions) while often also demonstrating average to above average abilities in rote memory, concrete thinking, oral expression, decoding and reading, and using computers.[17]

It is also important to mention that the motor difficulties that all children with ASD experience affect significantly their ability to express and apply any information they have learned.[18] In summary, all children with ASD experience learning difficulties in many of the same areas (abstract reasoning, auditory processing, and comprehension), but it is the severity of their learning difficulties that greatly affects the type of educational interventions they need, as well as the location in which they need to be educated.

Social Interaction Skills

The social behavior of children with ASD is typically the deficit that people notice most often, it is the skill that parents are most concerned about in their child, and it is the most difficult skill for educators and parents to teach. Social interaction skills are the skills that children with ASD most often lack and that are the most difficult for them to gain.[19]

> ➡ The social behavior of children with ASD is typically the deficit that people notice most often, it is the skill that parents are most concerned about in their child, and it is the most difficult skill for educators and parents to teach.

Contrary to popular belief, many children with ASD do not necessarily lack the desire to interact with their peers and family members; rather, they lack the ability to interact with others *appropriately*. Because they are often unable to employ the cognitive skills of joint attention or perspective taking, they are unable to notice and understand, as well as provide, nonverbal social cues. Nonverbal social cues include facial expressions and body language, as well as tone of voice, prosody, and pauses within conversations. These are foundational social skills that people need to use and to understand as others use them.

Individuals with autism may appear completely isolated or aloof and not appear to show any interest in other children. Sometimes the only time a child with autism interacts with someone is to use that person physically as a tool to obtain something he or she wants. On the other side of the continuum, children with Asperger's syndrome may be highly interactive yet peculiar in their social behavior. They may interact with individuals frequently, but only to talk about subjects in which they are particularly interested, and they may completely dominate the conversation, not realizing that the other person lost interest a long time ago. Individuals with Asperger's syndrome may often upset another person with something they say or they may misunderstand things that people say to them. Words often used to describe these children are *stiff, inflexible, self-centered,* and *awkward* because such children do not use and understand nonverbal cues,[20] do not listen well to other people, do not want to talk about topics in which they are not interested, and make other people feel uncomfortable with their lack of eye contact or inability to maintain "personal space." It is also important to understand that many

> ➡ Many children with Asperger's syndrome are painfully aware of their social ineptness but lack the ability to recognize their particular social deficits.

children with Asperger's syndrome are painfully aware of their social ineptness but lack the ability to recognize their particular social deficits.

Overall, children with ASD display a broad range of social skill abilities. On one end of the continuum they may appear to have completely isolated themselves and to have attempted, at all costs, to remove themselves from the presence of all other children. In the middle of the continuum they may be totally passive, not caring if other children are around them or if they are touched, and they may initiate interaction only when they want something. On the far end of the continuum they may continually attempt to initiate interaction with others but do so inappropriately and without regard for the other person's feelings.

Play Skills

The play skills that children with ASD do or do not possess stem directly from the types and amount of social skills they possess. Children who have socially isolated themselves from others typically do not initiate play or share toys with their peers. Children with autism often perform perseverative (repetitive and unending) actions with certain objects. The objects that these children enjoy "playing" with may not be toys at all, and typically they do not use the object (such as a stick, plunger, fork, or string) in the way in which it was designed to be used. These children typically lack the skills to engage in symbolic as well as spontaneous, functional play.[21] It is not unusual to see these children become upset if someone else has "their" object or toy, and to see them exhibit aggressive behaviors in order to get the object back. Some children with autism or PDD-NOS exhibit parallel play behaviors in which they may tolerate children playing nearby but not interact with or show interest in them or their toys. Some may also be quite passive; if another child attempts to take their toy away they may show no reaction.

Many children with Asperger's syndrome typically play with toys but they often limit their interest to specific toys or games and can become obsessed with playing with them and with all the rules and aspects of play. Children with Asperger's syndrome typically are quite interactive in their play with others, but they can appear to be self-centered—dictating the actions of the other children or continually reciting the rules and pointing out the supposed wrongdoing of their peers. Sometimes these children do not pick up on the nonverbal and subtle verbal cues of their peers during games and may continually be confused or demonstrate exaggerated emotions about certain events.[22] Many people with Asperger's syndrome also display an extreme need to be first or to win or do something perfectly (or not at all), which often results in their peers not wanting to play with them.[23]

Play skills thus cover a wide continuum on which children with ASD may perseverate on certain objects and actions during isolated play, parallel play next to their peers while not caring which toys they play with, or continually initiate play interaction but only on their own rule-bound terms.

> ➔ Play skills cover a wide continuum on which children with ASD may perseverate on certain objects and actions during isolated play, parallel play next to their peers, or initiate play interaction but only on their own terms.

Communication Skills

"Troubles within the domains of communication and language are so prevalent in children with autism that they have been used as the central descriptors of the syndrome."[24] Lack of communication and language skills is so pervasive in ASD that it

> ➔ Lack of communication and language skills is so pervasive in the autism spectrum disorders that it significantly affects all of the person's skills in other areas.

significantly affects all of the person's skills in other areas. Children on the spectrum of autism disorders display a significant range of abilities and disabilities, from completely nonverbal to excessively verbal.

A review of the literature[25] identifies the following three categories of communication and language characteristics of children with autism:

1. Nonverbal communication

2. Verbal delays

3. Echolalic speech

The nonverbal communication of children with autism has been described as "intentional nonsymbolic communication," which means they typically use few isolated and nonsophisticated gestures (such as reaching into the air for something but not pointing to a specific object) and they exhibit aggressive and self-injurious behaviors.[26] Children with autism who display verbal delays—that is, do not use sentences that are typical and appropriate for their age—use some speech, but they often exhibit significant developmental delays in phonology, syntax, and semantics as well.[27] The language of these children differs from the language of typical children both quantitatively—that is, in how many words they use—and qualitatively—that is, in how well they use language to communicate. Many verbal children with autism also exhibit echolalic speech; that is, they repeat vocal expressions they have heard in the near (immediate echolalia) or distant past (delayed echolalia); this behavior is also sometimes referred to as scripting. Overall, the communication deficits displayed by children with autism affect their ability to function and to behave appropriately within both their home and their school environment.

Many children with PDD-NOS display several of the same communication and language characteristics as children with autism, but they are often more verbal and use more functional, albeit repetitive, communication.[28] Children with Asperger's syndrome and some children with PDD-NOS do not demonstrate any developmental communication and language delays (a crucial component of diagnosis for Asperger's) but instead display abnormal expressive and receptive communication skills,[29] including the following:

- Inability to use appropriate conversation speech and skills (pragmatics)
- Literal interpretation of comments
- Inappropriate use of prosody (speech modifiers)
- Inappropriate use of pedantic speech (formal or precise speech)
- Idiosyncratic use of words (creative or original words)
- Excessive vocalization of thoughts
- Inability to discriminate auditorally between noises and voices
- Excessive speech or *selective mutism* (talking rarely and only to specific people or in specific environments)[30]

In summary, children with autism find it difficult or impossible to communicate their needs and desires effectively, and children with Asperger's syndrome and high-functioning children with PDD-NOS particularly display communication deficits in the context of social communication.

Adaptive Behavior Skills

One of the skill areas in which children with ASD display uneven development compared to their development in other areas is adaptive behavior skills, that is, self-care or self-help skills, including the following:

- Toileting
- Sleeping
- Eating
- Bathing
- Dressing

Development of these skills ultimately leads to children's acquisition of a repertoire of independent living skills and to success with social interaction skills. Not surprisingly, those children who are most severely affected with autism exhibit the least amount of adaptive behavior skills. What *is* surprising is that many children in the range of disabilities from PDD-NOS to Asperger's syndrome who are considered to be higher functioning often also display low levels of adaptive behavior skills.[31]

> ➜ One of the skill domains in which children with ASD display uneven development is that of adaptive behavior skills.

Children across the spectrum who have difficulty with self-care skills may

- Display significant delays in acquiring toileting skills (urination and bowel movements)
- Have significant sleep difficulties
- Have trouble feeding themselves
- Be interest in eating only a limited variety of foods
- Lack understanding regarding personal hygiene
- Have no interest in or show extreme aversion to washing themselves
- Exhibit delays in development of motor skills
- Have difficulty getting dressed
- Lack interest in fashion or appearance

Behavior Characteristics

The behavior problems exhibited by children with ASD are "among the most challenging and stressful issues faced by schools and parents in their efforts to provide appropriate education programs."[32] The problem behaviors that many children with autism and PDD-NOS display are significant barriers to effective social interactions as well as to educational placement and development. The range of these behaviors includes the following:

- Aggression toward others
- Self-injury
- Hyperactivity or underactivity (overstimulation and understimulation)
- Lack of compliance with instructions and ongoing routines and activities

> ➜ The problem behaviors that many children with autism and PDD-NOS display are significant barriers to effective social interactions as well as to educational placement and development.

- Destruction of property

- Disruption of classroom or family routines

- Obsession with specific objects, activities, or routines

- Excessive display of emotions (such as crying, laughing, and tantrums)

- Repetitive and self-stimulatory movements

- Inattention[33]

The frequency and intensity of these behaviors typically coincide with the severity of the person's cognitive deficits and the degree of development of their functional communication abilities. Many high-functioning children with autism, including those with PDD-NOS, may exhibit a few problem behaviors, but not to the degree of those whose cognitive deficits are more severe.

Children with Asperger's syndrome typically do not exhibit severe behavior problems and are able to function to a high degree within a typical educational environment. The problems that these children often do experience involve feelings of stress, fatigue, loss of control, anxiety, and depression, resulting in social misconduct, obsessive and single-minded pursuit of particular interests, and defensive panic reactions to seemingly benign events.[34] Overall, these behavior problems are connected with these children's inability to predict the outcomes of their own and others actions.

Thus, the variety of behavioral characteristics displayed by individuals on the spectrum of autism disorders includes noncompliance, disruptiveness, destructiveness, aggressiveness, self-stimulatory and stereotypical behaviors, and talkativeness (asking questions and telling people how to do things, for example), excessive fidgeting, and self-injurious behaviors.

Motor Skills

One of the more mystifying characteristics of children with ASD is their motor and physical challenges, that is, their difficulties with both gross and fine motor skills. Due to the severity of the manifestations of disability in children with autism, little is known about their motor skills other than what can be observed. Many children with autism display uneven motor development, with significant delays in some skill areas and considerable advancement in others. For example, they may exhibit advanced fine motor skills in using their fingers (such as in picking up small objects

> ➡ One of the more mystifying characteristics of individuals with ASD is their motor and physical challenges, that is, their difficulties with both gross and fine motor skills.

or drawing), yet may not be able to catch a large ball or walk with a typical gait. Some children with autism may either lie on the ground or stand at a table as though they lack the muscle strength to sit and hold their upper body in an upright position.

There is much more knowledge about the motor difficulties of children with Asperger's syndrome. The words used most commonly to describe the motor coordination of such children are *clumsy* and *awkward*. The areas in which these children experience motor coordination difficulties include the following:

- Locomotion (walking and running)
- Ball skills (catching and throwing)
- Balance
- Manual dexterity (coordinating the use of both hands for one action)
- Handwriting
- Speed of movement (rapid and impulsive versus slow and smooth)
- Rhythm (synchronizing movements)
- Imitation of movement (posture, gestures, body language)
- Executive functions (planning actions and carrying out planned actions)[35]

Motor difficulties in these areas affect the ability and opportunities of children with Asperger's syndrome to engage in sports, acquire typical leisure skills, perform simple motor actions, engage in fluid conversations, and communicate effectively through writing.

Because the development of motor skills in children with ASD is uneven, these children may display a wide range of skills that do not necessarily appear to correlate with their cognitive abilities. For example, even though they may not be able to perform the simple action of stacking blocks, they may be able to put together a thousand-piece puzzle without assistance; even though they may be unable to coordinate their movements in order to dress themselves, they may be able to operate a joystick and keypad at the same time while playing a complicated computer game.

Sensory Sensitivities

One distinctive characteristic of all children with ASD that many educators and parents attempt, often unsuccessfully, to understand is their sensitivity and abnormal reactions to various stimuli within their environment. This particular continuum of sensitivities—from hypersensitive to hyposensitive—does not correlate with the severity of the overall disabling condition, but it does indicate the degree to which a child with ASD is sensitive to his or her environment. It is not uncommon for a particular child with ASD to be hypersensitive to some stimuli and hyposensitive to other stimuli. In the typical envi-

> ➜ A continuum of sensitivities does not correlate with the severity of the overall disabling condition, but it does indicate the degree to which a child with ASD is sensitive to his or her environment.

ronment, individuals with ASD are sensitive to visual stimuli (sight), auditory stimuli (sound), olfactory stimuli (smell), tactile stimuli (touch), and taste as well as to texture, pain, temperature, proprioception (body position), and the vestibular sense (movement).[36] Visual stimuli include colors, brightness of light, and distorted perceptions. Auditory stimuli include pitch, volume, consistency of particular sounds, and sudden noises. Olfactory stimuli include the intensity or pungency of particular smells. Tactile stimuli include the texture of items touched, the amount of pressure applied to the body, and the location of touch on the body. The stimuli of food taste and texture include the types and intensities of tastes as well as the feel of the food while it is in the mouth. Many people with ASD are not sensitive to pain or temperature and may not react to typical sources of pain or to the temperature of their environment.

Proprioception stimuli are internal messages sent from a person's muscles, joints, tendons, and ligaments that tell the body what position it is in and where it is in space. Vestibular stimuli are generated from the inner ear as it responds to movements and to positions of the body, indicating whether it is up or down, balanced or unbalanced, fast or slow, and so on. Both of these systems can result in great variations in how students with ASD interact physically and socially with others during play activities, as well as in their ability to sit, stand, or participate in physical activity for any length of time.

Many of these stimuli (and sometimes combinations of them) cause overstimulation and hypersensitivity in some children with ASD; other children may not even register these stimuli, resulting in understimulation and hyposensitivity. Children who experience hypersensitivity often exhibit many problem behaviors, such as screaming, tantrums, and crying, in reaction to the stimuli, while those who experience hyposensitivity may not react to dangerous situations or experience pain and therefore may become seriously injured.

Summary

When assessing a child's abilities and planning his or her individualized educational intervention, professionals and parents must consider, measure, and plan according to the child's ability and disability levels within the nine skill areas: cognition, learning, social interaction, play, communication, adaptive behavior, behavior characteristics, motor skills, and sensory sensitivities. In order to plan and execute an appropriate IEP for a particular child or student with ASD, it

> ➜ When planning a child's individualized education plan, implement interventions that address the individual's ability and disability levels within the nine skill areas: cognition, learning, social interaction, play, communication, adaptive behavior, behavior characteristics, motor skills, and sensory sensitivities.

is important that educators and parents gain a clear understanding of the many complex characteristics of ASD through studying the spectrum of skill areas and their corresponding ranges of ability and disability. Subsequently they must generate and explain a comprehensive profile of the particular child or student with ASD. The informal method presented in this book of creating a profile that summarizes the child's abilities and deficits is unique to working with children with ASD. The profile must incorporate information on the child from all available sources (including assessment, observation data, and verbal reports).

Form 1.1, ASD Characteristics: Student Profile, can be used by educators and parents to create a comprehensive yet concise description that

> ✎ Use Form 1.1: ASD Characteristics: Student Profile

summarizes a particular student's skills and deficits across the skill areas. This tool is especially useful when an IEP team is planning to include the student in a general education environment. How to use the information contained in the profile in the inclusion program planning process is explained further in Chapter Four.

Student: _____   Date: _____

Form 1.1. ASD Characteristics: Student Profile

Cognitive Abilities	Learning Abilities	Social Interaction Skills
Strengths:	Strengths:	Strengths:
Difficulties:	Difficulties:	Difficulties:

Play Skills	Communication Skills	Adaptive Behavior Skills
Strengths:	Strengths:	Strengths:
Difficulties:	Difficulties:	Difficulties:

(Continued)

Form 1.1. ASD Characteristics: Student Profile *(Continued)*

Behavior Characteristics	Motor Skills	Sensory Sensitivities
Strengths:	Strengths:	Strengths:
Difficulties:	Difficulties:	Difficulties:

Comments:

Reviewing the Context of Inclusion for Students with ASD

2

Historical Context

Debate regarding the inclusion of students with disabilities in general education settings has remained strong throughout the past thirty years since the Individuals with Disabilities Education Act (IDEA; formerly known as Public Law 94-142) was passed in 1975. This law established a broad outline of principles for the development of educational services that would ensure that all children with disabilities would receive a free appropriate public education designed to meet each child's special needs. This was the first time that the U.S. federal government took a firm stand in setting criteria and procedures for the provision of education for children with disabilities. The law resulted in sweeping reforms in the way special education services were delivered and in how public education was viewed and delivered to all children. One specific requirement within this law had a unique and powerful impact on the educational services provided to children with disabilities. The least restrictive environment (LRE) provision mandated instructing children with disabilities within the general education setting to the maximum extent appropriate.

> ➔ The least restrictive environment provision mandated instructing children with disabilities within the general education setting to the maximum extent appropriate.

Throughout the late 1970s, the number of students with disabilities receiving their education within the general education environment multiplied, and the success in natural, integrated settings of students with independent functioning, skill generalization, and skill maintenance disabilities multiplied as well.[1] By the early 1980s, the Regular Education Initiative (REI) movement, which called for the merger of special education with general education with the intent of the *full* inclusion of students with disabilities, gained momentum and supporters.[2]

Then, in the mid to late 1980s, a division emerged among REI supporters. On one side were those who felt that REI should be aimed primarily at students with high-incidence mild disabilities and that a continuum of services and alternative settings outside the general education classroom remained the most appropriate placements for students with severe and profound disabilities.[3] On the other side were those who felt that *all* students with disabilities should be included in general education classrooms regardless of disability type or severity level.[4] The latter group asserted that if all students were not included, two separate systems of education (general and special) would be maintained and the needs of students with severe and profound disabilities would not be addressed.[5]

This division over the application of REI caused considerable tension in special education in the 1990s. Supporters of full inclusion called for a radical change that would alter the nature of special education; others called for a more cautious approach to change, basing their beliefs on empirical analyses and historical considerations.[6]

Debate continued, with those supporting full inclusion asserting that when students with disabilities are provided appropriate education experiences and support within the general education classroom, they are better able to learn, interact, communicate, and develop friendships than when they are placed in segregated settings.[7] Still others supported a continuum of services and placement options for students with disabilities, asserting that the general education classroom cannot accommodate all students with disabilities because some students require highly specialized care and education and much larger amounts of individualized attention, and that these needs are best met by specially trained teachers in settings other than the general education classroom.[8] Other placement options included a special education classroom at the student's neighborhood school or at another school in the district, a special education classroom at a private school for students with disabilities, an in-home one-to-one special education program, or a full-time residential care facility for students with disabilities.

Despite the controversy surrounding inclusion, the LRE provision in the IDEA has remained intact and has been promoted throughout subsequent revisions of the law. Under the current version (the Individuals with Disabilities Education Improvement Act of 2004), the LRE mandate has brought about structural changes to special education by making the general education classroom rather than the special education classroom the primary consideration for placement for each student with a disability.[9]

> ➔ The LRE mandate has made the general education classroom the primary consideration for placement for each student with a disability.

The issues surrounding inclusion are still debated among both general and special educators.[10] In an integrated system, special education can no longer act separately but must instead formulate policy and procedures in relation to the conditions, attitudes, perceptions, and behaviors of general education. Special educators must understand general education, and general educators must understand special education and all of its specialties. Thus, all supporters of inclusion, whether advocating for full inclusion or for inclusion as one option in a continuum of services, agree on the need to strengthen the capabilities of both special and general education teachers in order to meet the needs of students with disabilities, including students with ASD.

A Review of Current Research on Inclusive Education for Students with Disabilities and Students with ASD

The following exhaustive review of the literature examines and analyzes the findings of studies on inclusive education in general and of studies specifically on inclusion of students with ASD. The following topics are covered:

- Factors contributing to attitudes and resulting behavior toward people with disabilities and students with ASD

- Preservice and in-service training on inclusive education for both special and general educators

- Support of general educators to promote successful inclusion

- Inclusion of students with ASD

Factors Contributing to Attitudes and Resulting Behavior Toward People with Disabilities and Students with ASD

As inclusive education programs became more and more prevalent within the public school system, it became apparent that the success of these programs depended on the attitudes of educators and peers toward students with disabilities.[11] By studying these attitudes we can come to understand past experiences and then perhaps be better able to inform future

> ➜ It became apparent that the success of these programs depended on educators' attitudes toward students with disabilities, as well as on the attitudes of peers.

decision makers about inclusion and its impact on students with varying degrees of disability.[12]

In the late 1970s, when educators and administrators seriously began to educate children with disabilities in public schools, it became apparent that not everyone held the same attitudes toward people with disabilities. Although at that time research was available on the origins of attitudes and on how attitudes affect behavior, there was not a clear, specific understanding of the attitudes held toward people with disabilities.[13]

A turn-of-the century review of these studies found that teacher-student interactions differed significantly on the basis of the attitude that general education teachers had toward the students.[14] Attitudes toward specific students with disabilities who were included in their classrooms could be grouped as *attachment, concern, indifference,* and *rejection*. Students who were identified by teachers as *attachment* students were high achieving and hard working, and the teachers quickly became attached to these students.[15] Students who were viewed as *concern* students received more intense and personal attention from the teachers on their academic progress.[16] Teachers further reported that they tended to be indifferent toward students who were quiet and avoided social interaction.[17] Students who were identified as *rejection* students received less positive attention from teachers because of their social, attitudinal, and behavior problems.[18] The review concluded that the quality of students' educational experiences is directly affected by their general education teachers' attitudes (of attachment, concern, indifference, or rejection), because these attitudes affect the teachers' willingness to include students with disabilities in their classes, and are critical to the successful implementation of the inclusion program overall.[19]

Fisher, Sax, Rodifer, and Pumpian identified five critical factors that contributed specifically to attitudes toward individuals with disabilities:

- Contact versus no contact

- Adequate information versus misinformation or no information

- Peer status versus subordinate roles

- Training versus lack of competence

- Functional activities versus stereotypical behaviors[20]

Livneh further identified thirteen psychological and sociocultural influences (such as childhood influences, prejudice, and body image integrity) that contribute to the origins of attitudes toward people with disabilities.[21] His findings argue that attitudes are difficult to change and measure because they are learned and conditioned over many years. Nevertheless, it is now widely agreed that people's attitudes can change and become considerably more favorable toward individuals with disabilities if they

> ➜ People's attitudes can change and become considerably more favorable toward individuals with disabilities.

- Receive the appropriate amount and type of contact, information, and training on people with disabilities

- Establishing appropriate relationships with persons with disabilities

- Observe individuals with disabilities performing functional activities[22]

Studies conducted over the past forty years, including one by Salend and Duhaney, have noted that general education teachers have expressed a wide range of concerns about inclusive education, including the following:

- Negative attitudes of other people (such as colleagues, students without disabilities, and parents)
- Fear that the education of students without disabilities will suffer
- Inability to address the severe medical needs and behavioral challenges of some students with disabilities
- Lack of funds to support personnel and instruction
- Rigid requirements associated with general education curricula
- Limited time available for collaboration and communication among staff
- Limited financial resources[23]

Buell and colleagues also found that the majority of general education teachers reported that the factors most inhibiting to successful inclusion were lack of in-service training and lack of time to implement an inclusion program successfully (that is, to collaborate, modify materials, and so on).[24]

One particularly important factor that many inclusion supporters have omitted from their discussions of inclusion acceptance until recently is the nature of the student's disability. Full inclusion implies that students with a wide range of disabilities will be placed in general education settings, and research suggests that teachers' attitudes and expectations about such students vary according to the student's disability. One of the most consistent findings across studies of general education teachers' perceptions of inclusion is that their degree of willingness to include students with disabilities is directly related to the nature and severity of the students' disability. Specifically, general education teachers have expressed more favorable attitudes toward including students with learning disabilities (mild disabilities) and less favorable attitudes toward including students with severe disabilities, mental retardation, or behavioral challenges.[25] McNally and colleagues also found that general education teachers see the severity of disability as an important dimension when assessing their need for additional training and support for working with particular students with disabilities who are included in their classes.[26] Similarly, Scruggs and Mastropieri found that teacher willingness to teach students with disabilities is directly related to the nature and severity of the students' disabilities and to the required amount of additional teacher responsibility.[27]

➜ Teacher willingness to teach students with disabilities is directly related to the nature and severity of the students' disabilities.

Most recently, a small amount of research examined more specifically the attitude of general education teachers toward the inclusion of students with ASD. McGregor and Campbell investigated the training and support provided to general education teachers in Scotland, their resulting attitudes toward inclusion, and their ability to cope in their classrooms with the students labeled autistic.[28] Forty-seven percent favored full inclusion where possible, but 83 percent believed that the degree of severity of autism is more important to consider than the students' academic needs, social needs, and abilities. Further, 78 percent reported that successful inclusion depends on "staff attitudes." Another study conducted in the United Kingdom found teachers reporting that the most important negative factors in working with students with autism in integrated settings were "lack of knowledge about autism, and/or lack of access to consultation and practical advice."[29] Only 5 percent of general education teacher respondents had received training on autism, although 97 percent of the teachers surveyed had included a student with autism in their class. The researchers also found that teachers held many mistaken beliefs about students with autism, for example, that students with ASD have special abilities and do not have learning difficulties. This misunderstanding was attributed to lack of training.

As previously mentioned, the disorders on the autism spectrum are listed in the category of severe disabilities within IDEA. Yet students demonstrate a range of mild to moderate and moderate to severe degrees of the disability.[30] Furthermore, individual students with ASD manifest great variability in strengths and deficits, further compounding the challenge of working with this population.

It appears, therefore, that the attitudes of general education teachers toward particular students are influenced more by the individual student's specific disability and by the degree of the disability than by the teacher's attitude toward inclusion itself.[31] More specifically, as McGregor and Campbell found, the severity of a specific student's disability contributed more than the inclusive education process itself to a general education teacher's attitude toward inclusion and to the willingness of the teacher to include a specific student.[32]

It is not only general educators' attitudes toward students with disabilities that are important; for inclusion to be successful it is also necessary for special education teachers to have positive attitudes. Yet it has been found that special educators' attitudes about inclusion are slightly less positive than those of administrators and general educators. Special education teachers are the ones who are ultimately held responsible for the day-to-day implementation of inclusion, for ensuring that the needs of the students with disabilities are met and that the students are progressing toward their goals in all of their environments, not just in the special education class.[33] Special educators are specifically trained and certified to meet the needs of students with disabilities. They are viewed by administrators and general education teachers as knowledgeable advocates for students with disabilities.[34] They are uniquely positioned to shape schoolwide attitudes toward inclusion. A study by Fox and Yssledyke found that special education teachers are relied on to "sell" inclusion to general education teachers, who lack training and expertise.[35] As the experts, special education teachers are often sought to take responsibility for and to lead the implementation of inclusion reforms.[36] The attitudes of special education teachers are affected by how much support their administrators give to inclusion by allocating funds and resources to the school's inclusion program, especially what the administrators do to protect special education teachers as resources of support and services for the students with disabilities who are being educated in the general education classroom.[37]

In the 1980s and 1990s, researchers also investigated the attitudes of typical students (from elementary school through college) toward their classmates with disabilities. These studies confirmed factors that Fisher and colleagues proposed as contributing to changes in attitudes.[38] Staub and Peck, for example, identified five types of attitude and behavior changes among typical peers resulting from being educated with classmates with disabilities:

- Reduced fear of human differences accompanied by increased comfort
- Growth in social cognition
- Improvement in self-concept
- Development of personal principles
- Warm and caring friendships[39]

Studies conducted with preservice teachers and typical college students found that the factors that contributed most to favorable attitudes toward peers with disabilities were

- The amount of time that students spent with their peers with disabilities[40]
- The type of interactions in which they engaged[41]
- Their observations of the typical behaviors and thoughts of their peers with disabilities[42]

Preservice and Inservice Training on Inclusive Education for Both Special and General Educators

It has been established that because of the increasing frequency with which students with disabilities are being included,[43] it is extremely important for teacher preparation programs to train general education preservice teachers to teach students with disabilities effectively in general education classrooms.[44] Today, unlike as in previous years, general education teachers are being asked to do the following:

> → It is extremely important for teacher preparation programs to train general education preservice teachers to teach students with disabilities effectively in general education classrooms.

- Participate in the IEP process
- Collaborate with many types of special education personnel
- Adapt the curriculum
- Manage a wide range of student behaviors
- Implement specialized behavior intervention plans
- Modify materials for students with disabilities who are included in their classrooms

The training and skill development of both special education and general education teachers for inclusive education must include assessment, curriculum accommodation, instruction, problem solving, collaboration, consultation, and behavior management systems.[45] The training "should place a strong emphasis on theory, practice, and experience in collaborative planning, teaching, and problem-solving processes"[46] while highlighting collaboration, which many consider to be the most important skill for meeting the diverse needs of students.[47] Stanovich and Jordan have also asserted that general and special education teacher preparation programs should be based on current research on the components (such as consultation and collaboration techniques, curriculum modification, and paraeducator assistance) of successful inclusion programs for students with disabilities.[48]

To ensure that their graduates are able to implement these critical instruction, management, and collaboration strategies in an inclusive environment, universities have been focusing on improving their general and special education teacher preparation programs by

- Requiring general education teachers to take a specific course on special education
- Combining special education and general education coursework so that students graduate with dual credentials

- Infusing special education content and curricula into all of the general education courses

- Providing coursework on consultation and collaboration for special educators

- Requiring field experience in both special and general education classrooms[49]

The reality, however, is that many general education teachers graduate from their teacher preparation program having received little or no instruction in working with students with disabilities or in how to include students with diverse needs in their classrooms.[50] In the early 2000s, Wolfe and colleagues surveyed seventy-eight universities across the nation that have teacher preparation programs and found that 60 percent of those responding reported that they required only one course on inclusion and disabilities.[51] The remainder of the universities reported that either information about disabilities and inclusion was embedded in other coursework or no coursework on disabilities and inclusion was required. Further, of the 60 percent of university programs that required coursework on inclusion and disabilities, only 41 percent required any type of field experience in an inclusive setting.

> ➜ Many general education teachers graduate having received little or no instruction in working with students with disabilities or in methods for including students with diverse needs.

Research that I recently conducted with general education teachers in a large urban school district in California found that 47 percent of the participants had received some type of inclusive education training in college and 50 percent had received such training through professional development as part of their job.[52] No respondents reported receiving any training in inclusive education through online courses. The majority of respondents indicated that their inclusive education training covered behavior management (72 percent), curriculum modifications and accommodations (77 percent), and instructional techniques (72 percent). Fewer respondents indicated that they had received training in social interaction skills (53 percent) and language and communication skills (35 percent).

Because teacher preparation programs (both special and general education) have not been able to prepare teachers adequately to include students with special needs successfully, it has fallen to local school districts to provide such training through in-service trainings.[53] Many school communities, however, are not providing such training and support for teachers[54] because of continued federal and state cuts in both general and special education funding, because of increased accountability for student achievement in reading and math, and because of the growing range of responsibilities teachers that need to balance within a six-hour day (after which there is no monetary compensation for hours of work completed).[55]

In order for school districts to provide appropriate professional development opportunities for general and special education teachers in teaching students with disabilities and in inclusive education, significant changes in how schools are organized and in how teachers work are required.[56] McLeskey and Waldron found several principles to be effective when working with schools to create professional development activities to support inclusion programs:[57] these activities must be school-based, they must involve implementation of coaching and other follow-up procedures, they must be collaborative across educational disciplines within a school, and they must provide opportunities for continued growth—that is, they must be embedded in the daily lives of teachers.[58] Weiner developed the following list of approaches to implementing changes in general educators' teaching practices in order to serve all students, including those with disabilities:

- Edifying through experience

- Collaborating with colleagues

- Reflecting on past practices

- Understanding what the best methods are for meeting the needs of students individually[59]

Essentially, the ability of general and special education teachers to work together to solve problems associated with inclusive education has been identified as critical to the ongoing implementation of inclusion.[60] New special education teachers have noted that they did not

> ➡ The ability of general and special education teachers to work together in inclusive education has been identified as critical to the ongoing implementation of inclusion.

receive appropriate training in this area during their preservice education, and they have reported their great need for consultation and collaboration skills in their day-to-day work with general education teachers.[61] General education teachers are being prepared for the challenges that occur with typical students in general education classrooms, and special education teachers are being prepared for the challenges of meeting the needs of students with disabilities in special education classrooms, but these two operating systems can no longer exist separately. General and special education teachers must now be trained as partners and collaborators in the cooperative venture of teaching children with disabilities alongside their typical peers within the general education classroom.

Support of General Educators to Promote Successful Inclusion

Whether preservice training has been minimal (as has been shown to be the case in the majority of colleges) or extensive, surveys have delineated the need that general education teachers have for a variety of ongoing support to help them include students with disabilities in their classrooms. One such survey found the following four most critical support needs:

- Sufficient training
- Observation of other classrooms
- Availability of a team of professionals
- Assistance within the classroom[62]

Another survey of general education teachers found the following to be the best predictors of positive attitudes toward inclusion of students with disabilities:

- Collaborative consultation
- Co-teaching partnerships
- Shared accountability for educational outcomes
- Comprehensive preservice and in-service training
- Administrative support[63]

In all the literature read and in all the surveys reviewed, the strongest emphasis appears to be on collaborative problem solving between general education teachers and consultants (such as special education teachers, inclusion facilitators, and behavior analysts).[64] Collaboration within the inclusive setting has been characterized as a process for providing education to students with disabilities who have specialized needs by involving parents, general and special education teachers, related service providers, and administrators in the planning, implementation, and evaluation of instruction and progress in the general education classroom. Consultation between teachers and other IEP team members is an important process aimed at improving the performance of both the teachers and the students with disabilities, and it is a tool for managing the increased responsibilities associated with inclusive education.

This collaborative and consultative problem-solving relationship between general and special education teachers (as well as among teachers, parents, and administrators) involves sharing expertise, discussing problems and strategies, deciding jointly on intervention and assessment methods, and making decisions based on consensus.[65] This type of collaboration also stands out as one of the most frequently cited and most powerful predictors of positive teacher attitudes toward inclusion.[66] Teachers are more willing to include and accommodate students with disabilities in their classrooms when they perceive that their school fosters a supportive climate and when the culture of the school encourages teaming and collaboration. One study compared the results of school professionals (both general and special education personnel) collaboratively developing inclusion solutions rather than developing the solutions individually.[67] When these professionals addressed problems together, they were able to identify more problems, more antecedents and causes, more objectives, and more intervention plans than when they worked alone. In addition, Hobbs found that the collaboratively written planning outcomes developed by these professionals incorporated a larger number of actions associated with effective inclusive education than those written individually.[68]

The fact that the LRE mandate emphasizes that students with disabilities be included in the general education environment to the maximum extent possible with *appropriate* supplemental supports and services further underscores that supports are required. My own survey of general education teachers in California revealed that the most important factors in their experiences of including students with disabilities are the amount and type of support they received.[69] Seventy-nine percent of the teachers receiving any support

> ➡ My own survey revealed that the most important factor in teachers' experiences including students with disabilities is the amount and type of support they received while including a student with a disability.

reported that the most common support given was ongoing consultation and collaboration, 78 percent reported receiving information and materials on relevant disabilities and inclusion-related topics, and 67.8 percent received paraeducator assistance within the classroom. Nevertheless, general education teachers reported significantly low levels of support in all of the areas assessed for both themselves and the students with disabilities.

Inclusion of Students with ASD

Students with ASD vary greatly in their abilities and disabilities: some are nonverbal or noncommunicative, with accompanying severe cognitive or learning disabilities; others function at a level close to that of their typical peers in the general education classroom; the remainder fall somewhere between these two extremes. Educating students with ASD requires thorough knowledge and understanding of their unique cognitive, social, sensory, communicative, and behavioral deficits.[70] Thus, "without proper training specifically in autism, even well-intentioned professionals

> ➜ Educating students with ASD requires thorough knowledge and understanding of their unique cognitive, social, sensory, communicative, and behavioral deficits.

may generate curriculum models inappropriate for the child with autism and impair the child's ability to develop to his/her fullest potential."[71]

The thought of educating a student with ASD in the general education classroom can therefore be frightening for both the general education teacher and the parents of the student with ASD. Both recognize that working with these students can be unsuccessful if the appropriate educational program is not implemented, supported by the necessary supplemental aides and services, and accompanied by the proper training for the teacher. Simpson and Myles aptly addressed the education of students with ASD, stating that "instructional and management strategies must be explicitly taught to enable educators to be effective with students with autism, followed by modeling and practice in field placements with students with autism."[72] Moreover, staff at the University of North Carolina directly address the inclusion of students with ASD by maintaining that

> inclusion activities are appropriate only when preceded by adequate assessment and pre-placement preparations including appropriate training. Inclusion activities typically need to be supported by professionals trained in autism who can provide assistance and objective evaluation of the appropriateness of the activity.[73]

As a direct result of the 1994 reauthorization of IDEA, when autism became an identified disability, more and more students with ASD are being included in general education classrooms. As mentioned earlier, there are advocates for full inclusion of students with ASD, but there are many more supporters of the position that a continuum of alternative placements needs to be available for students with ASD.[74]

For almost two decades, and especially within the past decade, there has been a concerted effort to investigate specific intervention strategies used in the inclusion of students with ASD. This research has focused on the following topics:

- Antecedent procedures (priming, prompt delivery, pretask sequencing, and picture schedules)[75]
- Delayed contingencies (increasing independence)[76]

- Self-management strategies (reinforcing, evaluating, and monitoring one's own behavior)[77]

- Peer-mediated interventions (peer tutoring, utilizing peer supports, cooperative learning)[78]

- Multicomponent interventions (use of multiple research-based techniques)[79]

- Pivotal response training and naturalistic teaching strategies (incorporating choices, natural reinforcers and consequences, and using modeling and prompting)[80]

Altogether, these studies are a rich source of specific intervention strategies targeting specific skill areas for use with students with ASD in the general education classroom. These studies found, however, that each general education teacher received training in only one technique and were provided ongoing consultation and feedback in their implementation of that technique only, and in only a few of these studies were the general education teachers asked to provide feedback on the success of the technique. No studies were implemented to examine the success of inclusion as a whole.

The research I conducted revealed that 37 percent of all participants had received training in topics related to working with students with ASD. It also revealed that, overall, teachers perceive that there is a fairly high need for all types of training on ASD. The topics that teachers reported needing training in most were as follows:

- ASD in general

- Specific interventions for students with ASD

- Improving the social interaction and play skills of students with ASD

The training topic for which teachers reported the least need was environmental modifications. The additional supports that teachers reported needing most were ongoing consultation and collaboration with special education personnel and paraeducator assistance in the general education classroom.

The support most commonly provided by special education personnel to general education teachers on ASD were ongoing consultation and collaboration (81 percent), paraeducator assistance in the classroom (73 percent), and assistance in modifying and accommodating curriculum (73 percent). The kind of needed support that received the overall lowest ratings was release time for meetings. It is important to note that all of the general education teachers reported that receiving support while including a student with ASD in their classroom was much more needed and useful to them than receiving preservice or ongoing training, although the training provided information they needed to understand the over-

> ➜ General education teachers reported that receiving support while including a student with ASD in their classroom was much more needed and useful than preservice or ongoing training.

all inclusion process and to work with students with ASD. Other literature also states that in order for the inclusion of students with ASD to be successful, it is important to provide educational staff with the following:

- Information on the student's specific disability

- Training and materials on preplacement techniques, on the inclusion process itself, and on methods used to evaluate the environments, the child's ability, and progress within the general education environment

- In-class support for the student and for instructional personnel[81]

A significant gap exists, however, between the intent of the IDEA and actual practice. There is little evidence in the literature that effort is being made to research, develop, and disseminate materials and methods or to design, develop, and provide pre- and in-service training models to close that gap and address these important components of the inclusion process for students with ASD. As Simpson and colleagues concluded:

> Unfortunately, in spite of this trend [of increasing inclusion of students with ASD], few models and procedures have been advanced to facilitate the successful placement and maintenance of learners with ASD in general education classrooms. Thus, teachers, related service professionals, parents, and others are frequently faced with the daunting task of designing inclusion programs for learners with ASD in the absence of clear guidelines and procedural protocol.[82]

Summary

General education teachers are faced daily with the daunting task of including students with diverse and unique needs in their classrooms, even though the majority of such teachers have not been prepared for this task by either preservice or in-service training. Literature has revealed that general education teachers have identified important missing components that are necessary to ameliorate the challenges they face throughout the inclusion process.[83] It is only through training and experience with children with disabilities and with the inclusion process and through ongoing consultation, collaboration, and assistance from in-class special education personnel that general education teachers can successfully include students with special needs in their classrooms. Coupled with this need for training and experience is the special education teacher's need for the support of administrators in allocating funds and resources that will allow them time to provide support to general education teachers and to the students with disabilities who are being included in their classrooms.

Research has also revealed that attitudes are precursors to behavior[84] and that teacher preparation influences the instruction that new teachers subsequently deliver.[85] It follows, then, that a positive attitude toward inclusion among preservice general and special education teachers is one prerequisite to successful inclusion of students with disabilities.

To improve the attitudes of preservice teachers so that they will willingly and successfully include students with disabilities in their classrooms it is important to promote their competency to deliver appropriate interventions and instruction. This training would in turn increase the possibility that the students with disabilities, and specifically the students with ASD, who are included in their classes in the future will attain desired academic, social, and behavioral outcomes. This goal is accomplished through ongoing training and continued support. Likewise, special education teachers need training to facilitate collaborative and consultative problem-solving relationships among the IEP team members, and specifically between themselves and general education teachers. This training will equip special educators with the tools they will need to create, coordinate, and implement successful inclusion programs with their partners, general education teachers.

Findings in Europe have revealed that the needs and attitudes of general education teachers who are including students with ASD in their classrooms are similar to the needs and attitudes identified by research on students with disabilities in general.[86] Because of the unique and complex nature of ASD, the specific needs and attitudes of teachers who are including students with ASD in their schools and classrooms must be more thoroughly researched so that the training needs of special and general education teachers and the support needs of general education teachers can be understood more fully. It is only through additional research that educators in the United States will be able to combine the findings from current research on interventions for students with ASD in general education settings with what research has revealed about the types of training and support that educators need to implement successful inclusion programs for students with ASD.

Examining the Legal Guidelines for Appropriate Placement

3

Parameters for Inclusion of Students with Disabilities

As indicated in Chapter Two, it was through federal legislation in 1975 that inclusive education was established as a mandate for children with disabilities. The least restrictive environment (LRE) provision of the Individuals with Disabilities Education Act (IDEA) states:

> To the maximum extent appropriate, children with disabilities, including children in public or private institutions or other care facilities, are educated with children who are not disabled, and special classes, separate schooling, or other removal of children with disabilities from the regular educational environment occurs only when the nature or severity of the disability of a child is such that education in regular classes with the use of supplementary aids and services cannot be achieved satisfactorily.[1]

In passing this law it was the intent of Congress to make available to each child with a disability the opportunity to be educated with his or her peers in the general education environment. The law also makes clear, however, that for an IEP team to determine that the general education classroom is not the appropriate placement for a child with a disability, adequate evidence to support an alternative placement must be provided.

In the years since the LRE mandate was established, school district personnel and parents have asked difficult questions, such as the following:

- What are appropriate supplementary aids and services?

- What level of severity of a disabling condition prevents a child from being educated in a general education classroom?

- How do we determine if a child is benefiting from being placed in a general education classroom?

- How much time in a general education classroom is the maximum extent appropriate for each child?

- How much money and time should we spend trying to provide supplementary aids and services?

These questions have resulted in much litigation in the courts aimed at accurately defining this statute. Four cases in particular have established "tests" that an IEP team can use to determine if they have followed the intent of the law in the LRE placement of a particular student with ASD. The first case, *Roncker* v. *Walter* (1983), established what is known as

> ➡ Four cases have established "tests" that an IEP team can use to determine if they have followed the intent of the law in the LRE placement of a student with ASD: the portability test, the two-pronged test, the four-factor test, and the three-part test.

the *portability test*. An IEP team must determine whether the services that make a segregated setting more appropriate for a child with a disability can be transported to a nonsegregated setting.[2] If this accommodation can be made, the LRE mandate requires that it be done.

The second case, *Daniel R. R.* v. *State Board of Education* (1989), established what is known as the *two-pronged test*. An IEP team must determine two things:

- Can they satisfactorily educate a child with a disability in the general education classroom using supplementary aids and services?

- If they cannot, how will they mainstream the child into the general education environment to the maximum extent appropriate?

To answer the first question and to be in compliance with the LRE, the IEP team must consider three factors:

- Will the student benefit academically, nonacademically, or both from the general education placement?

- What is the overall benefit to the student of his or her experience in the general education classroom relative to his or her experience in the special education classroom? In other words, the IEP team must balance the benefit of each environment for the child while emphasizing the child's receiving as much education as possible within the general education environment.

- What effect does placement of the student with the disability in the general education classroom have on the other students in the classroom?[3]

If the team decides that they cannot determine whether the child will benefit from placement in the general education classroom, the second question is considered. The team's goal is to mainstream the child into the general education environment to the maximum extent appropriate.

The third case, *Sacramento City Unified School District* v. *Rachel H.* (1994), established what is known as the *four-factor test*. The court relied heavily on the two-pronged test when making its decision about Rachel H.'s educational placement. This case established that an IEP must consider the following four factors:

- The educational benefits of the general education classroom with supplementary aids and services relative to the educational benefits of the special education classroom

- The nonacademic benefits of integrating students with disabilities with students who do not have disabilities

- The effect of the presence of the student with a disability on the general educational environment and on the children in the classroom

- The cost of including the student with a disability in the general education classroom[4]

This test guides an IEP team in determining for a particular student whether each factor supports placement of the student in the general education classroom or in the special education classroom, and then helps the team to answer the general question of whether the child is in fact being educated within the general education environment to the maximum extent appropriate.

The fourth case, *Hartmann* v. *Loudoun County Board of Education* (1997), established what is known as the *three-part test*. The court decided that under the following three conditions mainstreaming is not required by the LRE mandate:

- The child with a disability would not receive educational benefit from being mainstreamed into the general education class.

- Any marginal benefit from mainstreaming would be significantly outweighed by benefits that could feasibly be obtained in a segregated special education class.

- The student with the disability is a disruptive force in the general education classroom setting.[5]

Thus the court decided that the LRE provision established a presumption but not an inflexible mandate.

These tests provide recommendations for an IEP team to follow to determine the appropriate placement for a student with a disability. Together they spell out the legal parameters for inclusion of students with disabilities.

First, a student has a *presumptive right to be educated within the general education setting*.[6] Both the LRE mandate and the litigated court cases have affirmed this important right. Thus the IEP team must make concerted efforts and provide evidence that they have used supplementary aids and services in their attempts to educate the child in a general education classroom. If they are unable to include the student in this manner and it is determined that the child will receive the majority of his or her education in a special education classroom, the team must still mainstream the child into general education classes or activities to the maximum extent possible.

Second, although the IEP team must first consider educating a child with a disability in the general education classroom, they must also ensure that their decision is *individualized* to meet the child's needs.[7] A decision about educational placement is made after the team has determined the child's needs and established appropriate goals and objectives to meet those needs. The team then determines whether all or most of those goals and objectives can be met in the general education classroom.

Third, the IEP team needs to determine *what services are appropriate* to provide for the child with a disability if he or she is to be educated in the general education program.[8] Again the decision about what services are needed precedes the decision about placement. Once the goals and objectives are determined, the team decides what services and what type of educational program the student must have in order to progress toward completion of those goals and objectives. Thus, when the IEP team looks at placement in the general education environment, they must determine whether in this environment the student can benefit both academically and nonacademically from the services he or she needs.

Fourth, if the IEP team determines that the supplementary aids and services that the child needs in order to benefit from his or her education cannot be provided to the child within the general education environment, the team must provide a *continuum of alternative and appropriate educational placements* from which to choose.[9] These placements would include a special education class on the same campus, a special education class on a different school campus, a special education class in a different school district, a private special education school, a home school, and so on.

Fifth, the IEP team must *consider problem behavior* when they are determining appropriate placement for a child with a disability.[10] The team must evaluate whether the student's behaviors detrimentally affect

> ➡ The legal parameters an IEP team must follow when determining appropriate placement for a student with a disability: the student has a presumptive right to be educated within the general education setting, the decision for placement must be individualized to meet the needs of the student, appropriate services must be determined, a continuum of placements must be available, and problem behaviors must be considered.

his or her ability to learn or detrimentally affect the ability of his or her peers to learn. Problem behaviors would include loud noises, destructive actions, oppositional and defiant language, self-injurious actions, aggressive actions, self-stimulatory actions, and so on. The intensity, duration, and frequency of these behaviors determine the effect they have on the student's or peers' learning.

Legal Parameters for Inclusion of Students with ASD

Although all of the legal parameters for including students with disabilities in general within the general education classroom apply to the inclusion specifically of students with ASD, specific litigation over the appropriate placement of students with ASD has been conducted and is worthy of discussion. As discussed in Chapter One, ASD encompasses many unique characteristics. The severity and pervasiveness of the disability within each child results in each child having different needs and needing different educational goals and objectives, educational programs and services, and finally, different placements. Because it was only about thirteen years ago that autism was recognized in the educational realm as a disability, educators have had to learn about and acquire quickly the skills to teach children with ASD in a variety of environments using a variety of intervention and instructional techniques.

Extensive research supports applied behavior analysis (ABA) in particular as the intervention methodology to use with children with ASD.[11] Although ABA teaching techniques can be utilized in a variety of environments, the best environment for early intervention programs and services for such children is often a segregated classroom or home setting because children with ASD need one-to-one instruction in an environment with limited visual and auditory distractions. When children with ASD enter elementary school and later middle and high school, different services, interventions, and environments are needed and available. Further information on interventions for children with ASD is included in subsequent chapters.

The varying needs of children with ASD over the span of their educational careers and the ensuing variety of programs, services, and placements that are available to children with ASD has resulted in much debate between school districts and parents over what is appropriate for these children. Thus, in the past ten years there have been more court cases on appropriate placement for children with ASD than on any other disability.[12] Analysis of these cases shows that most of them address appropriate early intervention (from birth to age five) and programs, services, and placement (such as in an inclusive environment or in a more segregated, restrictive environment). Rulings in these cases fall into four categories in which the LRE mandate was applied to the educational decisions made for children with ASD:

- Potential benefits of an inclusive program
- Readiness for inclusion
- Utilization of an instructional approach in placement
- A full continuum of placement options[13]

> ➜ Categories of rulings on appropriate LRE placement for students with ASD: potential benefits of an inclusive program, readiness for inclusion, untilization of an instructional approach in placement, and a full continuum of placement options

The courts involved in these cases utilized the Roncker portability test, the Daniel R. R. two-pronged test, the Rachel H. four-factor test, and the Hartmann three-part test.

Court decisions on the benefits that a child would receive from an inclusive education program were sought in order to determine whether a particular proposed program would be both academically and nonacademically beneficial, and therefore appropriate. Some decisions were made in favor of a specialized and segregated program, others were made in favor of an inclusive setting for a child with autism. One court ruled that a particular child needed to receive the majority of his education in a segregated special education class in order to get the appropriate academic benefit, but he was also to be included in the general education setting as much as possible.[14] Another court ruled that a particular child with autism must be educated within a general education classroom because in that setting he would experience greater nonacademic benefit and his academic needs could be met through the assistance of a paraeducator.[15]

Some cases addressed a child's academic and social readiness for an inclusive setting. Because children with ASD have such significant skill gaps and so many splinter skills (see Chapter One), it is often difficult to determine what environment will best address most of their needs. One court decided that a particular child with autism was not ready to be placed in a general education classroom because of his distractibility, perseverative behavior, and poor social interaction skills with peers.[16] Another court decided that a set of twins with autism should not be advanced to a general education kindergarten simply because they were the right age because they needed to learn more skills in the special education preschool before moving on to kindergarten.[17] In another case, a court decided that a student with autism and other disabling conditions was ready for placement in an integrated kindergarten that would provide him with appropriate role models and that was preferred over a classroom of children who all had significant delays.[18]

Some courts reviewed whether a particular type of instructional approach needed by a child with autism could be appropriately delivered in the general education environment of a specific school district. In these cases, the court investigated whether the appropriate methodology was available in the district, and if it was not, the court investigated where the child could receive the instruction he needed. One court decided that the need of a particular child with autism for both intensive one-to-one discrete-trial teaching (an ABA method) and an environment with minimal distractions warranted placing the child in the home and not in the proposed integrated preschool (which contained both typical children and children with disabilities).[19] Another court determined that although a private school classroom, a home-based classroom (proposed by the parents), and the public school special education classroom (proposed by the school district) offered the same instructional approach needed by the child, the public school classroom placement offered the child opportunities to interact with typical peers and was thus the appropriate placement.[20] These particular placement decisions took into consideration the Daniel R. R. two-pronged test, which states that if a child is not going to be educated in the general education classroom, he or she will still be mainstreamed to the maximum extent appropriate.

In decisions about whether a full continuum of placement options was available to a child with autism, courts focused on the fact that if the appropriate placement is not available at a particular school, placement in another school district or in a private school in the community must be considered. In two cases, the IEP or the Individualized Family Service Plan (IFSP, for children under age five) team had proposed an alternative placement outside the district for a student with autism.[21] In both cases, an administrator within the district (who was not a member of the IEP or IFSP team) attempted to nullify the decision, saying that his district offered an appropriate placement. Both courts ruled that the administrator was not considering the continuum of placement options that was available to address the child's needs, and both courts upheld the original decisions of the IEP and IFSP teams to place the child in an alternative situation in order to meet the LRE requirements.

Courts also emphasized the need of the teams to consider first a placement with nondisabled peers (general education or integrated), which must always be a part of the continuum of placement options. In one school district, two cases revealed that such a placement was not considered. In one of the cases, a district offered a student only a specialized setting; the court ordered the district to include among the options a placement with nondisabled peers that would serve the student's social and communication needs.[22] In the other case, the court determined that the school district had not considered placing a particular student in a general education classroom with supplementary aides and services.[23]

These various categories of court decisions on the placement of children with ASD have resulted in several recommendations from researchers and practitioners for improving and promoting placements that meet the requirements of the LRE mandate. First, early intervention and elementary school educators need ongoing professional development (in-service) opportunities in order to gain and improve the skills they need to provide appropriate services and instructional methods to children with autism in less restrictive environments. Research has found that new practitioners have difficulty understanding, adapting, and using inclusive environment practices in their work with young children with disabilities.[24] Educators should receive adequate training to ensure that they are competent in applying the instructional techniques that will enable children with autism to develop both academically and nonacademically in inclusive settings.[25] Overall, an emphasis on professional development for educators that focuses on meeting the needs of children with severe disabilities, particularly children with autism, may lessen resistance to inclusion of children with ASD and build the capacity of educational programs to provide appropriate inclusive learning environments for these children.

Second, a child's social and academic readiness for an inclusive education placement needs to be considered.[26] In many situations, the behavioral challenges presented by a child with autism may lead to a more restrictive placement. It is important, however, to balance the services that will help a child address his or her social and academic needs with services that will address the child's behavioral challenges. Federal IDEA regulations clearly state that a child's social and behavioral readiness for an inclusive setting must be considered within the context of providing adequate support. "If the child can appropriately function in the regular classroom with appropriate behavioral supports, strategies, or intervention, placement in a more restrictive environment would be inconsistent with the least restrictive environment provisions."[27] Educators in general education classrooms must therefore facilitate and plan to include appropriate behavioral supports, which may include social skills training, self-monitoring and reinforcement systems, alternative discipline (behavioral intervention) plans, and so on. IEP teams must thus carefully consider a child's readiness for a general education placement not as a criterion for exclusion but rather as a factor in planning the necessary behavioral or academic supports that must be continually monitored to ensure the appropriateness of placement.

Third, school districts need to coordinate and expand their efforts to provide a full continuum of placement options for children with autism, from early childhood intervention through elementary school and beyond.[28] Service coordination among early childhood agencies and school districts is essential in providing seamless, inclusive early childhood education and transition into elementary school. Lack of skills, involvement, communication, time, and funding resources contributes greatly to difficulties in coordinating services.[29] Because of these difficulties, there is often conflict between providers over what services are appropriate and what methods should be used to delivery them to children with disabilities, in particular children with autism. Many early childhood educators report that the LRE requirement is difficult to fulfill because their school district does not provide preschool services for typical children and therefore there is no general education environment in which to mainstream a child with a disability.[30]

> ➔ Recommendations for improving and providing appropriate placement of students with ASD in order to meet the LRE mandate: educators must receive professional development to help them provide appropriate services and instruction, IEP teams must consider children's social and academic readiness for inclusive education placement, and school districts must provide a full continuum of placement options.

Summary

Meeting the needs of children with disabilities, in particular those with autism, in an inclusive environment, as expressed by the federal government in the IDEA (law) and in the U.S. Court of Appeals (litigation) continues to be a priority. By using the tests developed in the courts and by increasing professional development opportunities, differential instructions, behavioral supports, and coordinated efforts to expand the capacity and feasibility of inclusive programs, it may be possible to implement appropriate services and enhance the quality of services provided to children with autism in inclusive environments.

Handout 3.1 provides a list of user-friendly guidelines for IEP teams to use to determine the appropriate placement of a child with autism. This one-page document summarizes all of the information presented in this chapter. It can be used as a measuring tool for establishing and implementing an inclusion program for students with ASD.

> ☞ Use Handout 3.1: Legal Guidelines for Appropriate Placement of Students with ASD in the General Education Classroom

☞ Handout 3.1. Legal Guidelines for Appropriate Placement of Students with ASD in the General Education Classroom

Appropriate Instructional Methods and Supports for General Education Classrooms

- Supplementary aides and services to be provided to help the student benefit from instruction within a general education placement may include but are not limited to the following:
  - Assistance from a paraeducator who has received appropriate training on and had experience with students with ASD, with inclusion, and with language intervention techniques
  - A behavior intervention plan
  - Different or modified instruction materials, additional time to complete tasks, alternative communication devices, visual supports, and so on
- Training and supports to help the general education teacher provide effective instruction to the student may include but are not limited to the following:
  - Information on the disabilities of ASD, and consultation and collaboration with special education staff on instruction techniques, behavior intervention strategies, and curriculum modifications and accommodations

Readiness for the General Education Classroom

- The student has acquired and continues to acquire many of the necessary skills (such as attending to the teacher, sitting for longer periods of time, and using some kind of communication system) that are needed to participate in and receive instruction within the general education classroom.
- The student displays increasing ability to generalize the use of his skills within the general education classroom without continuous prompting from adults.
- The student does not consistently need one-to-one instruction from the teacher or paraeducator in order to follow instructions and participate in class assignments and activities.

Appropriate Participation in the General Education Classroom

- The student contributes to a safe learning environment for all students by not consistently hitting, biting, or kicking people; throwing objects; engaging in self-injurious behavior; or destroying school property.
- The student does not hinder the successful delivery of instruction by the teacher and receipt of instruction by the other students by consistently making loud noises, running around, talking incessantly, or handling objects inappropriately within the classroom.

Benefits from Participation and Education in the General Education Classroom

- *Social*: The student uses a functional form of communication, shows awareness of peers, imitates actions of adults and peers, responds to interactions initiated by peers, shows attempts to initiate interaction, seeks social reinforcement for appropriate display of behavior and completion of tasks, and so on.
- *Academic*: The student participates in academic activities at increasingly independent levels (requiring less assistance or modifications over time), progresses toward goals and objectives, demonstrates acquisition of new skills, displays generalization of known skills, attends to group instructions, and so on.
- *Inclusive*: The student is included and accepted as a full member of the classroom, participates in all of the same activities as other students according to his ability, is spoken to by and interacts directly with the teacher and peers.

PART II

Considerations Before Creating an Inclusion Program

Determining Least Restrictive Environment Services and Placement for Students with ASD

4

ONE of the most difficult things for parents and educators of a child with ASD to do is to determine the appropriate educational placement for the child, a placement that best addresses the child's specific needs. Autism spectrum disorders manifest so uniquely in each child who has the disability that even after the IEP team develops goals and objectives and determines appropriate instructional services, an appropriate placement to address those goals and implement those services can still be elusive. Further complicating this placement decision is the fact that many children with ASD have average to above average cognitive abilities yet demonstrate great delays and challenges in language, play, and social and behavioral skills. The team then struggles with the challenge and desire to meet the child's academic needs in the general education classroom while providing specialized services and interventions in the special education classroom to address his nonacademic needs. The opposite situation might also exist, in which a child with ASD whose cognitive abilities are below average needs the specialized academic instruction of a special education classroom but would also benefit from the social interaction opportunities available with typical children in the general education classroom. As difficult as it is to do so, in the end the IEP team must make a decision about the child's placement.

There are specific steps that a team can take to facilitate making an informed and accurate decision The first step is the completion by the team of the profile of student ASD characteristics that was explained and provided in Chapter One (see Form 1.1: ASD Characteristics: Student Profile). This form captures the skills and deficits displayed by a particular child in each of nine skill areas described in Chapter One using information gathered from all those who are working with the child. This information is compiled into one form and distributed to each member of the team; it is then reviewed to gain an overall picture of the child's level of functioning.

In the second step the team meets to review together all of the characteristics of the student in order to determine his strengths and prioritize his problem behaviors and needs. The team methodically reviews and discusses each of the nine skill areas by answering the following five questions:

Questions Used in Analysis of Student Characteristics

- What are the child's greatest strengths and how does the child use these and other skills to overcome his deficits?
- What motivates the student?
- How independent is the student in the school environment?
- What are the predominant problem behaviors displayed by the student?
- What are the greatest needs affecting the student's ability to function appropriately, learn new skills, and participate independently in his environment?

What are the child's greatest strengths and how does the child use these and other skills to overcome his deficits? Sometimes these questions result in overlapping answers. The team should evaluate all of the skills listed in all of the skill areas and decide which skills are the child's greatest strengths. At the same time the team needs to consider which skills they have seen the child use across environments and with different people to compensate for his lack of skills in other areas.

What motivates the student? The team must consider what motivates the child when he or she is alone and free to choose an object or activity, and what motivates the child to do something that a teacher or parent requests. An important aspect of educating a child with ASD and intervening in his or her problem behaviors is the child's motivation: What is the child always trying to gain access to or avoid?

How independent is the student in the school environment? The team needs to evaluate how much assistance the student needs from adults to perform the skills he currently displays, as well as how much assistance the student needs to behave appropriately within the school environment.

What are the predominant problem behaviors displayed by the student? Problem behaviors typically are a function of the deficits the student displays in each skill domain. Determining the reasons for such behaviors may require relating the child's behavior skill deficits to the deficits in the other skill areas and analyzing whether there is a relationship between each skill deficit and the problem behaviors. The team should consider how the problem behaviors impede the student's learning and how they affect the learning of peers and the safety of others in the education environment. If a functional behavior assessment has previously been performed and a behavior intervention plan has been written, the information in the assessment and plan is used during this decision process.

What are the greatest needs affecting the student's ability to function appropriately, learn new skills, and participate independently in his environment? The team must review all of the skill deficits across all of the skill areas and decide which are the top two greatest needs at this point in time. The team needs to determine whether significant changes would be accomplished in the student's ability to function in his environment and to consider the effect on the student's overall quality of life if he were to gain the skills needed in these high-priority areas. To assist the IEP team, this information can be recorded and summarized at the top of the LRE Services and Placement Determination form provided at the end of this chapter (Form. 4.1).

> ✎ Use Form 4.1: LRE Services and Placement Determination

In the third step, after all of this information has been collected, the team establishes goals and objectives to address the student's primary needs and problem behaviors while taking into account his unique strengths and motivating objects and activities. It is important for goals and objectives to be measurable (to gather data that can be collected), attainable (the student can realistically achieve the goal) and observable (the student can be seen performing the skill). Many goals and objectives may need to be revised if they are to be addressed in the general education classroom. That is, the team needs to take the time to ensure that all goals and objectives are appropriately written for the placement in which they will be addressed. The following example illustrates a goal and subsequent objectives for a student with ASD who will be included in a first grade general education classroom for the reading period.

> *Annual Goal*: By [date], given thirty minutes to participate in the second grade general education classroom's reading class, the student will independently engage in the specified reading activities while sitting on the carpeted floor in the reading area for at least fifteen minutes of the thirty-minute period in four out of five days as measured by the teacher-charted records.
>
> *Short-Term Objective*: By [date], given that the teacher or a peer is reading a book out loud, the student will look at and turn pages of the same book with no prompting for at least five minutes on four out of five days as measured by teacher-charted records.
>
> *Short-Term Objective*: By [date], when given two audiotapes with picture cues, the student will independently select between the two tapes and listen to the tape for up to ten minutes on four out of five days as measured by teacher-charted records.

Short-Term Objective: By [date], given the opportunity to select a free-reading book, the student will do so without interrupting his peers and will look at the book appropriately for ten minutes on four out of five days as measured by teacher-charted records.

In the fourth step, the team will use the goals and objectives of both the IEP and the LRE Services and Placement Determination form to determine and record the interventions and services that are appropriate for meeting the goals and objectives based on the student's primary needs and behaviors. To establish these interventions and services, the IEP team needs to consider the unique skills and deficits displayed by a student with ASD. As the team completes the LRE Services and Placement Determination form, they may need some guidance on the different methods that can address the child's primary needs and problem behaviors in the general education classroom or in another LRE placement. Following is a brief description of the questions and intervention and service considerations relevant to each skill domain listed and described in the ASD Characteristics: Student Profile form provided in Chapter One. More details on specific interventions are provided in subsequent chapters.

Cognitive Abilities

Understandably, the cognitive abilities of a student with ASD directly affect his or her ability to receive academic benefit from being educated in the general education classroom. If the student's cognitive abilities are below average, the team must evaluate whether he or she is able to participate in the academic activities of the general education classroom or would benefit more from specialized academic instruction in a special education setting. Because the team's first consideration is the general education classroom, they need to determine which available types of curriculum accommodations (such as modifications to classwork and alternative grading) and other services (such as paraeducator assistance) the student might need in order to participate in the class at the most independent level possible while making progress and coming to need less support over time. It is also important to remember that a student with below-average cognitive functioning eventually plateaus the learning of new skills and the application of previously acquired skills. Throughout the student's school career, his or her inclusion in the general education classroom for the sake of nonacademic benefit needs to be balanced with the need to learn functional living skills that will enable him or her to operate as independently as possible in his or her community.

> ➜ Inclusion in the general education classroom for the sake of nonacademic benefit needs to be balanced with the need to learn functional living skills.

If the student's cognitive abilities are average to above average, the team needs to evaluate the student's current level of academic performance relative to the grade level in which he would be included. It can then be determined whether special instructional techniques and accommodations are needed to help that student participate in class activities. Many students' academic skills may be at or above grade level, but because they lack the ability to attend to a teacher in a large group, sit for long periods of time, or complete an activity within the time allocated in the general education classroom, accommodations are needed to help them participate and progress in the class's academic activities. There are also students with ASD who have average to above-average cognitive abilities but have been diagnosed with a specific learning disability in reading, math, written language, or auditory processing, to name a few. To address that specific learning challenge, these students may need to be provided services similar to those provided to children with mild learning disabilities (such as being pulled out of the classroom to a resource room for special instruction).

Whether a child has average or below-average cognitive abilities, the IEP team needs to reconsider each year whether the academic focus in a particular grade coincides with the child's goals and objectives. At each successive grade level the academic material becomes increasingly abstract. For many children with ASD the transition from concrete concepts in grades K through 2 to more abstract concepts in grade 3 and beyond can be quite difficult and cause a child to fall behind his or her peers.

Learning Abilities

As discussed in Chapter One, the unique learning characteristics of children with ASD can greatly affect their ability to learn and function in a typical classroom environment, specifically the general education classroom. The team needs to consider four main aspects of learning for children with ASD:

- How the child learns new skills (which instructional strategies must be used)

- How independently the child learns new skills

- How well the child uses the skill he has learned (generalization)

- What motivates the child to participate in learning activities

Many children with ASD need to be provided specialized instruction (such as discrete-trial teaching) in a segregated setting using a one-to-one teacher-to-student ratio with a highly trained special educator in order to learn new skills. Such a setting provides the intensity, structure, task analysis, low level of distraction, and high level of adult attention that the student needs to be motivated to attend appropriately to the stimuli presented and respond to the adult intervention. Thus, early intervention with children with ASD is extremely important because it can take many years for a particular child *to learn how to learn* before he or she can begin to gain the skills needed to function in a classroom and in the community. The IEP team needs to consider whether a particular child needs this highly intense and structured teaching method and environment in order to learn new skills; if so, the general education classroom may not yet be appropriate for this child.

One of the most important aspects of learning is the ability of the student to learn new skills with the least amount of individualized assistance as possible (that is, with a minimum of additional visual, verbal, or physical prompts or curriculum or environmental accommodations). Most students with ASD begin their experience in the general education classroom with many accommodations and modifications. These supports are important and necessary for such children to learn to function in that environment. Over time, however, their ability to learn independently is a crucial indicator of their learning abilities in general and of their possible future success in a general education classroom. Tracking the progress of a student's ability to learn more independently entails monitoring the following elements:

- The types and amounts of prompts provided during the teaching of different types of skills

- How quickly prompts are able to be faded from use during teaching

- If and how quickly a student is able to learn in increasingly larger groups

- If and how quickly a student is able to generalize the skills learned

As a student's ability to learn independently increases, he is learning to learn and is thus able to learn more quickly and more typically. If a student is not becoming more independent in his or her learning over time, then inclusion (learning) in a general education classroom may not be the appropriate placement.

A child's ability to use the skills he has learned is directly related to how the child learns new skills. The IEP team needs to consider the student's ability to generalize skills that he or she has learned with specific instructors in specific environments. If the materials are different, if peers or other adults are present, if the room is different, if the instructions are provided with different words, or if the reinforcers are different or not presented in the same manner, is the child still able to use the skills he has learned? If he has difficulty generalizing skills he has learned (and thus has trouble increasing his independence), his ability to participate in general education classroom activities is greatly impeded, which typically means he needs small-group or one-to-one instruction, and that he needs skills to be broken down and taught in smaller increments in order to learn them. The large teacher-to-student ratio and the greater quantity of instruction provided at one time to all the students in a general education classroom thus makes it difficult for this student to learn new skills and use acquired skills in this environment.

It can be difficult to find ways to motivate the child with ASD to participate in activities or learn new skills in the general education classroom, because many students with ASD often are not motivated by the same things that motivate typical children, such as age-appropriate toys, items, or activities, and they also are not socially or intrinsically motivated by such things as wanting to please the teacher and receive praise for appropriate behavior or for doing a good job, by finding satisfaction in the challenge of a difficult task or in completing a task, in enjoying learning new things, in being able to wait till the end of the day or week for reinforcement, and so on. Some students with ASD may initially need an alternate and more frequent reinforcement system that utilizes visual tokens to maintain their motivation throughout a task or activity and provides a tangible reinforcer that interests them. Thus, it is important to consider how a particular student is motivated.

Overall, it is a child's cognitive and learning abilities that will have the greatest effect on the services and interventions he needs and on his subsequent educational placement. The IEP team needs to monitor and assess the child's progress carefully

> ➔ It is a child's cognitive and learning abilities that will have the greatest effect on the services he needs and on his educational placement.

because over time the child's needs may need to be addressed in different environments than the environment in which they are currently being addressed. Around age six or seven, cognitive and achievement testing are often beneficial in assisting the IEP team in understanding a child's abilities and deficits and in planning for educational interventions and placement.

Social Interaction Skills

Because social skills are so difficult to teach and because most students with ASD display a significant delay in development of social skills, this skill area can be particularly difficult to address in any placement, whether special or general education. The IEP team needs to consider the difference between the interactions the student has with adults and those he or she has with same-age peers. Typically children with ASD interact more frequently and in a variety of ways with adults before they use the same skills with their peers, because many children with ASD are educated in early childhood programs through instructional strategies involving one-to-one teacher-student interactions. This pattern can cause difficulties in the general education classroom because the large student-to-teacher ratio in such classrooms will allow the student to have very little one-to-one interaction with the teacher. Also, children with ASD are often more comfortable interacting with adults because adults are more accommodating to their social awkwardness and will continue to show interest in and maintain a game or conversation with the child even though the adult may not actually be interested in what the child is talking about or doing. Peers will more quickly discontinue interaction with a child with ASD because to them that child will be "different," because they will not understand that child's humor or find the same things to be funny, because they will not be interested in that child, or because they will not want to play what that child wants to play.

The IEP team will need to evaluate how aware the student with ASD is of his or her peers. Does he watch his peers as they play and work? Does he look to his peers for clues about what to do? Does he attempt to initiate interactions with his peers to get something he wants? Some students with ASD are very interested in their peers and initiate interaction frequently, but they may not initiate that interaction appropriately or maintain appropriate interaction skills, or they may not want to discuss things or play with toys and

> ➡ Some students with ASD are very interested in their peers and initiate interaction frequently while others act as though their peers are not present.

games in which they are interested. Other students with ASD act as though their peers are not present. Regardless of the environment in which the IEP team places a child, the IEP team will need to consider what services they will need to provide in order to teach that child new social interaction skills and then promote and facilitate the child's social skill interactions with peers. These services could include pulling the child out of the classroom for a social skills group with typical peers or with a trained adult facilitating social interaction and play with peers during specific ongoing interactive activities.

It is also important to note that many children with ASD are highly motivated to be in the general education classroom because they are socially motivated to be with their same-age typical peers. Many problem behaviors exhibited by children with ASD disappear when they are in a general education classroom because they want to stay there but they are soon pulled out when they are disruptive or uncooperative.

Play Skills

Although social skills and play skills are closely related, a particular child may be significantly better in one skill area than in the other. One child may play well with toys but socially isolate himself from his peers whereas another child may attempt to interact frequently with adults and peers but be unable to engage in appropriate independent or interactive play skills. It is therefore important to note whether a child is able to engage in play with toys and games as they are designed to be played with, and to note how much and how well he or she engages in independent and interactive play. Preschool and kindergarten are excellent times to implement interventions for teaching and developing appropriate play skills. During these years a lot of time is allocated to free-choice play, which provides excellent opportunities for educators to facilitate appropriate play with toys and games and for children with ASD to engage in peer play with one or two typical peers. Peers are also often more tolerant and accepting of others' differences during these early years.

> ➔ It is important to note whether a child is able to engage in play with toys and games as they are designed to be played with, and to note how much and how well he or she engages in independent and interactive play.

The IEP team should also notice whether the child engages in particular self-stimulatory behaviors (such as hand flapping, making noises, rocking, and so on) when he or she is left alone for periods that are not structured or adult directed. If a student engages in such behaviors repetitively when he is unengaged, the IEP team will need to plan services and accommodations that will help replace those self-stimulatory behaviors by engaging the student instead in appropriate leisure and play activities. Because the child does inherently gain enjoyment from playing with a particular toy or a certain game, he or she is initially given tangible reinforcement for engaging in appropriate play and not engaging in self-stimulatory behaviors for certain periods. It is important to choose replacement play skills and behaviors that match the function of the self-stimulatory behaviors.

Communication Skills

For young children with autism or PDD-NOS, communication skills are often the primary area of need. These children typically display significant delay in talking and may interact with people only to use them as tools to get what the child wants. Lack of functional communication skills can elicit severe problem behaviors such as yelling, screaming, crying, tantrums, aggression toward others, self-injurious behavior, and destruction of property. Children engage in such behaviors when they are frustrated over not being able to communicate effectively what they want to communicate, such as when something hurts, when they are hungry or thirsty, or when they do not want something.

If a child does not have a functional communication system in place when the IEP team is attempting to determine placement for the child, the need for such a system should be identified as *the* primary need for the child. The child's goals and objectives, the services he receives, the intervention program he utilizes, and the placement he needs to support this priority should all be focused on and tailored to meet this functional communication need. The team needs to consult with language and communication development specialists to determine which communication system would be acquired most easily by the child. Although the goal is for the child eventually to talk, sometimes a system that uses sign language or pictures or an electronic output device may be needed initially.

> ➜ If a child does not have a functional communication system in place when the IEP team is attempting to determine placement, the need for such a system should be identified as *the* primary need for the child.

For children with ASD who use only one- or two-word phrases or whose speaking skills have not developed typically, it is important to attend to articulation, prosody, pace, and volume, and to their ease or difficulty with which others understand what they are saying. This communication difficulty greatly affects these children's social interaction skills with peers, who will not try as hard as adults to understand or continue interacting with a child with ASD who is not easily understood and who may also not have good eye-contact skills. It is also important for educators to attend to the types of words a student with ASD uses, and to determine whether those words are age appropriate, whether they mean what the child intends them to mean, and whether they are in the correct order within the sentence. A child with ASD may display difficulty with all of these skills, and if interventions are not implemented to change or improve these deficits, the child's ability to communicate and interact with his teachers, family, and peers appropriately and successfully, as well as his or her ability to learn and use new skills, will be greatly affected.

Adaptive Behavior Skills

Self-care (or self-help) skills are crucial to a student's ability to participate in activities in the general education environment as independently as possible. Toileting skills in particular are important for young children with ASD. Many preschools for children with disabilities will tolerate changing diapers and even assisting parents in teaching the child to use a toilet, but once the child enters a general education classroom in elementary school, he needs to be using the bathroom and toilet independently.

The teaching of adaptive behavior skills (such as eating, sleeping, dressing, bathing and personal hygiene and toileting) is largely up to parents because some of these skills (such as dressing, sleeping, and bathing) are used only at home and are focused on at an early age, often before a child enters school. If the child is in an early childhood intervention program, the teachers and parents need to maintain careful communication and to collect and share data on the child's progress in acquiring these skills to be sure that they are using the same interventions.

> ➜ The teaching of adaptive behavior skills is largely up to parents because some of these skills are used only at home and are focused on at an early age, often before a child enters school.

For children who are older and who have acquired the basic self-care skills, it is important to continue to focus on the subtle self-care skills of personal hygiene (body odor, breath odor, and cleanliness of hair, body, and clothes), hair and clothing style (age and fashion appropriateness), and table manners so that they are polite and do not cause others discomfort by their eating habits and so on. These more refined adaptive behavior skills will make a major difference for children in the general education environment, especially those who want to interact successfully with their peers and make friends.

Behavior Characteristics

Behavior characteristics are particularly crucial for the team to consider when determining whether placement in a general education classroom is appropriate. First, there are many *classroom behavior skills* that all children need to have in order to function appropriately and learn within the general education classroom. These behavior characteristics can also be called *learning readiness skills* and they include but are not limited to the student's ability to do the following:

- Sit appropriately for up to twenty minutes
- Wait for reinforcement or in a line or to be called on by the teacher
- Share toys
- Choose from a variety of activities
- Attend to a teacher in a group setting

These and other classroom readiness skills help students greatly to be included in the general education environment for extended periods and to learn in that environment. Although they are not mandatory for entry into a general education class, they are skills that are expected and will eventually be necessary. These skills are listed, described, and discussed further in Chapter Eight.

Second, there are many inappropriate classroom behaviors that prevent a student from being included in the general education environment, such as making frequent or loud noises; engaging in excessive talking, walking, or running around the classroom; hitting others; engaging in frequent physical or verbal self-stimulatory activities; or displaying self-injurious behaviors. If any of these problem behaviors occur with such a frequency and to such a degree that they disrupt the classroom, this particular skill deficit needs to be one of the primary needs addressed in the IEP goals and services. It is important that a student with ASD learn appropriate classroom behavior skills so that he or she can ultimately integrate into the general education class.

> ➜ It is important that a student with ASD learn appropriate classroom behavior skills so that he or she can ultimately integrate into the general education class.

A functional behavior assessment (FBA) and resulting behavior intervention plan (BIP) may also need to be developed or updated. The FBA and BIP enable the IEP team to identify the functions of each problem behavior, suggest appropriate replacement behaviors, and offer methods for decreasing the problem behavior. The team needs to be sure that the BIP employs appropriate supports for positive behavior that can be implemented in the LRE appropriate for the child. Many children with ASD can be included in the general education classroom when a BIP is implemented. More specific methods for implementing a BIP within the general education classroom are provided in subsequent chapters.

Motor Skills

The motor skill deficits that children with ASD exhibit affect their ability to participate in many common, daily classroom activities. A particular child often exhibits specific (rather than global) gross or fine motor difficulties, which may be underlying reasons for some of their problem behaviors. One particular and fre-

> ➜ If motor difficulties are preventing a child from functioning appropriately in the educational environment, the IEP team should consider obtaining an occupational therapy or physical therapy evaluation.

quently occurring motor deficit for many children with ASD, and especially for children with Asperger's syndrome, is significant fine motor difficulties with writing. Such children may write all over the paper with apparent disregard to the lines provided, and the letters and words can all be different sizes and illegible. The child may either take a long time to write something or not take the time to write it carefully. Many behaviors are the result of a child's despair over not being able to write or draw something properly or over how quickly he or she becomes fatigued when given a particular writing activity or assignment and therefore cannot complete it within the time allocated. Such behavior may at first be attributed to the child's being off-task or inattentive rather than physically fatigued and frustrated. Many children with ASD benefit greatly from being able to use a word processor to complete writing assignments.

Other gross motor difficulties may be evident when a child is playing with toys or on the playground. A child may not have the coordination to throw or kick a ball, climb the play equipment, or use both hands to build with blocks or Legos. The child's frustration over being unable to perform such play activities at which other children are successful may result in the inability to play with age-appropriate games or toys or to socially interact with their peers, and thus lead to problem behaviors. If motor difficulties are preventing a child from learning or functioning appropriately in his or her environment, the IEP team should consider obtaining an occupational therapy or physical therapy evaluation with recommendations for ongoing intervention services.

Sensory Sensitivities

The extensive array of sensory sensitivities that can possibly affect a child with ASD, and the resulting comprehensive influence of these sensitivities, can be daunting to understand and address effectively. An IEP team needs to take into account a child's particular sensitivities and determine how they might interfere with the child's ability to pay attention to the teacher, interact with others, participate in activities, or remain on task. Examples of sensory inputs to which children with ASD might have sensitivities include the following:

- Noises inside and outside the classroom
- Type of lights used in the classroom
- Talking in the classroom
- Location of the child's desk in the classroom
- The type of clothes worn by the child

There are many accommodations that an IEP team may make to help a particular child deal with the various auditory and visual distractions. An occupational therapist who has been trained in sensory integration techniques (physical intervention strategies used to assist students with hyper- or hyposensitivity) can be a valuable resource to the team as they evaluate and determine appropriate accommodations for a particular child.

Once the team has determined which interventions and services can address a child's primary needs and resulting goals and objectives, it is time for the fifth and final step: determining the appropriate placement for the child. It is a difficult process to collate all the information gathered and decide what types of instruction and curricula are needed. These data, along with the necessary modifications and accommodations that take into account the child's current learning abilities, social and play skills, motor skills, sensory sensitivities, adaptive behavior skills, and problem behaviors, are essential to the determination of effective placement. The team needs to complete the LRE Services and Placement Determination form by filling in the placement that best meets the child's needs and provides the best services, and then decide which placement (that is location or locations) is best overall.

Occasionally, a further complication in this step is the parents' strong desire to have their child attend the neighborhood school. Although this school would be the first LRE consideration, it may not offer the supports and services that children with ASD typically need. The parents may want this placement because the child's siblings attend this school, because it is convenient to drive or walk to, or because they do not want their child to ride a bus (which is difficult due to his behaviors, communication difficulties, or both). They may also want their child to be able to make friends in his neighborhood. These parents need to be informed of the factors that must be considered first before their child can be placed in the neighborhood school. These considerations would include whether special education personnel who have experience working with students with ASD are available on the site to provide support to the general education teacher and to the student with ASD, and what experience the administration and the general education teachers have and how willing they are to accept students with relatively severe disabilities into an inclusive placement. Although it might appear that placing a child in his neighborhood school would be the LRE placement, the resources that are or are not available at the school to meet the child's individual needs would be the determining factor.

The word *placement* may be misleading when a team attempts to determine in what classroom a student will receive his education. It might sometimes mean one location at which services can best be provided to meet the student's primary needs. It might also mean different locations where the child might go throughout the day to receive instruction and participate in various activities. The child might spend one portion of the day in a general education classroom to address his grade-level math abilities or have the opportunity to interact with typical children who are the appropriate models for language and play. Another portion of the day might be spent in a resource room or self-contained special education classroom where he would receive the specialized instruction he needs to learn how to read, develop his writing skills, participate socially appropriately, or use language in a manner commensurate with the language of his peers. At specific times on other days the child might remain in the classroom and receive "push-in" services; for example, a speech and language therapist or an occupational therapist might work with the child on a certain activity in order to provide the child with assistance and instruction in the context of a common and ongoing activity. Of course some children with ASD are able to spend their entire day in the general education classroom and receive their instruction along with their typical peers.

Although an IEP team might consider a variety of locations for a child's placement, and although such consideration might mean that the child would go to different classrooms and work with different service providers, it is important also to consider how changing locations throughout the day will affect the child. Sometimes the disruption of changing classes and teachers can cause difficulty for the child with ASD and detract from the benefit the child would receive from instruction in the various locations. It is also important to consider that the more people there are who are working with the child throughout the day, the more probable it is that the interventions and services will not be delivered with accuracy and consistency and in accordance with what was determined in the IEP. Although it is important for a child to learn and demonstrate skills with different instructors and in different environments, it is also important to remember that ASD affects the child's ability to learn and generalize across instructors and environments.

Summary

Overall, the IEP team must remember that the most important placement considerations should be the child's top priorities in needs and skill deficits. These priorities may mean that sometimes other needs cannot be addressed until the child's higher needs have been met. For example, if a child does not have a functional communication system for expressing his needs, it is more important that the placement considerations center on that specific need rather than on making sure that the child has access to typical peers to learn appropriate social interaction skills. It is possible that both of these needs could be addressed in the same placement, or that part of the child's work in developing communication skills is to generalize those skills with typical peers.

From this point on I will provide information and methods for developing a successful inclusion program, and considerations and suggestions for how to address a child's skill abilities and deficits within the general education environment. All of the information already provided is designed to assist the team in deciding whether inclusion in a general education classroom is appropriate for a particular child with ASD. It is my firm belief that placement in a general education class is one of many options on a continuum that should be available to all children with ASD.

Student: _____ Date: _____

Form 4.1. LRE Services and Placement Determination

Main strengths: _____

Important motivators: _____

Independence hindrances:

Difficulty: _____ Level and type of assistance: _____

Difficulty: _____ Level and type of assistance: _____

Difficulty: _____ Level and type of assistance: _____

Significant problem behaviors:

Behavior: _____ Intervention: _____

Behavior: _____ Intervention: _____

Behavior: _____ Intervention: _____

Needs	Intervention and Services	Placement
Primary need:		
Secondary need:		
Other important needs:		

Designing an Appropriate Inclusive Education Program

5

FOR an IEP team to create an effective and successful inclusive education program for a particular child with ASD, major inclusive education components need to be in place schoolwide. This chapter discusses these components. The implementation of an inclusive education model, like the implementation of any schoolwide model, requires that foundational ideas and viewpoints be accepted by administrators, educators, school personnel, and parents. It is important for readers to understand that the inclusive education program model for children with ASD provided in this book is based on the belief that the best inclusive education model provides a *continuum* of placement and service options; inclusion is not simply enrollment in the general education classroom. Although this book does focus on an education model for students with ASD within the general education classroom, the underlying belief that a continuum of services and placement options should be provided applies to all students with disabilities, and

> ➔ The inclusive education program model for children with ASD provided in this book is based on the belief that the best inclusive education model provides a *continuum* of placement and service options.

the components of this model apply to all inclusive education models implemented within a school.

To begin developing an appropriate and effective inclusive education program for students with ASD, the school's administration, its teaching staff, and its parents will need to adopt the following underlying, proactive assumptions that will directly affect the success of the program:

- Students with ASD and their typical peers benefit greatly from planned interaction with each other in a general education setting.

- Change needs to occur in the traditional structure of the school environment and in the delivery of special education services.

- Development and implementation of an inclusive education program requires a collaborative team approach.

Given these assumptions, a school needs to develop a team to plan, aide in the implementation of, and follow the implementation process of the inclusive education program for students with ASD through all of its stages, including evaluation of the program over time. It must also learn to adjust the program according to the needs of the administration, staff, students, and parents.

As this team begins its planning process, it must understand *what inclusion is* and *what it is not*. Following is a list of, first, factors that encourage and, second, factors that discourage effective inclusion of students with ASD in the general education environment.

Factors That Encourage Effective Inclusive Education for Students with ASD

- All students in a school building are included and considered in the planning and problem-solving process.

- Every attempt is made to include students with ASD in their neighborhood school.

- All students are accepted as full members of their classroom, school, and community.

- Appropriate supports are provided to students with ASD within the general education classroom.

- Appropriate supports and training are provided to general education teaching staff.

- Services provided and placement decisions for students with ASD are based on their individual needs.

- Implementation of the inclusive education program involves the input and cooperation of all staff and administration, as well as parents.

- Time is allocated for planning and problem solving among administration and special and general education staff.

- Special education teachers and their resources are protected and maintained for students with ASD even though they are being utilized within the general education classroom.

Factors That Discourage Effective Inclusion for Students with ASD

- Only certain general education teachers include students with ASD in their classrooms.

- Special education services within a school are being reduced because more students are being included in the general education classrooms.

- Students with ASD are considered the responsibility of the special education teacher and not members of the general education class.

- Special education teachers become assistants in the general education classrooms.

- Academic expectations for typical students have decreased.

- Students with ASD are isolated in a certain location in the general education classroom and receive separate instruction from a special education teacher or paraprofessional.

- Students with ASD are "dumped" in the general education classroom without prior planning and appropriate supports.

- Inclusion of students with ASD in the general education classroom is viewed as a cost-saving measure for special education.

As discussed previously in Chapter Two, the attitudes of special and general education teachers greatly affect the success of inclusion. It is therefore crucial that any team

> ☞ Use Handout 5.1: Benefits of Inclusion of Children with Autism Spectrum Disorder

implementing an inclusive education program for students with ASD be cognizant of the attitudes, beliefs, and viewpoints currently held by the administration and teaching staff at their school. If the current general attitude toward inclusion of students with disabilities, including those with ASD, is not positive, it is important that time be allocated for discussion and training. Change of attitudes can take time, but it does not need to impede the progress and implementation of an inclusive education program. Helpful to changing attitudes is direct presentation of how the inclusion of children with ASD benefits not only the children with ASD and their families but also their typical peers and the general education staff.

The Inclusive Education Program Model

The inclusive education program model for students with ASD provided in this book has eight components. They are the scaffolding on which the structure of the model—it's inclusion roles, responsibilities, and practices—are built. This structure ensures that a school is able to implement a comprehensive and effective inclusion program that addresses the needs of its staff and students. The components of the scaffolding are briefly described here. In subsequent chapters the coinciding practices are described in detail to complete the structure.

Administrative Leadership

There are different levels of leadership in the process of implementing inclusive education programs. At the district level, directors of education and special education set policies and allocate funding that can establish a general tone and attitude in favor of or against the inclusion of students with ASD. It is principals, however, who have a unique role in the implementation of an inclusive education program within their school.

They directly determine school policy and resource allocation, as well as supervise the personnel on their site. Therefore, a principal's support and leadership of an inclusive education program exercises a significant influence on the schoolwide structure, on policy implementation, and on ongoing operations.

> ➡ A principal's leadership of an inclusive education program exercises a significant influence on the schoolwide structure, on policy implementation, and on ongoing operations.

It is important for principals to recognize their leadership role in the school restructuring process and in the implementation of the inclusive education program. Because principals are more distantly involved in the day-to-day inclusion practices, it is crucial for them to seek input from influential and knowledgeable school personnel and to recognize the need for strategic allocation and protection of resources. The principal also needs to be responsible for removing barriers that arise during the implementation process. Fostering positive attitudes among staff and students is key to the sustainability of the program during the inevitable difficult times (such as during conflict with parents, lack of needed funding and resources, disagreement among school personnel, and so on). Consequently, without appropriate support and leadership from a principal, an inclusive education program cannot be implemented successfully or with lasting effect.

Allocation of Funds

The implementation of an inclusive education program within a school requires funding for personnel and material resources, but it is the fiscal issues that are often thought to be the greatest obstacles to inclusive education. Administrators often feel intimidated by the daunting task of determining how to budget for one more "program" in their school.

Interestingly enough, research has begun to report that although the initial startup of an inclusive education program may require additional funds, over time there is no increase in costs.[1] The Special Education Expenditure Project (SEEP) reported that in 1985–1986 the average

> ➡ Research has begun to report that although the initial startup of an inclusive education program may require additional funds, over time there is no increase in costs.

expenditure on a student with a disability was $9,585 and in 1999–2000 it was $12,474. (Average cost of educating a student without a disability in 1999–2000 was $6,556.) This growth in expenditure is deceiving. Since the Individuals with Disabilities Education Act (IDEA) was passed in 1975, the number of students with disabilities enrolled in special education programs has increased from 8.5 percent to 13 percent—more than a 50 percent increase. SEEP determined that in 1985–1986 the cost to educate a student with a disability was 2.28 times higher than the cost of educating a student without a disability, and that in 1999–2000 the cost to educate a student with a disability was 1.90 times higher than the cost of educating a student without a disability. This decline in cost per student is due to several factors, the most significant one being that today more students with disabilities are educated in less restrictive settings than previously. Thus, there are now more students with disabilities receiving special education services (thus there is an increase in overall expenditures), but less money is spent overall per student with disability because more students with disabilities are educated in less restrictive environments, including the general education setting. Less money was spent on transporting students with disabilities to school sites other than their neighborhood school, thus allowing more money to be allocated to providing services for those same students at their neighborhood school or in another school within their district.

Although inclusion of students with disabilities, and in particular students with ASD, should not be viewed as a cost-saving venture, it is conceivable that by establishing an effective inclusive education program within a school, funding can be adjusted and reallocated to follow the students with disabilities as they are educated more and more in the general education setting.

Collaboration and Cooperative Team Commitment

Special education and general education have historically functioned as independent systems. Thus special educators have historically assumed responsibility for students with disabilities while they are in special education settings, and general educators have assumed responsibility for students without disabilities. But when students with disabilities are included in the general education setting, who takes responsibility for these students? Some schools assume that the general education teacher is the primary teacher for all of the students, and some assume that the special education teacher maintains all of the responsibility for the students with disabilities, no matter what classroom they are in.

This configuration would mean that the special education teacher also has primary responsibility (without adequate input from the general education teacher) for determining the following:

- Whether and when the needs of students with disabilities can appropriately be met in the general education setting
- Which general education programs and teachers will best meet the students' needs
- How inclusion may be accomplished most effectively.

Not surprisingly, this system, in combination with other imprudent inclusion policies and activities, has weakened many general educators' motivation for inclusion. Improvements in the way students with ASD are integrated into general education can be expected only with the support of and only through close working relationships between general and special educators.

Thus a major component of an effective inclusive education program is shared responsibility for students with ASD by general and special educators. That is, general educators must accept that students with ASD who are included in their

> ➜ A major component of an effective inclusive education program is shared responsibility for students with ASD by general and special educators.

classroom are their responsibility, and special educators must also accept that they continue to be responsible for their students' education even when their students are in the general education classroom. In return, general educators can expect full participation by special education teachers in decision-making processes associated with inclusion (including input on which students are appropriate for inclusion) along with appropriate support (that is, training and consultation). This approach results in shared decision making and interdisciplinary management (including related services providers, such as speech language pathologists, occupational therapists, adaptive physical education teachers, behavior specialists, and assistive technology teachers, and administrators) of each student with ASD who is included in the general education classroom.

An important step toward effective inclusion is to organize schools so that they require and reinforce coordination and communication between faculty and staff. Coordination in this context requires clear definition of roles and responsibilities for all IEP team members, along with clear understanding by each person of their own as well as of others' duties and responsibilities. This approach enables team members to have appropriate expectations of one another and of themselves, which will help them to make appropriate implementation decisions and to follow through on tasks and responsibilities in a timely fashion. As previously noted, much of the discontent among general education teachers over inclusive education programs stems from lack of orchestration and clarification (of organization and roles, for example) by the school's personnel. Hence, a logical step in dealing with this problem is to establish clear responsibility guidelines and boundaries.

Communication is the basis for developing the collaborative relationships that can achieve coordination. Communication is the basis for involving all inclusion stakeholders, including administrators, parents, teachers, support personnel, and students. Effective communication ensures that all involved persons are working toward the same goals and that each person follows established procedures. It is therefore important that team members have the time they need to collaborate and problem solve on issues related to the students with ASD with whom they are working. Principals have the ability to adjust the typical daily school schedule (for example, by providing one early-release day per week, and by providing roaming substitute teachers to release general and special education teachers) in order to provide IEP teams with the time they need to meet regularly and receive training.

Training and Support for Students and Personnel

As was noted in Chapter Two, training on inclusive education and ASD as well as the provision of supports within the general education classroom when including a student with ASD are critical to the success of an inclusive education program. Although all components of an inclusive education program are important, the success of the program can hinge solely on this particular component. General educators have most often not received the necessary background training that would enable them to understand the characteristics of ASD the way to communicate with persons with limited verbal skills, or the academic procedures that have been proven effective for this population.[3] Accordingly, it is essential that schools provide ongoing in-service training as well as consultation and coaching for general educators who work with students with ASD. Group trainings may be useful in providing a body of general information on the characteristics and needs of students with ASD, and individual consultation and coaching would focus on specific instructional techniques, intervention methods, and behavioral strategies. This training and consultation for both special and general educators needs to focus not only on information about ASD but also on collaboration and consultation skill training to prepare these educators for their new roles as team members of an inclusive education program, and ultimately to ensure that students with ASD receive the most appropriate services in the most appropriate placement.

It is important for an inclusive education program to recognize that paraeducators play an important role in supporting students with disabilities, especially students with ASD.[4] Paraeducators must therefore, to the extent possible, be available in general education settings to support students with ASD; consequently, they will need the same ongoing training and consultation as the teachers. They will require knowledge of the following:

> ➜ It is essential that schools provide ongoing in-service training as well as consultation and coaching for general educators who work with students with ASD.

- Characteristics of children with ASD

- Communication skills

- Behavior management techniques

- Instructional methods

- How to arrange the educational environment[5]

Once they have been trained, paraeducators may assist with a variety of tasks, including the following:

- Helping students practice previously taught academic and social skills

- Documenting student performance and progress

- Assisting teachers with daily planning, materials development, and curriculum modification[6]

Most important is that it is not appropriate for paraeducators to be assigned exclusively and consistently to a student with ASD for the purpose of translating teachers' instructions and implementing all programs. In many instances, it is preferable to have a paraeducator assist all of the students in a classroom, not just the students with ASD. In many situations, students with ASD are able to complete tasks without the assistance of a paraeducator. When this is the case, the student should be allowed to work independently while the paraeducator supports other students in the classroom. Nevertheless, paraeducators are considered an essential resource for effectively serving students with ASD in the general education classroom.

Many states and researchers have observed that the efficiency of our educational system could be significantly improved by reducing the size of the average general education class.[7] For students with ASD, a class size smaller than the usual (the twenty-to-one ratio seen in grades K–3 in many states) is of paramount

> ➔ For students with ASD, a smaller-than-usual class size is of paramount importance.

importance because these students typically require high levels of teacher-student interaction and classroom structure. Researchers have found that these students learn best when student-to-teacher ratios are small.[8] In addition, behavioral excesses and deficits are most easily controlled when the student has access to adequate teacher support, which is often unavailable in classrooms containing large numbers of students. It is thus important for IEP teams to consider the size of the general education class in which a particular student with ASD will be included. The class size may significantly affect the general education teacher's ability to respond effectively to the individual needs of all students, with and without disabilities.

Allocation of Resources and Space

As previously mentioned, it is important for special education resources to be protected and continually provided for students with ASD who are being included in the general education classroom. This means that the special educator who has been designated case manager for a particular student with ASD must have time in her schedule to observe the student in the class, to meet with the general education teacher and paraeducator, to develop materials the student needs, and to assist in making accommodations to curriculum, among other needed assistance. Ideally, a special educator at a given school site is designated inclusion facilitator and his or her entire caseload consists of the students with ASD who are being included in the general education classrooms. This special educator would have a staff of paraeducators who would be used solely to support the students with ASD in the various general education classrooms. It is my experience that the most effective student-to-teacher ratio for such an inclusion program is one special education teacher and two to three paraeducators to no more than eight students. If more than eight students with ASD are included in the general education classrooms on a given school site, it is best to have two special educators with paraeducators serving the students in specific grade ranges (such as kindergarten through second grade and third grade through fifth or sixth grade).

It is also imperative that a classroom or other space on the school site be designated for the sole use of inclusion facilitators, paraeducators, and students. This is where the teachers and paraeducators have their desks and where they meet with general education staff and parents and develop materials and accommodations for curriculum. This space also provides a place for students with ASD to come for lessons in specific skill areas in which they need specialized instruction, such as social skills, math, reading, science, and social studies. Most important, this is also a place where students with ASD can go to take breaks and where they can be taken if their behavior becomes too disruptive for the general education classroom. This space is often called the inclusion classroom, but it is still a special education classroom and is operated similar to a resource room.

Accommodations and Instructional Methods

Using appropriate instructional methods with students with ASD within the general education environment contributes to the success of their programs and to their progress. As stated earlier, students with ASD lack many of the language, learning, and social skills they need to function and learn within a typical education environment. There are proven teaching techniques, intervention methods, and curriculum and environment accommodations that can be used to enhance the ability of a student with ASD to receive and learn from instruction provided in a general education classroom.

The information gained from the LRE Services and Placement Determination form (completed by the IEP team prior to the child's inclusion in the general education classroom; see Chapter Four) greatly assists both general and special education teachers in knowing what intervention and teaching methods each student has benefited from, as well as what specific services need to be delivered and possibly modified in the general education classroom. It is important that an IEP team understand that initially there is no way to know exactly how many and what types of accommodations and modifications the student needs, and initially he or she may need more accommodations and modifications until he or she adjusts to the new learning environment and curriculum. This is why it is particularly important to have a paraeducator assisting the teacher while the student is in the class. During the first month of inclusion it is important for the team to keep detailed records of how the student is performing in the new environment, including data on the changes that were made for his or her benefit and how successful these changes were for the student. It is also important for the special education teacher to observe the classroom frequently, and specifically to observe the general education teacher, the paraeducator, the student, and typical students, in order to obtain a baseline for performance and behaviors, and to provide feedback for needed changes. Further information on teaching techniques, methods, and accommodations is provided in subsequent chapters.

Recurrent Evaluation of Inclusion Procedures and Student Progress

"Assessment is a key component of any program serving children with exceptionalities, and acts as an ongoing part of the instructional strategy."[9] Once the IEP team has developed a student's goals and objectives and determined that some of the goals and objectives can be met within the general education environment, the team needs to develop strategies to assess the student's progress. Ongoing evaluation of the progress of a student with ASD within the general education classroom is an integral part of the IEP. Unfortunately, it appears that a school or IEP team can put great amounts of effort, time,

> ➜ Ongoing evaluation of the progress of a student with ASD within the general education classroom is an integral part of the IEP.

and resources into starting an inclusive education program, but then forget the important component that will ensure that the program continues to be successful and continues to meet the needs of students with ASD: continual evaluation.

The team must continually reevaluate the appropriateness of addressing the student's needs (goals and objectives) and providing appropriate services within the general education environment. Writing goals and objectives that are very specific helps the team to develop detailed data collection methods and checklists for evaluating the student's progress.

Ultimately the student's progress or lack thereof determines whether he or she is benefiting from the educational program within the general education classroom. A particular student's progress thus depends not only on his or her own performance but also on the performance of the teacher and the paraeducator, and on the structure of the inclusive education program that was set up by the IEP team and school. Ongoing use of the four main components of a successful inclusion program that are listed in the Legal Guidelines for Appropriate Placement of Students with ASD in the General Education Classroom (Handout 3.1 in Chapter Three) assists the IEP team in evaluating the overall inclusion program for the student with ASD.

In order to determine whether the student's inclusive education program is being successfully implemented and whether he or she is benefiting educationally and socially from being included in the general education classroom, educators need to observe, record data, and maintain a portfolio of the student's work. In subsequent chapters, further information is provided on the key components that contribute to the success of a student in a general education classroom, and on the methods used to facilitate an objective and measurable evaluation.

Parental Involvement

The IDEA not only guarantees the right to a free and appropriate education for all students with disabilities, it also ensures the continuous involvement of parents in educational planning, decision making, and implementation. Current policies and practices not only allow and encourage parent involvement in educational matters that affect their children but also mandate and ensure the right of involvement for all parents. Thus, the meaningful participation of parents in activities that facilitate the successful inclusion of students with ASD is essential; such involvement must be crafted for individual parents and is an indispensable part of an effective inclusive education program.

> ➡ Participation by parents in inclusion-related activities is an indispensable part of an effective inclusive education program.

Several basic elements have been identified as necessary for effective parent-school collaboration,[10] including the following:

- Development and maintenance of a collaborative home-school environment

- Application of a collaboratively oriented administrative arrangement

- Willingness on the part of professionals to train parents and family members to participate as effective members of an IEP team

Creating the conditions for a collaborative home-school environment begins with recognizing that parent-professional cooperation extends beyond legislation and that interpersonal, not legislative, conditions are the bases for meaningful parent and family involvement. Simpson and Fielder have specifically noted that such a relationship must be founded in professionals' willingness to listen, to recognize that trust is a basic element of cooperation, to have knowledge of and accept individual values, and to demonstrate willingness to accommodate a partnership relationship.[11] That parents of children with ASD and professionals have often had less than optimal interpersonal relationships underscores the importance of these elements as salient ingredients of effective parent-professional relationships.

Administrative arrangements and policies also help to determine effective parental involvement. Indeed, meaningful involvement between parents and professionals is likely to occur only when suitable administratively supported conditions are in place. Such support from administrators includes encouraging and reinforcing participation, and demonstrating willingness to share information and procedures. Thus program and building leaders should make it clear to parents that they have access to documents on their child, that they are free to review program information and data, and that school professionals will assist them in locating problem-solving resources. Such willingness to inform on the part of leadership not only provides parents with valuable information, but more importantly establishes trust and communicates the willingness of school personnel to accommodate parents and share decision making with them.[12]

Training parents to be partners in the educational and inclusion process is also a requirement of developing an effective parent-school relationship. This component recognizes that many parents of students with ASD will want to participate in the decision-making and evaluation processes. Without suitable training, however, parents' ability to understand and make meaningful contributions may be limited. Accordingly, educators must offer to train parents in the relevant data collection procedures and instructional methods, and encourage them to participate in IEPs and other conferences. Such training of course varies in accordance with the parents interests and abilities. Nonetheless, appropriate parent training must be recognized as a fundamental element of forming and maintaining an effective and collaborative parent-professional partnership.

> ➜ Appropriate parent training must be recognized as a fundamental element of forming and maintaining an effective and collaborative parent-professional partnership.

Summary

As stated earlier, when developing and implementing an inclusive education program for students with ASD it is important to remember that full-time inclusion in the general education classroom is not appropriate for every student; a continuum of placement options must be available and individualized for each student with ASD. Also, each student with ASD benefits in different ways and to different degrees from being included in the general education classroom. One student may receive great academic benefit but continue to struggle with his social skills while another student may show great progress in his or her social and play and language skills but struggle with the academic expectations of the general education environment, and still others may show steady progress in all of these skill areas but be unable to display those skills at the same level as their peers in the classroom. It is thus imperative that IEP teams be able to individualize and constantly adjust and accommodate instruction, curricula, and environments through ongoing evaluation of the inclusive education program and of student progress in it.

A successful inclusive education program also requires ongoing training and collaborative consultation for general and special education teachers, paraeducators, administrators, and parents. Autism spectrum disorders are unique and affect a student so comprehensively that years of education and experience are required to work successfully with such children. In order to educate and work with such students effectively, all those involved with the students need training and follow-up collaborative consultation with experts on ASD and inclusion.

A school's startup of an inclusive education program for students with ASD and the ongoing process of providing an inclusive education program for each individual student with ASD takes more time and resources initially than are needed later in the ongoing maintenance of the program. Implementing a new program always takes more than maintaining a program once it is in motion. The situation is the same as that of a school district that is deciding to invest in an effective and extensive early intervention program for students with disabilities; more money is spent and more resources are provided in the beginning because it is understood that the investment will allow students to be successful earlier and to make more progress and need less special education services in the later years of their education. Thus investing in setting up an effective and comprehensive inclusive educational program for students with ASD will allow the students to learn the skills they will need to progress, and by receiving as much of their education as is appropriate within the general education classroom, they will need fewer special education services.

> ➜ Investing in setting up an effective and comprehensive inclusive educational program for students with ASD will allow the students to learn the skills they will need to progress, and by receiving as much of their education as is appropriate within the general education classroom, they will need fewer special education services.

Finally, effectively implementing an inclusive education program is always a challenging and demanding process. Because students with ASD are so different from one another, an IEP team can never expect to implement a program for one child that was implemented for another. IEP teams need to celebrate the small successful steps that a student makes, as well as those that teachers make. In order to maintain a healthy outlook on the process of including students with ASD in the general education environment, teams should plan for the best but expect the worst. This approach will enable them to prepare wisely and work hard to implement both proactive and consequential procedures, but also to recognize the small steps and progress that a student makes.

☞ Handout 5.1. Benefits of Inclusion of Children with Autism Spectrum Disorders

Benefits for Children with ASD

The children will

- Be provided with the opportunity to learn appropriate social, behavior, play, and communication skills from their typically developing peers, who will serve as models
- Be provided with opportunities for growth in academic learning
- Learn to function and work in a typical environment through the realistic life experiences they have in the general education environment
- Be provided with increased motivation and natural reinforcers
- Learn to understand the natural consequences of actions (both positive and negative)
- Have opportunities to develop friendships with typical peers

Benefits for Typical Peers

The peers will

- Learn about and become comfortable with children and people with disabilities by gaining a more realistic educational experience alongside their peers with disabilities
- Grow up with people with disabilities, which may lead them to be accepting employers and employees of people with disabilities
- Be able to use their strengths in assisting a child with autism, which may build self-esteem and leadership qualities and lead to a career option

Benefits for General Education Staff

The staff will

- Learn to use a variety of teaching modalities
- Gain experience working with children with ASD and other disabilities
- Learn additional teaching techniques to use with all children
- Gain a better understanding of the development of a child

Benefits for Families of Child with ASD

The family may

- Feel less isolated from the rest of their community
- Allow their child to become more independent
- Develop relationships with families of typically developing children who could provide them with meaningful support
- Gain a better outlook on their child's future

Defining Roles and Responsibilities of Inclusive Education

6

IEP Team Members

An IEP team of administrators, school personnel, and family members is convened to determine the needs, services, and then placement of a particular student with a disability. Certain people are mandated to be a part of the IEP team: the principle, the special education teacher, the general education teacher, and the child's parents or guardians. The same people are required for any IEP team, whether it is for a student receiving speech and language instruction, a special day student, a resource specialist student, or a special education student being included in the general program. Other members of the IEP team can be the paraeducator, the speech and language pathologist (SLP), the occupational therapist (OT), the adaptive physical education (APE) teacher, the school psychologist, the inclusion facilitator, the behavior specialist, other school and special education administrators, other special and general education teachers, other family members, and the student with the disability.

Some IEP teams can be very large and some can be quite small, but ultimately the team is brought together by law and not by choice. This often means that the members of the IEP team do not know each other well, which can sometimes create an awkward or difficult situation, because these people, all of whom bring their different experiences, viewpoints, beliefs, and expertise to the team, must work together to establish a program for a particular student. The concept of inclusive education for students with disabilities, and in particular for students with ASD, is quite controversial, and this can also add to the difficulties that an IEP team encounters when its members come together to work. The ASD Characteristics: Student Profile form provided in Chapter One, the Legal Guidelines for Appropriate Placement in General Education Classroom for Student with ASD handout provided in Chapter Three, and the LRE Services and Placement Determination form provided in Chapter Four provides the IEP team with a step-by-step process for collaborating effectively and deciding what are the primary needs of the student with ASD, and what are the appropriate goals and objectives, services, and placement that will meet those needs. If the team has reached the point in its decision process when it has decided that some of the student's needs would best be met in the general education classroom, it now needs to establish how the inclusive education process will occur for this particular student.

The first and foremost step in this process is to establish what each IEP team member's roles and responsibilities will be throughout the process. Taking the time to discuss, collaborate on, and establish clearly defined responsibilities for each person on the team will greatly increase the success and effectiveness of the student's inclusive education program by providing clear expectations for each member. It will ensure efficient follow-through on tasks and that unnecessary delays do not occur, because such delays would inhibit the success of the program and the student's progress. It will also help to maintain open channels of communication and enable team collaboration to continue without frustration and conflict.

This chapter discusses the roles and responsibilities of the key members of an inclusive education program team for a student with ASD. These are the members who have crucial decision-making or day-to-day implementation responsibilities, or both. It is also important for other team members (those who are less-involved or involved for a single purpose) to have clearly defined roles and responsibilities. These are outlined only briefly here, but they should be discussed and clearly defined by the team. It is assumed that one responsibility of all team members is to attend every meeting that is held about the student's IEP for the inclusive education program. There are of course other times outside of the IEP meeting setting and throughout the school year when specific team members will meet to collaborate and discuss concerns and strategies.

The roles and responsibilities of the following personnel are defined and described in this chapter:

- Administrator or principal
- Special education teacher or inclusion facilitator
- General education teacher
- Paraeducator
- Parents or guardians
- Other related service personnel

An easy-to-use checklist has also been created for the team to use on an ongoing basis for reference.

Administrator

The administrator provides the impetus and the ongoing financial and logistical support for the inclusive education program. Without someone playing this supportive role, the inclusive education program does not succeed. The administrator helps to organize the school environment, the teaching schedules, and the finances in such a way that an attitude of inclusiveness and acceptance of students with ASD in the general education classroom permeates the school. The administrator helps the IEP teams overcome any difficulties and removes any barriers that may arise at the beginning of and during the process of including a student with ASD.

> ➜ The administrator helps the IEP teams overcome any difficulties that may arise at the beginning of and during the process of including a student with ASD.

There are many different ways that an administrator can provide support to his or her staff and students in order to establish and maintain a successful inclusive education program at the school site. The administrator can be part of a team of school personnel who plan the implementation of on-site professional development (training) or off-site workshops or seminars. Professional development topics would include the following:

- Understanding autism spectrum disorders
- Understanding inclusive education
- Handling challenging behaviors
- Facilitating social and play interactions among children with and without disabilities
- Collaborating and consulting with the general and special education staff in regard to service provision for students with ASD in the general education classroom

The administrator can develop a school schedule that would allow release time for the general and special education staffs to meet to collaborate and consult on students' inclusive education programs.

The administrator has an integral role in behavior intervention plans and behavior management strategies, including providing reinforcement for appropriate behavior of all students, including students with ASD. This role promotes ongoing contact between the administrator and the students with ASD and their parents, and it establishes trust in and understanding of the needs of both the students and their parents. The administrator also supervises and assists in the hiring of support staff (that is, paraeducators) and in contracting with outside consultants (such as an autism consultant, a behavior specialist, or an inclusion facilitator) if needed. He or she helps to delegate to various school staff any new inclusive education program duties (such as providing medication, assisting with making materials, supervising recess, and so on). The administrator also meets occasionally with individual staff to monitor progress, attitudes, and needs among staff and other IEP team members. The administrator attends all IEP meetings and helps the special education teacher or inclusion facilitator to ensure that each IEP team member's responsibilities are implemented. A list of the administrator's role and responsibilities is provided in Checklist 6.1.

> ✓ Use Checklist 6.1:
> Administrator: Roles and
> Responsibilities

Special Educator

Typically the special education teacher who has the student with ASD in his or her class is the person who becomes the facilitator for including the student in the general education classroom. Occasionally a school district will have an autism consultant or inclusion facilitator on its staff and this person may become a part of the IEP team in order to assist in facilitating the student's inclusion in the general education classroom. Also, at school sites where there is not a special education day class, the special education teacher may be the resource specialist. The special education teacher may therefore also be the inclusion facilitator, or there may be two separate special education personnel—the special education teacher and the inclusion facilitator.

One of these people (hereto referred to as the special educator) has the role of case manager of the student's IEP. He or she supervises and is responsible for ensuring the implementation of the student's inclusive education program. This person must ensure that all of the team members understand their roles and responsibilities and follow through on their individual tasks and duties. He or she facilitates ongoing communication and collaboration among the team members, with the goal that all members will be well-informed and not be unprepared or lack the necessary information or support they need to accomplish their roles and responsibilities.

Once an IEP team has decided that a student with ASD will be included in the general education classroom, the special educator is responsible for instigating the inclusion process. The next chapter describes the complete process of establishing and maintaining an inclusive education program for a student with ASD. The special educator also works with the administrator to provide trainings for the general education teachers and paraeducators. This role may entail providing workshops on specific topics or holding successive meetings to provide information and discuss specific teaching or behavior intervention strategies.

The special educator also provides ongoing training and support
to the general education teacher, to
the paraeducator, and to the student with ASD in the general education classroom. This role entails such
activities as the following:

> ➡ The special educator provides ongoing training and support to the general education teacher, the paraeducator, and the student with ASD.

- Establishing ongoing forms of communication among school staff

- Performing ongoing observations in the general education classroom

- Assisting with accommodation of curriculum for the student, model-ing and training others on the use of specific teaching and behavior intervention methods

- Performing functional behavior assessments

- Establishing behavior intervention plans with the general education teacher and paraeducator

- Developing a play and social interaction plan,

- Creating a data collection system for tracking goals and objectives and monitoring its implementation

- Setting up an emergency plan for any behavior, allergy, or injury situation that might arise with the student

- Creating visual supports for the student to assist him or her in following daily routines and activities

- Establishing an ongoing communication system with the parents or guardians

More information on the ongoing support and consultation that the spe-cial educator provides to the general education teacher and paraeducator is provided in Chapter Eight.

One of most important and time-intensive responsibilities of the special educator is training and supervising the paraeducator who is assisting the general education teacher and the student in the general education classroom. Sometimes this paraeducator has previously worked with the student in a home program or in another special education class, other times a new paraeducator may be hired. It is important that the special educator allocate time prior to the first day that the paraeducator works in the general education classroom to provide information and training on ASD, teaching techniques, behavior management techniques, accommodation of curriculum, and facilitation of the student's social and academic inclusion within the classroom. Time also needs to be allocated for the paraeducator to become acquainted with the student and establish a rapport, as well as to become acquainted with the general education teacher and establish a foundation for their day-to-day working relationship. The most important training that a special educator can provide to a paraeducator is how to facilitate the independent learning and participation of the student with ASD in the general education classroom. Details on the process of training the paraeducator are discussed in Chapter Seven.

It is also important that the special educator establish with the other IEP team members a continual collaborative working relationship that promotes ongoing mutual feedback throughout the inclusion process. The general education teacher, special educator, and paraeducator all need to have regular meetings to discuss ongoing student progress and well as concerns and plans for future changes, activities, and events.

The special educator is also responsible for writing the IEP goals and objectives in a manner that makes them measurable, attainable, and observable within the environment to which they are addressed. This person is responsible for tracking the student's goals and objectives within the general education classroom and needs to establish a data collection system that allows the general education teacher, the paraeducator, and the special educator to monitor accurately the student's progress with the goals and objectives. This role entails creating a binder for the student that includes copies of the following pertinent information:

- The student's goals and objectives
- Teaching procedures
- Behavior intervention plans
- Use of communication and visual support systems
- Data collection sheets with explanations

This information will also be important as the child transitions from one school year to the next and a detailed transition plan is developed with the IEP team.

Another important responsibility of the special educator is to involve the student's parents or guardians in the inclusion process, thereby empowering them. This involvement can make a significant difference in the progress the student makes socially, behaviorally, and academically. It helps the parents to trust the special educator as the case manager of their child's inclusive education program, to trust the general education teacher's ability to teach and include their child in his or her classroom, and to trust the importance of the paraeducator and his or her ability to assist their child in learning and in participating in the ongoing classroom activities. A cooperative and respectful relationship with the student's parents can also greatly improve the general education teacher's attitude and motivation to handle difficult behaviors the student may display, and to implement different and challenging teaching techniques.

Involving the parents in the inclusive education process begins with establishing an ongoing communication system between the parents and school staff. Each party informs the other of changes in skills or behaviors, about significant events (whether positive or negative) that occurred before the child got to school or went home, about changes in schedules, and so on. It is important to invite the parents to observe their child during class time or to volunteer to assist with special events or regularly occurring activities. The special educator and general education teacher also need to seek feedback from the parents on teaching techniques, generalizing skills, handling difficult behaviors, and so on. This communication allows all parties to express their viewpoints and learn from one another's experiences while coming to a mutual decision on the best method for proceeding. Shared and informed decision making promotes consistency between home and school. All educators and family members using consistent intervention and teaching techniques across all environments is critical to facilitating a student's progress in an inclusive education program. Checklist 6.2, provided at the end of this chapter, summarizes the special educator's roles and responsibilities.

> ✓ Use Checklist 6.2: Special Educator: Roles and Responsibilities

General Education Teacher

The general education teacher's primary role is to accept the student with ASD as a full member of his or her classroom and to create an environment that enables the student with ADS to learn new skills and interact with his or her peers. The general education teacher partners with the special educator to ensure that the student receives the appropriate supplementary aides and services that he or she needs to make progress on his goals and objectives.

> ➡ The general education teacher's primary role is to accept the student with ASD as a full member of his or her classroom and to create an environment that enables the student with ADS to learn new skills and interact with his or her peers.

Just as the principal sets the tone for the school's positive or negative attitude toward including students with disabilities in general education classrooms, a general education teacher sets the tone for the positive or negative attitude of the general education students toward including a student with ASD in the classroom. The typical students watch their teacher's interactions with the student with ASD and pattern their responses to the student after the patterns they observe in those interactions. These observations show them how to accept and respect the student as a part of their class. This means that the teacher needs to behave as if the student with ASD is able to understand and participate in the class just as all the other students would; it means that the teacher needs to speak to the student without condescension and to speak to the student directly and not through the paraeducator. It also means that the general education teacher must work with the paraeducator to facilitate appropriate and productive social and play interaction between the student with ASD and his or her peers. Further strategies for this process are provided in subsequent chapters.

The general education teacher partners with the special educator and paraeducator in developing and choosing appropriate curriculum adaptations, behavior intervention plans, visual supports, data collection methods, methods for ongoing communication among staff and IEP team member, specific and additional teaching strategies to assist the student, and so on. It is important for the general education teacher to view the paraeducator as a trained and valuable member of the student's IEP team and seek input from this person and accept suggestions for implementing teaching strategies (such as prompting, ways of phrasing instructions, methods for facilitating interaction with other students, and so on). The general education teacher also partners with the special educator to involve the student's parents in the inclusion process by promoting ongoing communication about the student's progress and by seeking input from the parents.

One responsibility of the general education teacher that can be difficult to implement is adjusting the academic grading process for the student. This is a change that needs to be decided on by the IEP team while remaining in accordance with the district's procedures for grading students with disabilities who are unable to use appropriate supplementary aides and services to attain grade-level achievement. Many students with ASD are able to participate at grade level and can be graded on the same scale as their same-age peers. A list of the roles and responsibilities of the general educator is provided in Checklist 6.3.

> ✓ Use Checklist 6.3: General Education Teacher: Roles and Responsibilities

Paraeducator

If the IEP team decides that the general education teacher and the student need a paraeducator to assist in the day-to-day inclusion process, the paraeducator then becomes a valuable and crucial member of the IEP team. Depending on the needs of the student, the paraeducator often is the person who works most directly with the student with ASD. This means that the paraeducator needs to be trained to assist the general education teacher in teaching the student and to assist the student in learning in the general education classroom.

The primary responsibility of the paraeducator is to facilitate the independent learning and participation of the student in the general education classroom. Essentially the paraeducator's goal is to work himself or herself out of a job so that the student no longer needs the paraeducator to assist him in learning and in interacting with his peers, and the general education teacher no longer needs the paraeducator in order to teach the student and handle challenging behaviors.

> ➡ The primary responsibility of the paraeducator is to facilitate the independent learning and participation of the student in the general education classroom.

It is important for IEP team members to understand that working with a student with ASD is a challenging job that always requires training. It is a specialized skill to be able to work successfully with a student with ASD. The appropriate person for the position of inclusive education paraeducator needs to

> ✓ Use Checklist 6.4: Qualifications for the Inclusive Education Paraeducator

- Be experienced in working with students with disabilities, preferably students with ASD

- Have demonstrated in previous positions that he or she has the ability to establish a rapport with children with whom he or she works

- Interact with the students as an instructor, to follow through on difficult teaching and behavior interventions, and not interact in a parenting or mothering manner

- Agree with the inclusion of students with disabilities—in particular, students with ASD—in the classroom

- Exhibit collaborative teaming skills

- Communicate well

- Demonstrate an understanding of his or her role as a paraeducator in the general education classroom, and agree with the accompanying responsibilities

- Be able to use data collection systems for tracking goals and objectives

- Receive ongoing training, consultation, and supervision willingly from the special educator

- Able to adjust his or her schedule to allow time for being in the general education classroom

The paraeducator will need to be able to begin working prior to the days when the student with ASD will actual be in attendance in the general education classroom. This time needs to be spent

- Receiving training from the special educator on ASD, teaching techniques, behavior intervention methods, using visual supports, facilitating social and play interactions, data collection, and so on

- Establishing rapport with the student with ASD (that is, playing with the student, working in the special education classroom with the student, and so on)

- Meeting with the general education teacher

- Observing the general education classroom during class time

- Meeting with the student's parents

As previously stated, more information on the process of training the paraeducator is provided in Chapter Seven.

Once the paraeducator is in the general education classroom, he or she assists the student with ASD to participate appropriately in the ongoing learning, social, and play activities in the classroom and in the larger school environment. With the goal of fostering the student's independent learning and participation, the paraeducator should as much as possible facilitate interaction between the general education teacher and peers and the student with ASD, and spend less time interacting with the student himself or herself. The paraeducator also needs to use teaching methods that require the least intrusive prompts possible so that they can be quickly faded from use (see Chapter Eight for more detailed discussion of prompting and fading). The paraeducator does not hover around or sit next to the child unless it is necessary to assist him or her during a specific activity. As much as possible, and under the supervision of the general education teacher, the paraeducator also needs to interact with and assist the typical students in the class. This interaction helps to give the appearance that the paraeducator is there to assist the whole class and not just one student. The paraeducator also helps the student with ASD attend to and interact with the teacher and peers, to remain on task during independent work periods, and to participate in ongoing activities both inside and outside the classroom. He or she needs to use natural reinforcement and correction procedures in the student's environment. The paraeducator assists the general education teacher and the special educator in making appropriate curriculum accommodations and visual supports to help the student with ASD follow routines and schedules.

One important responsibility of the paraeducator is to implement goals and objectives by using agreed-upon procedures throughout the child's time in the general education classroom. While doing this, the paraeducator needs to maintain data on these goals and objectives, as well as on anything else on which the team has agreed information needs to be collected. This can be the most difficult task to learn and implement. It requires the person to multitask—to attend to the needs of the student while simultaneously recording information on the student's responses to and progress on specific tasks and skills. This is one responsibility that relies heavily on the ability and understanding of the paraeducator, because he or she is the person who works most directly with the student, and is the only person whose job is dedicated solely toward servicing this student's inclusive education program.

The paraeducator is also responsible for providing constant feedback to both the general education teacher and the special educator on the progress or lack of progress of the student with ASD. Information for this feedback may come from data collected on the student's activities that relates to the student's performance on goals and objectives, or it may come from a log the paraeducator keeps on daily classroom occurrences involving the student. This is often also an excellent opportunity for the paraeducator to offer suggestions for getting the child to participate in activities and on adaptations for the curriculum.

Finally, it is important that the paraeducator accept feedback from the general education teacher, including information provided on formal evaluations and suggestions for improvement. This feedback might cover suggestions both on how to improve the program for the student with ASD and on how to improve the paraed- ucators skills in working the student in the classroom on a daily basis. A list of the paraeducator's roles and responsibilities is provided in Checklist 6.5 at the end of the chapter.

> ✓ Use Checklist 6.5:
> Paraeducator: Roles and
> Responsibilities

Parents and Guardians

As stated in Chapter Five, the parents of the student with ASD are an integral part of the IEP team. Many times it is only through the parents' insistence that a child is being included in the general education classroom; at other times it is with great reservation that the parents allow their child to be included in the general education classroom. Regardless of the situation, the success of the inclusive education program depends on the parents' involvement and assistance.

The parents' primary role is to assist the IEP team in maintaining the "big picture" of their child—to establish long-term goals and priorities for their child that include interests, home and family life, and extracurricular activities. This means that the parents need to provide accurate information on events that occur at home and in the community. They also need to attend IEP meetings and come prepared with questions, concerns, and ideas about goals and objectives and services.

Parents also need to maintain an objective viewpoint on their child's abilities and disabilities. It can sometimes be difficult to accept the challenges their child experiences and how their child compares to typical children of the same age and grade. Although it is important for a child with ASD to be included in the LRE, it is also extremely important that he or she be able to continue learning. Sometimes, however, the level at which the child is able to learn inhibits him from being able to learn new and relevant skills in the general education classroom. It is crucial that parents maintain realistic goals for their child and understand that the rate of accomplishing those goals may sometimes need to change on the basis of a student's progress or lack of progress during his school years. This also means that each year the IEP team needs to reevaluate whether placement in the general education classroom is still the most appropriate and least restrictive placement for the child. Although fully including the child in the general education classroom in kindergarten and in first and second grade may have been appropriate, because of changes in the curriculum this may not be the case when the child is in third and fourth grade.

> ➡ Parents need to maintain an objective viewpoint on their child's abilities and disabilities.

An important responsibility for the parent at the beginning of the inclusion process is to work with the special educator and general education teacher to develop an ability awareness activity that can be carried out with the typical peers in the general education classroom prior to the inclusion of the child with ASD. Depending on the severity of the child's ASD, more or less information would need to be provided to the peers about the differences and similarities they can expect. Being involved allows the parents to share with the other students the special interests of their child and the activities and games he or she likes to play. More information on the ability awareness activity is provided in Chapter Seven.

One of the most important ongoing responsibilities of parents is to set up and maintain regular open communication with the special educator, the paraeducator, and the general education teacher. Parents need to be informed of upcoming changes in schedules, routines, or events or about any classroom themes or topics that are being explored and discussed so that they can prepare their child and engage in ongoing discussion with him or her. The parent also needs to provide accurate information on any changes in the family's life at home, about schedules and routines, and about any positive or negative events that may affect the child's behavior and performance in class. They should also ask for suggestions for effective in-home activities, for homework, or for specific strategies for handling behavior or social interactions that will help reinforce the work that is being done in the classroom. Establishing a reliable and regular communication system between home and school also means that both parties need consistently follow through on handling the changes that have occurred at home or in school, and parents and teachers need to be able to rely on the other to implement similar strategies for behavior, social and play interactions, and completing academic work.

If the child is not distracted by the parents' presence, then the parents should volunteer to assist in the class for a once-a-week activity or event (while having as little contact with the child as possible). This involvement will allow the parents to be a part of the ongoing class activities in the same way as the parents of other general education students are; it will allow them to observe their child's behaviors, social and play skills, academic skills, and so on; and it will help the parent to develop a stronger relationship with the general education teacher and paraeducator.

Another important responsibility of the parent is to provide ongoing feedback to the IEP team, in particular to the general education teacher, the special educator, and the paraeducator, on their work with the student with ASD. The parents can expect the same feedback from these people. This feedback should include expressions of appreciation for each other's hard work and for small steps in progress that the student is making, as well as constructive feedback about teaching strategies and behavior intervention strategies that need to be changed in order to be more effective. Checklist 6.6 provides a list of the roles and responsibilities of the parents.

> ✓ Use Checklist 6.6: Parents:
> Roles and Responsibilities

Related Service Providers

Other service providers who commonly work with students with ASD are SLPs, OTs, and APE therapists. These providers vary in the amount and type of therapy they provide on an ongoing basis (typically thirty to ninety minutes are provided each week in one to two sessions). It is important for these service providers to consider that when an inclusive education program is established for a student with ASD, there need to be changes in the service delivery methods to address the student's goals and objectives. For example, if the SLP has two sessions a week with the student and is working on social communication skills, one therapy session could be provided within the general education classroom during a free-choice play time. The therapist could use typical peers to help the student generalize skills within the setting in which he or she would typically use them. This activity could also be done with the OT or APE specialist; one session could be provided during recess with a small group of typical peers or during an activity in class.

Because these service providers are often itinerate (that is, they often travel from school to school to provide services for children with varying disabilities), their communication with the student's IEP team can be difficult. It will be important for the team to develop strategies to keep these service providers in the loop on any important changes in the student's skills, and particularly in behaviors and behavior intervention strategies. Consistency across instructors is basic to success for students with ASD; therefore, when service providers take the time to communicate with each other about the student, it is worth the effort. Because these service providers are often not readily available to answer questions, they need to provide information about the student's progress regularly to the general education teacher, the special educator, and the paraeducator. It is also important that these service providers attend the IEP meetings so that they can provide information about the student to help the team gain a comprehensive view of the student's abilities and ongoing challenges.

Summary

The common thread that runs through all of the responsibilities of the IEP team members has been regular communication and collaboration on the student's progress in the inclusive education program. For the team to implement any activity with success, collaboration and communication must happen and be the foundation for the program. It therefore falls within everyone's realm of responsibility to maintain regular and open communication channels. When everyone participates and there is open communication, people build trust and are able to rely on one another to fulfill their roles and responsibilities.

> ➜ It falls within everyone's realm of responsibility to maintain regular and open communication channels.

It is also important that the special educator, as the case manager of the student's inclusive education program, be a competent, cooperative, and reliable leader for the IEP team. First implementing an inclusive education program within a school and then implementing individual inclusive programs for specific students with ASD is rigorous. Although the inclusive education program may be thought of as "just another special education program" on the site (like the speech and language program, the special day class, the resource specialist program, and so on), it is not. It is in this program that a previously special-education-only student becomes an inclusive student in the general education program. Implementing this total crossover of general education and special education requires the minutia of preplanning, training (both preservice and ongoing), implementation, collaboration, and so on to establish a program of shared responsibilities for all involved that is built for the successful inclusion of the student with ASD.

Student: _____

✓ Checklist 6.1. Administrator:
Roles and Responsibilities in the Inclusion Process

Primary Role:

Provides impetus and ongoing support to both the general education programs and the special education programs that can make inclusive education successful.

Responsibilities:

✓ Removes barriers to change and is an instigator of change within the system

✓ Assures every parent that their child is welcome in the school

✓ Organizes school environment, teaching schedules, and finances to incorporate inclusion program

✓ Attends all IEP meetings

✓ Assists special educator in ensuring implementation of the IEP team's task

✓ Supervises hiring of support staff and contracting with outside consultants

✓ Assists special educator in delegating inclusive education duties to staff

✓ Meets with staff to monitor progress and attitudes

✓ Ensures that general education teachers and paraeducators have the opportunity to attend workshops and conferences specific to ASD so that they can gain knowledge and training in the necessary skills

✓ Ensures that the appropriate supports and resources are available for all students, as well as for those that are specific to students with ASD

✓ Participates on the collaborative planning team for the inclusive education program established for students with ASD on that site

✓ Provides release time for lesson preparation and collaboration for teachers

✓ Has an integral role in establishing behavior intervention plans for students with ASD

✓ Reinforces appropriate inclusive behavior of typical students

Student: _____

✓ Checklist 6.2. Special Educator:
Roles and Responsibilities Throughout the Inclusion Process

Primary Role:

As the case manager for the student's IEP, provides ongoing support and consultation for the general education teacher and the paraedcuator on the student being included in the general education classroom

Responsibilities:

✓ Instigates inclusion process

✓ Sets up meeting times with IEP team—initial, reviews, annuals

✓ Writes and creates a tracking system for IEP goals and objectives that are measurable, attainable, and observable in that environment

✓ Provides ongoing information and training for the general education teacher

✓ Provides initial and ongoing training, support, and evaluation for the paraeducator

✓ Sets up reliable and consistent forms of communication (maintaining a binder of pertinent information on the student) to ensure collaboration among IEP team members

✓ Ensures understanding, implementation, and completion of tasks related to team members' roles and responsibilities

✓ Sets up a communication system for conveying information to parents and for involving parents in the inclusive education program

✓ Sets up emergency steps so that a plan for obtaining immediate assistance exists for handling extremely disruptive behavior and other emergencies when needed within the general education classroom

✓ Provides adapted materials for the teacher, paraeducator, or both for the student to use during specific activities, keeping records of adaptations that are made

✓ Performs functional behavioral assessments

✓ Establishes a behavior intervention plan with implementation supports for the student

✓ Creates visual supports to assist the student in routines, transitions, and social interactions.

✓ Develops a play and social interaction skill plan and provides assistance for implementation.

✓ Performs ongoing observations in the classroom and evaluates the program implementation with suggestions and supports for changes.

✓ Sets up and implements a transition plan for each school year

Student: _____

✓ Checklist 6.3. General Education Teacher: Roles and Responsibilities in the Inclusion Process

Primary Role:

Accepts the student with ASD as a full member of the classroom and creates an environment that enables the student to benefit from learning new skills and interacting with peers

Responsibilities:

✓ Attends IEP meetings

✓ Models acceptance and respect for the student with ASD to the general education students

✓ Encourages and facilitates peer and social interactions

✓ Includes and communicates with the student with ASD as a typical member of the class

✓ Maintains open communication with IEP team members

✓ Works collaboratively with the paraeducator and special educator

✓ Implements suggestions from the paraeducator and special educator

✓ Assists the special educator in evaluating the paraeducator

✓ Meets regularly with the special educator to enact ongoing changes

✓ Develops visual supports

✓ Assists in data collection methods

✓ Provides feedback on teaching strategies to the special educator and the paraeducator

✓ Uses accommodations and modifications of curriculum as appropriate

✓ Provides modified grading for student when necessary

✓ Involves the student's family in class activities

✓ Consistently implements the student's behavior intervention plan

✓ Provides appropriate encouragement and reinforcement to the student

✓ Uses structured and consistent classroom management strategies

Student: _____

✓ Checklist 6.4. Qualifications of Inclusive Education Paraeducator for Students with Autism Spectrum Disorders

Following is an ideal set of qualifications for the position of inclusive education paraeducator to work with a student with ASD in the general education classroom. The person:

✓ Is experienced in working with students with disabilities and preferably students with ASD

✓ Demonstrates the desire and ability to establish rapport with children with whom he or she works

✓ Interacts with students as an instructor and does not interact in a parenting or mothering style (that is, follows through objectively with difficult teaching and behavior interventions)

✓ Agrees with the inclusion of students with disabilities, in particular, students with ASD

✓ Exhibits and uses collaborative teaming skills

✓ Demonstrates good communication skills

✓ Demonstrates an understanding of his or her role as a paraeducator in the general education classroom and agrees with the responsibilities

✓ Is experienced in utilizing data collection systems for tracking goals and objectives

✓ Willingly receives ongoing training and supervision from the special educator and general education teacher

✓ Is able to set up a flexible work schedule to allow for time adjustments (increasing and decreasing) for being in the general education classroom with the student (that is, may work in a different classroom for part of the day)

Student: _____

✓ Checklist 6.5. Paraeducator: Roles and Responsibilities in the Inclusion Process

Primary Role:
Facilitates the independent learning and participation of the student within the general education classroom

Responsibilities:

✓ Establishes rapport with the student with ASD

✓ Receives training from the special educator

✓ Assists the general education teacher in interacting with student

✓ Assists the general education teacher in providing effective instruction to the student

✓ Assists the general education teacher with adaptations of and modifications to the program

✓ Assists the general education teacher and special educator with the whole class and with all students whenever possible

✓ Provides constant feedback to the special educator and general education teacher on the student's progress or lack thereof

✓ Offers suggestions on student participation in activities and adaptations for curriculum

✓ Assists the student in paying attention to the general education teacher

✓ Uses the correct prompting and fading instructional procedures

✓ Consistently implements the behavior plan and reinforcement system

✓ Uses natural correction procedures for the general education environment

✓ Facilitates social and peer interactions and friendships within the class and during recess, physical education, lunch, and so on

✓ Provides naturalistic reinforcement for the student

✓ Fades his or her presence near the student

✓ Maintains data and records on the implementation of goals and objectives and the behavior plan

✓ Implements goals and objectives by using appropriate teaching procedures while in the general education classroom

✓ Maintains a daily log of all occurrences and of progress or lack of progress

✓ Accepts and implements feedback on evaluations and suggestions for improvement from the general education teacher and the special education teacher

Student: _____

✓ Checklist 6.6. Parents and Family: Roles and Responsibilities in the Inclusion Process

Primary Role:

Assists the IEP team in maintaining the "big picture" of their child, establishing long-term goals and priorities for their child that include interests, home and family life, extracurricular activities, and academic education.

Responsibilities:

✓ Attends meeting with special educator prior to inclusion to review the transition and inclusion process; offers suggestions, obtains information, answers and asks questions

✓ Attends IEP meetings

✓ Is a part of the ability awareness activity or inservice for the general education staff and students in the classroom into which the child will be going

✓ Maintains an objective viewpoint on the child's abilities and disabilities

✓ Is consistent with various in-home activities suggested by the special educator or by the teacher to reinforce general education classroom activities and lessons

✓ Volunteers time in the general education classroom

✓ Constantly expresses appreciation to the team members for their involvement and efforts in implementing the child's inclusion program

✓ Maintains open communication throughout the school year

    ✓ Asks to be informed of upcoming changes, events, classroom themes, or topics to be discussed

    ✓ Provides any information on the child that may be important for the general education teacher to know, including the child's interests

    ✓ Assists in maintaining communication and a collaborative teaming process between the general education teacher and themselves (being assertive yet friendly and cooperative)

    ✓ Provides accurate information on changes in home life, or on any events that may affect the child's behavior

    ✓ Provides ongoing feedback to staff team members about perceived effectiveness and implementation of instruction techniques, about curriculum adaptations, and about behavior, social, and play skills interventions

PART III

Establishment of the Inclusion Program

Initiating the Inclusion Process

7

ONCE a school site has established the structure of a successful inclusion program, beginning the inclusion process for a specific student with ASD entails all of the individualized preparation activities previously discussed—identifying the student's unique characteristics; determining the priorities of the student's needs, goals, and objectives; and deciding on the appropriate placement. Thus every student with ASD who is being included in the general education classroom has his own specific inclusive education program. To position the student for success, this program must encompasses much proactive work on the part of the special educator, along with the efforts of the IEP team. This chapter discusses the four stages through which the special educator will need to lead the team to begin and establish the inclusion process:

- Observing and finding the appropriate general education classroom

- Planning for the first days of inclusion

- Training and preparing the general education teacher and paraeducator

- Facilitating the first days of inclusion

These four stages are broken down here into more manageable steps with the ultimate goal of systematically setting the stage for successful

> ✓ Use Checklist 7.1: Initiating the Inclusion Process

inclusion. An easy-to-use checklist that includes these four stages and their steps has been provided at the end of the chapter. Other useful forms and checklists for specific processes have also been noted throughout the text and included at the end of the chapter.

Observing and Finding the Appropriate General Education Classroom

In the first step of the first stage of the inclusion process, if the special educator (the person acting as the inclusion facilitator and case manager) is not currently the primary special education teacher for the student being included, the special educator needs to become familiar with that student. This step may be eliminated if the special educator has already been the student's primary special education teacher. Because the special educator has most likely already been involved in the IEP team and in the decision-making process that has led the IEP team to begin including the student with ASD in the general education classroom, he or she already has a clear understanding of the student's abilities, challenges, specific needs, and goals and objectives. Therefore, at this point the special educator needs to observe the student in his or her current education environment (in-home program or special education classroom) and to attend specifically to how the student participates in the ongoing

The Observation of Student in Special Education Program form (Form 7.1) has been created and placed near the end of this chapter for use by the special educator to compile pertinent

> 🖋 Use Form 7.1: Observation of the Student in the Special Education Program

information about the instructional techniques currently being used with the student, about the student's interactions with the teacher, with other adults, and with the other students; about the student's need for ongoing support, and about the student's participation throughout the day in ongoing activities and routines. This information assists the team in planning for the student's transition to the general education classroom for part or all of the day

The second step of this first stage is to decide which general education classroom and which teacher best match the student's needs and characteristics. Sometimes an IEP team may already have in mind a particular teacher and classroom in which they would like to include the student, but often they do not yet know which is the best placement. Therefore, the special educator and, usually, the parents will observe all the general education classrooms at the appropriate grade level (or sometimes the *only* classroom available at that grade level). The Observation of General Education

Classroom form (Form 7.2) guides the special educator through the process of obtaining information on the salient features and components of

> 🖋 Use Form 7.2: Observation of the General Education Classroom

the classroom, on the teacher's management style, and on characteristics of the typical student in that classroom. The special educator is attempting to answer the following questions:

- Is the classroom environment one to which the student with ASD adapts well and that can be adapted (if needed) to help the student?

- What are the typical routines and the schedule for the day and week?

- What types of curricula are used for the main academic subjects?

- With what types of ongoing activity does the student with ASD do well and with what types does he not?

- How do the typical students interact with each other?

- What is the teacher's management style with the class as a whole and with individual students?

- What are potential difficulties that the student might encounter when starting to be included?

This information helps the special educator make an informed recommendation to the IEP team on the appropriate classroom and teacher for the student with ASD.

The parents do not need to use this form or any other special form when they observe, but the special educator should give them basic ideas about what they might pay attention to and consider. They might observe, for example, the main characteristics about the class in general and about the teacher with whom they see their child possibly struggling (at least initially), and the activities and aspects of the class and characteristics of the teacher and typical students with whom they see their child doing well. These observations assist both the IEP and the inclusion process.

While the team is in the classroom, it is important for them to consider how much time the student spends in the general education classroom. Most students with ASD do best when the amount of time they are initially included in the general education classroom is less than the amount of the ultimate goal and is gradually increased over time. This process allows the student (as well as the general education teacher) time to adjust

> ➡ Students with ASD do best when the amount of time they are initially included in the general education classroom is less than the amount of the ultimate goal.

as he or she transitions to the new classroom. This is a crucial aspect of being proactive in the success of the inclusive education program. In the beginning, the team wants the time that the student spends in the general education class to be reinforcing for both the student and the general education teacher, and they want the daily inclusion time to begin and end on a positive note so that the student will want to go back to that class and the general education teacher will have a positive attitude toward the student and his inclusion in his or her class.

One of the most difficult aspects of the inclusion process takes place when the student has a negative experience in the classroom and then decides that he does not want to go to that class. Typically he often then learns that if he becomes disruptive he will be taken out of the classroom (so that the teacher can continue teaching he other students). The educator has little power to change this pattern of inappropriate behavior and must avoid reinforcing it, because the student cannot be allowed to continue disrupting the class indefinitely. Conversely, if the student initially has positive experiences in the classroom and looks forward to being in the general education class, the educators are able to pull him or her out of the classroom if he or she becomes disruptive because this response is now an appropriate consequence for an inappropriate behavior rather than a reinforcer of an inappropriate behavior. In this situation the student learns, "If I want to stay in the classroom I like, I cannot engage in this inappropriate, disruptive behavior or I will be taken out of that classroom." Thus, the inappropriate, disruptive behavior typically decreases. Of course if the inclusive education program is going to be successful in the long run, the student needs to learn to engage in the less-desired activities (such as listening to the teacher's lectures), but initially the goal is for the student to find the classroom reinforcing and to desire being there where he is learning and interacting with his typical peers.

So, during the initial observations in the general education classroom, the special educator and the parents need to identify the specific activities in which the student will be included, the specific time that is optimal to include the student, and the manner in which the time will be increased from that point. During the observation it is important to note the beginning and ending times and the resulting length of each activity. If someone believes that the student will enjoy a particular activity most, it is important to determine if it would initially be difficult for the student to maintain the appropriate behaviors of attending, sitting, and being quiet for the whole time of that activity. For example, in a preschool or kindergarten class, the circle time that involves music and a storytelling might be identified as an activity the student would enjoy; but the circle might time lasts for forty-five minutes and include talking about the weather, checking the calendar, and so on. These activities might be of interest to the student, but the length of time they last might cause the student to tune out, become distracted and agitated, and so on. It is therefore best to plan for the student to initially be involved in the circle time during the activities he would enjoy and for a period in which he is able to sit, pay attention, and participate appropriately. This participation may involve a change in the order of the activities during the circle time so that the singing and music and storytime all occur in a sequence. Another example might be that the student particularly enjoys and is good at math, so the team decides to start his inclusion time in the general education classroom during math time. The team needs to analyze how long math class takes and whether the student would be able to sit and listen appropriately through the math lesson while a new computation is taught and then while an activity or worksheet is given to the students to complete. Initially it may be appropriate to preteach the math concepts to the student before he goes into the general education classroom. The student will then enter the classroom and only participate in an activity or complete a worksheet. When, how, and how much to increase or decrease inclusion time will be discussed during the fourth stage of the inclusion process: facilitating the first days of inclusion. What is important during this third step is to decide for how long and during what activity the student will initially be included.

> ➜ It is important to decide how long and during what activity the student will be initially be included.

During the observation of the general education classrooms, each general education teacher's instructional and classroom management style, as well as his or her attitude toward inclusive education, is further analyzed. These approaches and the teachers' attitudes are ultimately the main factors in deciding which classroom is the best match for the student. The principal typically has valuable input into the different teachers' personalities, their attitudes toward students with disabilities, and their instructional and management styles, and this is helpful information to have when observing the teachers. The principal can also provide information about the other students with disabilities who may be included in some of the general education classrooms. This is especially important because it is not best for all or most of the students with disabilities to be included in the same class.

Ultimately, two factors are most important when deciding which general education teacher will be the best fit for the student with ASD:

1. Does the teacher have a positive attitude toward the inclusion in his or her class of students with disabilities in general and of the student with ASD in particular?

2. Does the teacher conduct his or her class with consistent and appropriate structure and behavior management?

The first factor—the positive attitude—does not indicate how many years of experience the teacher has as a teacher or how many years of experience the teacher has including other students with disabilities. This accords with the research presented in Chapter Two that found that a positive attitude on the part of the teacher was paramount to the success of the inclusion of students with disabilities. A positive attitude and willingness to include students with disabilities motivates a teacher to learn quickly and work cooperatively with the IEP team, particular with the paraeducator and the special educator. The second factor—structure and management—is important because research has proved that students with ASD need to be in a structured education setting in order to benefit from teaching. This also means that the teacher must have a predictable and consistent behavior management plan that she implements both class-wide and individually with each student (adjusting the plan according to various students' needs). Any pertinent information on the various general education teachers can be recorded on the observation form for the general education classroom (Form 7.2).

It is possible that there are not several teachers from which to choose and that only one classroom is available in which to include the student with ASD. In that case, it is important to rate where the general education teacher falls on the scales for positive inclusive attitude and maintenance of a structured classroom, and then to note any possible difficulties that may arise related to these factors. This assessment may then require that extra measures be taken to improve the teacher's attitude or to provide more structure in the classroom before the student is included.

The third step in this first stage of finding the appropriate general education classroom is to perform an overview of the school environment in terms of the locations to the student might go, the activities in which he may be involved, the classrooms he may attend, and the people with whom he may interact. This overview will help the IEP team to gain the logistical information on the arrangement of the school and on ongoing activities that is necessary to prepare additional supports to meet the student's needs. Information is collected on the physical features of the buildings, the playgrounds, the classrooms, and the cafeteria; on the movement routines that occur during transitions to and from important locations such as the office, the bathrooms, the playground, and so on; on the types of extra classes the student will attend (such as classes in the library and computer, art, and music classes); and on the number of adults present in the different locations of the school and on the types of interactions these adults have with the students. The Inclusive Education Environment Review form (Form 7.3) was created for the special educator to fill our and use during this review process.

> ✐ Use Form 7.3: Inclusive Education Environment Review

The fourth step in this stage in the inclusion process is to decide what changes need to occur in the student's current program to prepare him or her for the transition to the general education classroom. There may need to be changes in some of the instructional methods being used with the student in the special education classroom in order to make those methods similar to what he will encounter in the general education classroom. One example of this may be that in many special education classrooms, because they are so small, students are not required to raise their hand and wait to be called on to ask a question or make a comment. In the general education classroom, however, it is not appropriate for him to speak whenever he desires. Another example is that the teacher in the special education classroom may sit at a table with the students while he or she is instructed them and thus the student is most comfortable receiving instruction from a teacher who is sitting at his eye level and who doesn't move around or away from him. When he enters the general education classroom, however, he is instructed by a teacher who usually walks around or stands quite a distance from him.

Other changes may need to occur in the behavior intervention strategies currently being used with the student that may not necessarily be appropriate for the general education

> ✏ Use Form 7.4: Suggestions for Changes to the Special Education Program

classroom. For example, although in the special education classroom the student might frequently receive a particular food item (such as a cookie or Jelly-Belly) as a reinforcer for appropriate behavior, it is not appropriate for the student to frequently receive these items for appropriate behavior in the general education classroom. Therefore, establishing a token economy system that allows a larger, more desired reinforcer to be delivered less frequently and at a more appropriate interval is a better strategy for the general education classroom. Also, using other age-appropriate items as reinforcers helps the student to stand out less as different. Further information on implementing a behavior intervention plan in the general education classroom is provided in Chapter Nine. Other changes that may need to be addressed are revisions to curriculum presentation methods and accommodations for the student, to visual supports used throughout the day, to the types of toys and games that are available to the student, and to the child's behavior as he interacts with his classmates.

At the end of this first stage, the special educator and the IEP team should have compiled enough information to make a decision on

- Which general education classroom and teacher will be the best match for the student with ASD

- What changes need to be made to prepare the student for the inclusion process

- In what activity and for how long the student will first be included in the general education classroom

The IEP team must then meet to reach a consensus on these factors. Following that meeting, either the principal or the special educator should speak to the general education teacher of their choice about their decision. The process of selecting a paraeducator to work with the student in the general education classroom also begins. All of the qualifications listed in the previous chapter and in the roles and responsibilities checklist can be used at this point to advertise for the job and when interviewing candidates. The team is now ready to move to the next stage of instigating the inclusion process.

Planning for the First Days of Inclusion

Having chosen the classroom and the general education teacher, the team is now ready to enter the second stage, in which specific plans are made to include the student in the general education classroom. The IEP team, including the related service providers, should meet again but this time with the newly chosen general education teacher. The main purposes for this meeting are to

- Familiarize the general education teacher with the student's ASD characteristics, abilities and needs, and goals and objectives, and with the decision process for placement in the general education classroom

- Plan the logistics of the activities that need to occur *before* the first day of inclusion

- Plan those first days of inclusion

This meeting enables all members of the IEP team to be an integral part of the decision-making process about the early days of inclusion, as well as to plan for ongoing service implementation, support, and collaboration.

Prior to this planning meeting it can be helpful to provide the general education teacher with the student summary forms *ASD Characteristics: Student Profile* (see Chapter One), and the *LRE Services and Placement Determination* (see Chapter Four), and with the latest IEP goals and objectives so that he or she may become familiar with the student. The beginning of the meeting should be spent reviewing the student's needs and the current goals and objectives (specifically those to be met in the general education classroom). The roles and responsibilities of the general education teacher should also be reviewed. This is an excellent opportunity for the general education teacher to ask questions and express any concerns she may have about the student and his inclusive education program, and to explain her teaching and classroom management style and philosophies. The team also needs to discuss with the general education teacher the role and responsibilities of the paraeducator (if one is going to be hired to work with this student). This is an important discussion because some general education teachers may feel uncomfortable having another educator in their classroom on a regular basis. The general education teacher should be invited to be part of the training of the paraeducator so that she understands and has input into the paraeducator's role and feels she has some authority over the paraeducator's actions in the classroom.

The IEP team then begins planning the activities that need to occur next in the inclusion process. They decide when the first day of inclusion will be for the student with ASD. A plan for the transition on that first day takes the following factors into account:

- The changes that are going to be put in place in the student's current program to help prepare him, and how much time that preparation will take

- The time that will be needed for training the general education teacher

- When the paraeducator can begin working and what training he or she will need prior to starting to work with the student in the general education classroom

- The materials that need to be prepared for use with the student in the general education classroom

- The activity into which the student will initially be included

- The amount of time that will be allowed for the initial inclusion activity

- The tentative plan for increasing the inclusion time

The team also needs to decide if ability awareness activities are to be carried out for the personnel at the school site and for the typical students in the general education classroom before the student attends the class. The Ability Awareness Checklist (Checklist 7.2) is provided at the end of the chapter for the special educator and IEP team to use

> ✓ Use Checklist 7.2: Ability Awareness Checklist

in planning for both the staff and the students. The purpose of the ability awareness activity for school personnel is to enable them to become familiar with the student with ASD (particularly if he is new to the school) and to see how ASD is manifested in him (that is, in his behaviors, in his communication and interaction abilities, and in his needs) and thus to dispel the myths about ASD and assist everyone in accepting the student as a member of the school. The special educator uses this opportunity to help other school personnel, such as those who work in the cafeteria, in the office, and on the school playground, to understand how they can support the student, and to implement specific behavior intervention strategies if needed. The purpose of the ability awareness activity for the general education students is to enable them to understand the differences and similarities between the student and themselves and to become comfortable interacting with the student. It should be noted that most general education students are very accepting and accommodating of a student with ASD and are often better at ignoring inappropriate behaviors than are the adult educators. Two forms—Form 7.5: Summary of Student's Abilities and Interests, and Form 7.6: Student Interest Survey—have been created for use in conjunction with the ability awareness activities if the parents and the IEP team feel they would be helpful.

> ✎ Use Form 7.5: Summary of Student's Abilities and Interests, and Form 7.6: Student Interest Survey.

The team also needs to develop an emergency plan for handling any unexpected inappropriate behaviors (such as aggressiveness, destructiveness, and ongoing loud noises), anxiety episodes, allergic reactions, or injuries. It is particularly important for the team to prepare and plan for these extremes so that one unexpected and difficult incident does not significantly disrupt or alter the student's inclusive education program. The Emergency Plan for Inclusive Education Program (Form 7.7) was created for the team to use to plan and prepare all members for possible emergencies. This preparation will also

> ✎ Use Form 7.7: Emergency Plan for the Inclusive Education Program

make the paraeducator and general education teacher aware of the difficulties they could face, and help them feel more confident in handling any unexpected events that occur. It is wise to expect that there will be some unexpected occurrences of inappropriate behaviors, because it is in the nature of people with ASD to display such behaviors, both appropriate and inappropriate. Further information on how to handle such behaviors is provided in Chapter 9.

The IEP team also needs to plan for the student to visit the general education classroom and the teacher when the other students are not present. Such a visit allows the student to become familiar with the new instructional environment and meet his new teacher in that context. He sees where he will sit and with what toys and games he will be able to play. It can also be helpful for the student's current special education teacher to accompany him on this visit to help alleviate any fears or anxieties that may arise from being in the new environment. Some students may also benefit from more than one visit prior to the first day of inclusion.

The team needs to decide what type of training the general education teacher and, if applicable, the paraeducator will need prior to including the student in the class, and what ongoing supports are to be provided for the teacher, the paraeducator, and the student once he or she begins attending the general education class. This training includes discussing the type of communication system that will be most effective for the team as a whole, and what more frequently-used communication system will be best for the special educator, general education teacher, paraeducator, and parents.

At this point, dates need to be chosen for the following events:

- Observation of the student in his or her current placement

- Teacher trainings for both the general education teacher and the paraeducator

- Ability awareness activities, if applicable, for all of the school personnel and for the typical students in the general education classroom

- Meetings for the paraeducator, general education teacher, and special educator to plan the first days of inclusion

- Visits by the student with ASD to the general education classroom when only the general education teacher is present

The dates for these events can be written on the Initiating the Inclusion Process Checklist (Checklist 7.1) to help the special educator keep track of the upcoming activities and events prior to the first day of the student's inclusion

Training and Preparing the General Education Teacher and Paraeducator

By this third stage in the process the IEP team has hired or selected (from paraeducators already within the district) an appropriate paraeducator to work with the student in the general education classroom. How much knowledge and experience the paraeducator has of ASD, of working with such students in special education programs (at home or in a special class), and of working with students with disabilities in the general education classrooms will determine how much training this person needs. Prior to beginning training, the paraeducator is given a copy of the student summary forms ASD Characteristics: Student Profile (see Chapter One) and LRE Services and Placement Determination (see Chapter 4) and a copy of the student's IEP goals and objectives. He or she should already have observed the student in his current placement (in-home or special education class). It has happened, although rarely, that the inclusive education paraeducator who is hired has already been working as a paraeducator for the student in his current special education program. This circumstance significantly lessens the amount of training and preparation activities that are needed for the paraeducator. Typically an initial meeting is set up for the general education teacher, the paraeducator, and the special educator to get to know each other and to discuss what ASD is, the specific characteristics of the student, and any concerns or questions they might have. The main purpose of the meeting is to discuss and finalize the roles and responsibilities of the three educators (specifically how each person supports the student in the class, and how they will communicate and collaborate with each other). The roles and responsibilities checklists provided in the previous chapter can help with this process, but each team varies somewhat in what they decide are their own responsibilities, which are based on their unique abilities, interests, and time availabilities. Later, if time permits, and before the inclusion starts, another meeting should be held with the same educators and with the parents so that the parents can become aware of the team members' responsibilities toward their child and how they communicate on a regular basis. Several forms have been created for the IEP team to use to communicate with one another. The Comments and Questions for Special Educator forms (one for the paraeducator and one for the general education teacher) can be kept in the classroom in a special folder to which all three have access at any time, or in a simple spiral notebook in which notes can be written. The Daily Home-School Communication form can be adjusted to fit the

> ✐ Use Form 7.8: Comments and Questions for the Special Educator (Paraeducator), Form 7.9: Comments and Questions for the Special Educator (General Education Teacher), and Form 7.10: Daily Home-School Communication

specific needs of the student, or again a spiral notebook that goes back and forth between school and home can be used. It should be noted that the team needs to decide who is to be the primary person communicating with the parents, and how frequently that communication should occur (a minimum of two times per week is desired).

Training the paraeducator involves discussing the research-based applied behavior analysis teaching and behavior intervention strategies, modeling the use of these techniques, and observing the person using them with the student. Thus, before working with the student, the special educator needs to explain these procedures and role-play the techniques with the paraeducator. It is also important that the paraeducator spend time with the student in his or her current special education program, establishing a rapport and building his or her instructional control in working with the student. The Training an Inclusive Education Paraeducator Checklist (Checklist 7.3) has been created for the special

> ✓ Use Checklist 7.3: Training an Inclusive Education Paraeducator

educator to use while training and preparing the paraeducator to work with the student with ASD in the general education classroom.

As previously discussed in the section on the paraeducator's role and responsibilities, the main purpose of using a paraeducator to assist the student with ASD in the general education classroom is to facilitate the student's eventual independent learning and participation in that setting. All of the procedures the paraeducator is taught to use with the student should include an explanation of how to provide the least intrusive prompts and how to fade prompts, how to facilitate more interaction with the typical students and general education teacher, and how to reinforce independent completion of tasks and participation in activities. The para-educator also has the important role of recording data on the student's progress on his or her goals and objectives; thus, training is provided on assisting the student in implementing the goals and objectives, and on using a data collection system that tracks the student's skills.

Once the paraeducator's preliminary training has been completed, and depending on how much experience the paraeducator already has, the special educator needs to schedule time to be in the classroom (during the first couple of weeks of inclusion) with the paraeducator and student to model the teaching and behavior intervention strategies, as well as to monitor goals and objectives and take data. The special educator frequently needs to observe the paraeducator working with the student. After the paraeducator has worked for several weeks in the general education classroom with the student with ASD, the paraeducator and special educator should meet to review the activities that took place in those weeks and any possible changes or improvements that need to occur. At this time it is also beneficial to set up goals for the paraeducator to achieve, such as improvements in implementing certain strategies or techniques. Such goals help both the paraeducator and the special educator to remain accountable for improvements that need to be made and for further training that needs to be provided.

It is important to note that one uncommon, although possible, occurrence in some schools is having two paraeducators work with the same student in the general education class at different times during the day. This arrangement can be due

> ✐ Use Form 7.11: Goal Sheet for the Inclusive Education Paraeducator, and Form 7.12: Observation and Evaluation of the Paraeducator

to the inability to find a paraeducator who is able to work in the classroom all day, or to the philosophy that using different paraeducators will decrease the possibilities of prompt dependence on the part of the student. If an IEP team does plan to have two paraeducators assist the student on a regular basis, it is important to train both of them at the same time and to schedule ongoing communication and meetings so that they can share information and communicate changes in behaviors or use of intervention strategies.

While the general education teacher and paraeducator are being trained, the team is also implementing the preparation activities that were mentioned earlier (ability awareness activities, student visits to the classroom, and changes in the special education program). The team is now ready to move on to the final stage of facilitating the first days of the student's inclusion in the general education program.

Facilitating the First Days of Inclusion

In this fourth and final stage of instigating the inclusion process, the first days of inclusion are actually planned. In my experience, it is often best to plan for the first day of the

> ✓ Use Checklist 7.4: First Days of Inclusion Within the General Education Classroom

student's inclusion in the general education classroom to be a Wednesday. This schedule allows the typical students to begin their week as they would regularly do, and it allows the special education staff who are currently working with the student with ASD to have a couple of days to discuss the upcoming change with the student and prepare him or her for it (without a weekend of two days in between for him to forget about the change). It also means that there are three days in a row—Wednesday through Friday—for the student to be included in the general education classroom—enough for him to become accustomed to the change in his routines and yet not too much for the novelty to wear off and for him to start displaying inappropriate behaviors. Also, many students with ASD are very aware that they are in a class with typical peers, and they like this and thus work hard to "keep it together" so they can behave appropriately and do well in the class. Thus, only three days of "keeping it together" followed by a weekend break of two days provide the student with time to process the new activities in which he is involved, and relieve the stress developed from the changes to his educational program and routines. During the first days of inclusion, the special educator either acts as the paraeducator for the student (modeling for the paraeducator) or the special educator observes during the inclusion time and is available if any difficulties or emergencies arise.

If the team has decided that at the beginning of the inclusion process the student is going to be included for only part of an activity, it is best to plan a "backward chain" for his inclusion time rather than a "forward chain." This means that the student joins the activity for the predesignated and appropriate amount of time at the end of the activity so that he or she participates in the natural completion of the activity with his or her peers. This approach prevents the student from being pulled out of an activity in the middle of its occurrence, causing it to appear to him or his peers that he did something wrong and needed to be taken out of the class. It allows the student to begin to be a part of the natural end of activities and to become accustomed to the way transitions occur between activities. Also, the student can be removed more discretely during that transition period while he can still sense the accomplishment of completing the activity. The objective next time (possibly in several days or the next week) is to increase the time of inclusion. The time is added to the front and the student joins the activity sooner (closer to when the activity began).

The way to decide when or how much to increase the amount of time the student is included is to ensure that for several days or up to a week the student has appropriately participated in the activity and demonstrated that he enjoys being in the class and wants to go back. If he struggles with being appropriate during the time already allocated, the team needs to consider shortening the time he is there or changing the activity during which he is included. It is up to the team to determine the time increase, but they should start by moving gradually in the beginning (with less time), and then after several weeks have gone by and the overall process has gone well, the team can add larger time increments and more activities.

After the first day of inclusion, the special educator needs to allocate time to check in with the general education teacher, the paraeducator, and the parents to discuss how everything has proceeded. It is also important for the educators to communicate with all of the IEP team members about the progress that has

> ➜ After the first day of inclusion, the special educator needs to check in with the general education teacher, the paraeducator, and the parent to discuss how everything has proceeded.

been made during the first several days of inclusion. The three main inclusive educators should also plan to meet three to five days after inclusion has started to discuss the inclusion time and make appropriate changes for the future. After the first week of inclusion, data on the student's progress with his goals and objectives should be collected. It is hoped that by this time the student has settled into the new routine, is displaying appropriate classroom behaviors, and is gradually increasing his time in the classroom. The team continues to facilitate the student's progress in learning new skills, generalizing acquired skills, and interacting and playing with his peers.

Summary

There may be variations in the stages through which a particular team goes and in the steps that a team takes to instigate the inclusion process, but the stages and steps in this chapter provide a logical outline for all the activities and procedures that are needed to maximize the possibility of the student's success of the student. There is only one opportunity to begin with a clean slate. The time prior to and during the first weeks of inclusion are most important because this is when the team can invest in proactive measures to prevent negative events and promote positive occurrences related to the student's inclusion in the general education classroom.

Most challenges and concerns reveal themselves after the first weeks of the inclusion process and the IEP team is aware of the predominant issues with which they will continue to deal. The team needs to plan proactively and immediately to decide how these difficulties are to be addressed so that no problem becomes a barrier in the student's inclusive education program. There are always some problems that could not be foreseen or responses that could not be planned until the student was included in the general education classroom. At this point the team needs to step back, reevaluate the student's needs and characteristics, reevaluate the present plan, and make changes to accommodate what is causing the difficulties. It is also possible that the timing for beginning inclusion will need to be interrupted until the student is ready to be in the general education classroom.

If on the other hand the inclusion process is flowing well at this point, it is of primary importance to maintain ongoing communication and collaboration among the special educator, the general education teacher, and the paraeducator (as well as with the parents) in order to continue to facilitate the successful education of the student. The special educator now needs to invest his or her time in providing ongoing training and support for the general education teacher and paraeducator, and in performing ongoing evaluations of the inclusive education program to ensure that the student is making progress with his goals and objectives through the use of appropriate teaching and behavior intervention strategies.

Student: _____

✓ Checklist 7.1. Initiating the Inclusion Process

✓ Observe student in current placement (Form 7.1): *Date/time*: _____

✓ Observe all possible general education classrooms (Form 7.2):

   Dates/times: _____

✓ Perform inclusive education environment review (Form 7.3): *Date/time*: _____

✓ Meet with student's current special education teacher and provide suggestions for changes to implement to prepare for transition to the general education classroom (Form 7.4): *Date/time*: _____

✓ Arrange for parents to observe general education classrooms:

   Date/time: _____

✓ Hire/select paraeducator (Checklist 6.4): *Interview dates*: _____

   Paraeducator: _____

✓ Meet with parents regarding new teacher/paraeducator: *Date*: _____

✓ Pick classroom teacher and invite to initial meeting: *Teacher*: _____

✓ Meet with appropriate members of team to discuss the following as it pertains to the student:

   Date/time: _____

   ✓ Classroom and teacher for student
   ✓ Final roles and responsibilities of team members
   ✓ Goals and objectives for general education classroom
   ✓ Strengths, weaknesses, and behaviors
   ✓ Transition to general education classroom
   ✓ Times for ability awareness activities before transition
      School personnel: *Date/time* _____   General education class: *Date/time*: _____

   ✓ First day of inclusion and appropriate time

      Date/time/activity: _____

   ✓ Emergency plan for student (Form 7.7)
   ✓ Staff and home-school communication systems (Form 7.10)

✓ Provide training for paraeducator (Checklist 7.3): *Date/time*: _____

✓ Provide training for general education teacher: *Date/time*: _____

✓ Provide ability awareness/training for general education teacher(s) and administration (Checklist 7.2)

(Continued)

✓ **Checklist 7.1. Initiating the Inclusion Process** (Continued)

✓ Bring student to class/school to meet teacher and explore environment:

    Date/time: _____

✓ Meet with staff immediately prior to first day of inclusion: *Date/time:* _____

    ✓ Finalize activity, time, and duration of inclusion (first week)

        Activity/time/duration: _____

    ✓ Establish transition process

    ✓ Review roles and involvement of staff

    ✓ Review staff communication methods

    ✓ Discuss questions and concerns

    ✓ Review behavior intervention plans

    ✓ Set meeting time for after first several days of inclusion: *Date/time:* _____

✓ Observe/facilitate student's first day of inclusion: *Notes:* _____

_____

_____

_____

_____

_____

_____

✓ Meeting after first day(s) of inclusion: *Date/time:* _____

Student: _____

✓ Checklist 7.2. Ability Awareness

School Personnel Preparation

✓ At school staff meeting, inform staff about upcoming inclusion of student and ability awareness activities

✓ Provide reading material prior to ability awareness activities

✓ Ability awareness activities for school personnel

  ✓ Develop purpose and agenda
  ✓ Show *How Difficult Can This Be? F.A.T. City* movie by Richard Lavoie
  ✓ Have parent of student talk at meeting

    ✓ Give parent specific topic and time frame ahead of time

  ✓ Show pictures or video of student
  ✓ Explain student characteristics and interests (Form IEA:17 and Form IEA:18)
  ✓ Explain to staff student's pending inclusion schedule and procedures
  ✓ Review ways that various staff can support student:
    ✓ Recess
    ✓ Lunch
    ✓ Hallways
    ✓ Coming to and leaving school
    ✓ Office

General Education Students Preparation

✓ Inform students about upcoming inclusion of student in class and ability awareness activities

✓ Ability awareness activities for students

  ✓ Have parent of student talk at meeting
    ✓ Give parent specific topic and time frame ahead of time
  ✓ Show pictures or video of student
  ✓ Explain student characteristics and interests (Form 7.5 and Form 7.6)
    ✓ Behaviors displayed by student
      ✓ Why
      ✓ Ways it is dealt with by adults
      ✓ Ways peers can deal with it
    ✓ Communication system
      ✓ Why
      ✓ Best ways peers can interact with student
  ✓ Explain to staff student's pending inclusion schedule (transition) and procedures
  ✓ Review ways that various peers can support student:
    ✓ Recess
    ✓ Lunch
    ✓ Class activities

Student: _____   Paraeducator: _____

Special Educator: _____   General Education Teacher: _____

✓ Checklist 7.3. Training an Inclusive Education Paraeducator

✓ Have an initial meeting to discuss student's IEP goals, inclusion process, and roles and responsibilities (Checklist IEA:9). *Date/time*: _____

✓ Schedule time for paraeducator to establish rapport and instructional control with student if he or she does not already know student.

✓ Have paraeducator participate in a team meeting with all team members (if possible).

✓ Set up schedule to train the paraeducator in the following areas:

   ✓ Reviewing the binder to be used for the student within the general education classroom

   ✓ Use of discrete trial teaching techniques in general education classroom (as appropriate)

   ✓ Use of functional correction procedures

   ✓ Implementation of any behavior intervention plans

   ✓ Implementation of reinforcement system

      ✓ Utilizing a token economy system

      ✓ Utilizing peers

   ✓ Demonstration by special educator and practice by paraeducator of the teaching procedures for goals and objectives

   ✓ Demonstration by special educator and practice by paraeducator of data collection of goals and objectives during class time

   ✓ Implementation of curriculum adaptations

      ✓ General procedures (least to most intrusive adaptations)

      ✓ Specific procedures for known adaptations to be made

   ✓ Process of using and fading prompts: demonstration by special educator and practice by paraeducator of different types of prompts to use for specific activities, ensuring that the least intrusive is used first and faded immediately (prompting hierarchy)

      ✓ Process of fading presence and improving student's attention to teacher

      ✓ Redirecting of questions to teacher

   ✓ Avoidance of eye contact and interaction with student while teacher is giving instruction

(Continued)

✓ Checklist 7.3. Training an Inclusive Education Paraeducator *(Continued)*

- ✓ Process of praising appropriate behavior and ignoring inappropriate behavior
- ✓ Methods for assisting teacher to be the one to have direct interaction with the student
  - ✓ Importance of student seeing teacher as the one to seek for information
  - ✓ Direction of student to teacher for directions or answers
  - ✓ Suggestions for crucial times to interact with student
  - ✓ Attention given to good and effective actions that teacher tries and does
- ✓ Methods for being an assistant for entire classroom (not hovering around student)
- ✓ Utilizing peers to help students during activities and instruction time
- ✓ Maintenance of ongoing log of occurrences throughout the day
- ✓ Discuss forms to be used for communication among staff (Form 7.8 and Form 7.9).
- ✓ Discuss how special educator will provide support to paraeducator and general education teacher (schedule of observations, modifications to curriculum, data collections, etc.).
- ✓ Discuss and review exact areas and activities in which student will initially participate in class and how inclusion will be increased.
- ✓ Set up ongoing goals for paraeducator to be working on (Form 7.11).
- ✓ Set up times for regular observations and evaluations of paraeducator performance (Form 7.12).
- ✓ Provide ongoing training as inclusion time increases and as student's skills improve and increase

Student: _____   Date: _____

✓ Checklist 7.4. First Days of Inclusion within General Classroom

Before the first day:

✓ Schedule for first week of inclusion: *Days/times*: _____

_____

✓ Reminders sent to all team members (parents, teachers, principal, etc.) to be sure they are aware of time and duration of inclusion

During the first day:

✓ Special educator present to facilitate first day of inclusion

✓ Special educator sends written note home or talks with parents to inform them of how the first day proceeded

✓ General education teacher, paraeducator, and special educator briefly meet at the end of the day to discuss any pertinent issues that arose and any immediate changes that need to be made

After the first week:

✓ Special educator meets and debriefs with general education teacher and paraeducator and makes appropriate changes and modifications (refer to strategies listed in Chapters Eight and Nine).

   Changes needed: _____

_____

_____

_____

✓ Set up time for next meeting in a maximum of two weeks.

   Date/time: _____

Student: _____   Date: _____

Teacher: _____   Time: _____

Observer: _____

✎ Form 7.1. Observation of Student in Special Education Program

Location of program/classroom: _____

Student-to-teacher ratio: _____

Typical daily schedule: _____

Related services provided: _____

Primary form of communication and social interaction:

Adults: _____

Peers: _____

Activity observed (with brief description) _____

_____

_____

_____

Student-to-teacher ratio: _____

Activity directed by: _____

Description of student's participation and interactions with others: _____

_____

_____

_____

_____

_____

_____

Method of instruction: _____

_____

Types of prompts: _____

_____

Supports and accommodations: _____

_____

Problem behaviors: _____

_____

Comments: _____

_____

_____

Questions: _____

_____

_____

Student: _____   Date: _____

Teacher: _____   Time: _____

School: _____

✎ Form 7.2. Observation of General Education Classroom

School: _____   Grade: _____   Classroom: _____

Size of classroom (brief description): _____

Number of students in classroom: _____   Length (times) of day: _____

Boys: _____   Girls: _____   Days per week: _____

Number of adults in classroom (ratio; volunteers, paraeducator, etc.): _____

Comments about classroom location on campus: _____

_____

Diagram of classroom arrangement:

Order of routine (lengths) for the day (activities): _____

_____

_____

_____

Comments about routine (Is this the normal schedule? Is it posted for all? Is it rigid or flexible? Does it provide a good amount of structure for the day? etc.): _____

_____

_____

_____

_____

_____

_____

(Continued)

Student: _____   Date: _____

Teacher: _____   Time: _____

School: _____

✐ Form 7.2. Observation of General Education Classroom *(Continued)*

Comments about specific classroom activities (appropriate and inappropriate activities for student with ASD, type of structure available, special activities occurring during the week, activities that could be difficult for the student):

_____

_____

_____

_____

Comments on typical students in class (interaction styles, cliques, possible peer helpers; Why? Who might cause challenges for the student?): _____

_____

_____

_____

Comments on general education teacher's attitude and outlook (teaching and inclusion of students with disabilities) and personality (soft-spoken, lively, affectionate, humorous, harsh): _____

_____

_____

_____

Comments about teacher's classroom management (rewards/consequences plan, system for transitioning to next activity, cooperative learning vs. direct instruction, responsibilities of children, methods used to get attention of class, cues used): _____

_____

_____

_____

Comments about curriculum used for main academic subjects (reading, math, handwriting) and how they compare to student's current curriculum and level of functioning: _____

_____

_____

_____

_____

(Continued)

Student: _____   Date: _____

Teacher: _____   Time: _____

School: _____

✎ Form 7.2. Observation of General Education Classroom *(Continued)*

Significant differences between general education classroom and special day/resource classroom (types of demands, delivery of instruction, classroom arrangement, time required to sit, breaks, methods of transition): _____

_____

_____

_____

_____

_____

_____

Ideas for accommodations to help student in the class: _____

_____

_____

_____

_____

Which activities (and times) work best to start inclusion in general education classroom:

Activity: _____   Length: _____

Description of activity: _____

_____

_____

_____

Activity: _____   Length: _____

Description of activity: _____

_____

_____

_____

Additional comments: _____

_____

_____

_____

_____

_____

Student: _____   Date: _____

School: _____

✎ Form 7.3. Inclusive Education Environment Review

CLASSROOM

General Information

Furniture type and size: _____

    Table and chair size: _____

    Desk size and type: _____

Toys and materials: _____

    Location and size: _____

Accessibility to outside: _____

Accessibility to bathrooms: _____

Other: _____

Additional comments: _____

Specific Physical Features

Notable hazards within or near classroom: _____

Type of lighting: _____

Specific types of possible distractions: _____

Availability of "private place" for student to go, if needed: _____

Areas of work and play (enough room, etc.): _____

Seating Arrangements (check if applies and fill in activity/activities or type(s) of instruction)

    ❏ Students in group on rug for _____

        ❏ Use carpet squares ❏ tape markers ❏ random seating

        ❏ Students sit at desks for _____

        ❏ Desks in groups ❏ desks in rows

    ❏ Students sit at tables for _____

        ❏ Specific seating arrangement by ❏ groups or ❏ individuals ❏ random seating

Movement Routines

Move in lines, pairs, or _____

Walk long distances to activities outside of class _____

    Distance traveled: _____   Time for travel: _____

Transition cues used by teacher/adults: _____

Transition cues given to group or individuals: _____

Diagram of Classroom:

(Continued)

Student: _____   Date: _____

School: _____

✐ Form 7.3. Inclusive Education Environment Review (*Continued*)

BATHROOM

General Information

Bathroom inside or outside of classroom: _____

Different or same facilities for boys and girls: _____

Height of sinks: _____

    Method of turning water on and off: _____

Toilet size: _____

Amount of space: _____

Items located near (arms length) toilet: _____

Access to soap and paper towels: _____

Other supplies and furniture: _____

Disposal of waste paper: _____

Other: _____

Additional comments: _____

Bathroom Routines

Students go in group or individually to bathroom: _____

Specific times for going to the bathroom: _____

Students ask for permission: _____

Use of bathroom pass: _____

Visual symbols used to identify bathrooms: _____

Unique bathroom routines: _____

LUNCH AREA/CAFETERIA

Lunch routine (standing in lines, passing out food, etc.): _____

Table and chair or bench size: _____

Utensils and dishes used and available: _____

Types of food and drinks served and available: _____

Routes around tables: _____

Number of students per table: _____

Space at table per student: _____

Supervision of tables: _____

Noise level: _____

Amount of time expected to sit: _____

Next event or activity after lunch: _____

Other: _____

Additional comments: _____

(*Continued*)

Student: _____ Date: _____

School: _____

✒ Form 7.3. Inclusive Education Environment Review *(Continued)*

Diagram of lunch area (use arrows for routes, if possible):

PLAYGROUND

Surface types: _____

Playground equipment (slides, jungle gym, swings, etc.): _____

_____

Toys available: _____

Location and surroundings (include boundaries, fences, roads, buildings, etc.): _____

_____

_____

Number of students or classes out at same time: _____

Supervision (type and amount): _____

Playground rules: _____

Time at recess: _____

Additional comments: _____

_____

Diagram of playground:

EXTRA CLASSES (Library, Art, Music, PE, Computer Lab)

Class: _____ Teacher: _____ Day: _____ Time: _____

Description: _____

_____

_____

Class: _____ Teacher: _____ Day: _____ Time: _____

Class: _____ Teacher: _____ Day: _____ Time: _____

Description: _____

_____

Class: _____ Teacher: _____ Day: _____ Time: _____

Description: _____

Student: _____   Date: _____

Teacher: _____

✎ Form 7.4. Suggestions for Changes to Special Education Program

Instruction
Visual supports, teaching strategies, transitions, following routines, following instructions, teacher-to-student ratio

Academic Curriculum
Accommodations, modifications, level of difficulty

Behavior Intervention
Antecedent and consequence interventions, reinforcers, replacement behaviors

Social and Play Interventions
Parallel and interactive play, making choices, length of play

Communication and Language Interventions
Adaptability of system, level of support, use with peers and adults

Student: _____   Date: _____

✐ Form 7.5. Summary of Student's Abilities and Interests

Notable strengths

Communication/language: _____

_____

_____

Motor abilities: _____

_____

Social/play skills: _____

_____

Behavior: _____

_____

Learning style (auditory, visual, tactile): _____

_____

Academics: _____

_____

Notable difficulties

Communication/language: _____

_____

Motor abilities: _____

_____

Social/play skills: _____

_____

Behavior: _____

_____

Learning style (auditory, visual, tactile): _____

_____

Academics: _____

_____

Special interests: _____

_____

_____

_____

Special aversions/dislikes: _____

_____

_____

_____

Name: _____   Special Educator: _____

Teacher: _____

✎ Form 7.6. Student Interest Survey

School: _____   Age: _____   Birthdate: _____

Grade: _____

My favorite thing to do is _____

because _____

I do not like to _____

because _____

My favorite toy or possession is _____

My favorite subject at school is _____

because _____

My least favorite subject in school is _____

because _____

The things I like best about my friends are _____

because _____

The things I like best about my teacher are _____

because _____

The things I like best about my family are _____

because _____

I do not like it when _____

_____

I really like it when _____

_____

Other things I want you to know about me are _____

_____

Student: _____   Special Educator: _____

General Education Teacher: _____   Paraeducator: _____

✎ Form 7.7. Emergency Plan for Inclusive Education Program

Allergies and Treatments: _____

_____

_____

_____

_____

Possible emergency situations (anxiety or destructive, disruptive, and aggressive behaviors):

1. _____

2. _____

3. _____

4. _____

5. _____

Procedures for handling each emergency:

1. _____

   _____

2. _____

   _____

3. _____

   _____

4. _____

   _____

5. _____

   _____

Contacts (names and phone numbers): _____

_____

_____

_____

Student: _____

Paraeducator: _____

✐ Form 7.8. Comments and Questions for Special Educator (Paraeducator)

Comments (occurrences within classroom, observations of behavior, progress or lack of, etc.)

Date: _____   Comment: _____

_____

_____

_____ Special educator's initials (read comment): _____

Date: _____   Comment: _____

_____

_____

_____ Special educator's initials (read comment): _____

Date: _____   Comment: _____

_____

_____

_____ Special educator's initials (read comment): _____

Date: _____   Comment: _____

_____

_____

_____ Special educator's initials (read comment): _____

Date: _____   Comment: _____

_____

_____

_____ Special educator's initials (read comment): _____

Date: _____   Comment: _____

_____

_____

_____ Special educator's initials (read comment): _____

Date: _____   Comment: _____

_____

_____

_____ Special educator's initials (read comment): _____

Date: _____   Comment: _____

_____

_____

_____ Special educator's initials (read comment): _____

(Continued)

Student: _____

Paraeducator: _____

✏ Form 7.8. Comments and Questions for Special Educator (Paraeducator) *(Continued)*

Questions (about occurrences within classroom, behavior, communication, techniques, procedures, changes that may be occurring, instructional assistant, etc.)

Date: _____   Question: _____

_____

Special educator's suggestions: _____

_____

Date: _____   Question: _____

_____

Special educator's suggestions: _____

_____

Date: _____   Question: _____

_____

Special educator's suggestions: _____

_____

Date: _____   Question: _____

_____

Special educator's suggestions: _____

_____

Date: _____   Question: _____

_____

Special educator's suggestions: _____

_____

Date: _____   Question: _____

_____

Special educator's suggestions: _____

_____

Student: _____

Teacher: _____

✎ Form 7.9. Comments and Questions for Special Educator (General Education Teacher)

Comments (occurrences within classroom, observations of behavior, progress, or lack of, etc.)

Date: _____   Comment: _____

_____

_____ Special educator's initials (read comment): _____

Date: _____   Comment: _____

_____

_____ Special educator's initials (read comment): _____

Date: _____   Comment: _____

_____

_____ Special educator's initials (read comment): _____

Date: _____   Comment: _____

_____

_____ Special educator's initials (read comment): _____

Date: _____   Comment: _____

_____

_____ Special educator's initials (read comment): _____

Date: _____   Comment: _____

_____

_____ Special educator's initials (read comment): _____

Date: _____   Comment: _____

_____

_____ Special educator's initials (read comment): _____

Date: _____   Comment: _____

_____

_____ Special educator's initials (read comment): _____

(Continued)

Student: _____

Teacher: _____

✐ Form 7.9. Comments and Questions for Special Educator (General Education Teacher) *(Continued)*

Questions (occurrences within classroom, behavior, communication, techniques, procedures, changes that may be occurring, instructional assistant, etc.)

Date: _____ Question: _____
_____
_____

Special educator's suggestions: _____
_____
_____

Date: _____ Question: _____
_____
_____

Special educator's suggestions:_____
_____
_____

Date: _____ Question: _____
_____
_____

Special educator's suggestions: _____
_____
_____

Date: _____ Question: _____
_____
_____

Special educator's suggestions: _____
_____
_____

Date: _____ Question: _____
_____

Special educator's suggestions: _____
_____

Date: _____ Question: _____
_____
_____

Special educator's suggestions: _____
_____
_____

Student: _____   Date: _____

✐ Form 7.10. Daily Home-School Communication

Progress Notes: (+) indicates much effort made, (/) indicates some effort made, (-) indicates no effort made

Classroom Conduct:

_____ Entered classroom quietly

_____ Stayed on task during activity/lesson

_____ Followed directions from teacher

_____ Asked appropriately for assistance appropriately

_____ Raised hand and waited until spoken to

_____ Sat appropriately during activity/lesson

_____ Stayed on task during individual work

_____ Cleaned up materials/toys after finished with task/playtime

_____ Transitioned appropriately to next lesson/activity

_____ _____

_____ _____

_____ _____

Social/Communication:

_____ Made transitions between lessons and activities appropriately

_____ Communicated appropriately with teacher and/or peers

_____ Kept hands, feet, objects to self appropriately

_____ Responded to behavior plan and warnings

_____ Responded appropriately to peer interactions

_____ Shared materials/items appropriately

_____ Played appropriately with toys

_____ Played appropriately on playground

_____ _____

_____ _____

_____ _____

Teacher's signature: _____   Parent's signature: _____

Comments: _____

_____

_____

_____

Student: _____   Supervisor: _____

Paraeducator: _____

✏ Form 7.11. Goal Sheet for Inclusive Education Paraeducator

Goal: _____
_____
_____
_____

Criteria: _____

Achieve by date: _____

Goal: _____
_____
_____
_____

Criteria: _____

Achieve by date: _____

Goal: _____
_____
_____
_____

Criteria: _____

Achieve by date: _____

Goal: _____
_____
_____
_____

Criteria: _____

Achieve by date: _____

Goal: _____
_____
_____
_____

Criteria: _____

Achieve by date: _____

Student: _____   Observer: _____

Instructional Assistant: _____

✏ Form 7.12. Observation and Evaluation of Paraeducator

Teacher: _____   Date: _____   Time: _____

School: _____

First activity observed: _____   Number of children involved: _____

Activity directed by: _____

Brief description of activity and paraeducator's role (involvement with client, other children, and teacher; amount and nature of prompting for specific tasks; etc.): _____

_____

_____

_____

_____

_____

_____

Comments and recommendations: _____

_____

_____

_____

_____

_____

Second activity observed: _____   Number of children involved: _____

Activity directed by: _____

Brief description of activity and paraeducator's role (involvement with client, other children, and teacher; amount and nature of prompting for specific tasks; etc.): _____

_____

_____

_____

_____

_____

Comments and recommendations: _____

_____

_____

_____

_____

_____

(Continued)

Student: _____   Observer: _____

Paraeducator: _____

✎ **Form 7.12. Observation and Evaluation of Paraeducator** (*Continued*)

Third activity observed: _____ Number of children involved: _____

Activity directed by: _____

Brief description of activity and paraeducator's role (involvement with client, other children, and teacher; amount and nature of prompting for specific tasks; etc.): _____

_____

_____

_____

_____

Comments and recommendations: _____

_____

_____

_____

_____

Fourth activity observed: _____ Number of children involved: _____

Activity directed by: _____

Brief description of activity and paraeducator's role (involvement with client, other children, and teacher; amount and nature of prompting for specific tasks; etc.): _____

_____

_____

_____

_____

_____

Comments and recommendations: _____

_____

_____

_____

_____

Binder upkeep (data, logging of comments, etc.): _____

_____

Additional comments and suggestions: _____

_____

Facilitating Students' Education Within General Education

8

ONCE a student with ASD is included in the general education classroom (part- or full-day), it is important for the special educator, general education teacher, and paraeducator to use teaching techniques and strategies that will effectively facilitate the student's education, both academic and social. One of the most important aspects of an inclusive education program for students with ASD is for them *to learn to learn*. This concept was previously discussed in Chapter Four in relation to the cognitive and learning abilities of the student with ASD, and it continues to be discussed in this chapter. It can be difficult to adjust teaching strategies for use specifically with a student who still requires special education services but is receiving his education within the general education classroom. Thus, it is important for ongoing support to be provided by the special educator for the student and teacher, and for the paraeducator to assist the teacher in the daily process of educating the student. This chapter discusses the following:

- The types of general education classroom behaviors that are the primary focus for students with ASD during an early intervention inclusive education program

- The types of teaching strategies to be used with the student with ASD in the general education classroom

- The consultation techniques for the special educator to use with the general education teacher and paraeducator.

General Education Classroom Behaviors

During the first year of his or her inclusion in a general education classroom, a student with ASD should primarily be expected to gain the skills needed to function appropriately and to learn within that environment. These skills are classified as *classroom behavior skills*. They are needed for the student to remain in the general education classroom and to benefit academically and socially from receiving his or her education in that environment. The IEP team should focus on these skills during the child's first year of inclusion in the general education classroom.

Ideally, when a student with ASD is between the ages of three and five, he is included for some time each week in a preschool class that has typical students and is focusing on school readiness skills. Then, when it is time for him to be included in a general education kindergarten classroom, there will be less differ-

> ➜ Ideally, when a student with ASD is between the ages of three and five, he is included for some time each week in a preschool class that has typical students and is focusing on school readiness skills.

ence between the types of activities and skills he will be expected to do in the kindergarten and the types of activities and skills he is already able to do; thus he will be enabled to participate more successfully. If an IEP team is debating about whether to keep a student with ASD who is five years old in a preschool for another year or to include him in a kindergarten class, it is more beneficial, I believe, for the student to have two years (ages five and six) in a general education kindergarten classroom than to have the another year in preschool. This approach would allow the inclusive education program to focus during the first year on classroom behavior skills and during the second year on gaining the needed academic skills. It is also more socially acceptable for a student to repeat kindergarten than to repeat preschool or a later grade, because some typical children repeat kindergarten, and many typical children are held out of kindergarten if their birthday is near September or if they are immature. Thus many typical children are six years of age upon entering or leaving kindergarten.

Classroom behavior skills can be categorized into the following five categories, which are essentially skill sets. Seeing these categories helps an IEP team to understand the various skills so they can determine if there are particular sets of skills in which the student is not progressing:

- Attention
- Participation
- Following classroom routines
- Social interaction and communication
- Play

All of these skills are included on the General Education Classroom-Behavior Skills handout (Handout 8.1) at the end of this chapter for easy reference.

> ☞ Use Handout 8.1: General Education Classroom Behavior Skills

Attention

One of the most important sets of skills that it is typically assumed every student has is the skills used to attend to pertinent stimuli in the environment, particularly the teacher. This is one set of skills that all children with ASD struggle with, and there is only one way to know if the student is paying attention: he or she performs an *expressive action* (that is, says something or does something) in response to what he or she was expected to pay attention to.

One early attending skill is *orienting to* a person who is initiating interaction with the student or with whom the student is attempting to initiate interaction. A typical child learns early to use eye contact to orient himself to a person who is interacting with (that is, speaking to) him or her. Eye contact is one skill that an individual with ASD may never be comfortable using, so requiring the student to provide eye contact when attending or listening to the person initiating interaction may be too difficult for him; but learning to orient to the person (that is, to turn body, head, and face toward the person) can help the student focus on what that person is saying or doing, and can help the person know that the student is both acknowledging the initiation of interaction and trying to interact with the person in return. This skill begins with attending to one person (that is, in a one-to-one teaching situation), who gradually moves farther and farther away from the student, followed by attending in a small group, and finally by attending in a large group. It is important to note that in any teaching situation the teacher should avoid repeatedly using the student's name to gain his or her attention, because this will inadvertently teach the student that he needs to attend only when his name is used. The skill of attending to a person then needs to expand to attending to other objects and events to which a teacher or other person is referring. This is called *joint-attention* and requires the student to attend simultaneously to what a person is saying and doing and to an object or activity to which that person is referring. This is an essential skill that aids the student's ability to learn from lectures and to play and interact socially with his or her peers.

To help a student gain attending and joint attention skills, it is important to develop the student's ability to imitate the actions of other people, first with his own body and then with objects. Reinforcing the student for imitating such actions teaches him

> ➜ Joint attention is an essential skill that helps the student learn from lectures and play and socially interact with his or her peers.

that this is a desired and important skill and increases his motivation to attend to his teacher and peers and to respond to instructions, questions, or comments directed to him. Other skills that help the student attend are as follows:

- Sitting for longer amounts of time through different types of activities and at different locations or settings (such as sitting at a table with three to four other students in order to complete a work assignment, sitting on the floor attending to a story being read, sitting at a desk, and attending to a lecture about adding numbers)

- Redirecting his attention back to a task or person after being distracted

- Remaining on task with independent work for longer periods

Participation

Both the amount of time a student is able to spend independently engaged in a given activity and the way in which he participates contribute to the success of his inclusive education program. To understand how well a student is able to do this and then to see if he is progressing in this skill, data need to be collected. It is easy to underestimate or overestimate how well the student is doing in independently and actively participating in activities without the data. Data should be collected on how long a student attends to and participates in the following:

- An independent work activity

- Adult-directed small-group activity (three to five students)

- Student-directed cooperative small-group activity (two to five students)

- Adult-directed large-group activity

Data should be collected on how many times the student needs to be prompted to continue participating (to remain on task) in each of these types of activities. Also, data need to be recorded on the on-task behaviors that are typical and necessary for each activity (that is, looking at materials and performing appropriate action with them, making appropriate comments about tasks or activities, quietly working on an assignment, and so on). It is only through reviewing this data that the educator can understand what skills need to be taught in order to increase the student's level of participation.

Another aspect of monitoring a student's participation is noting how motivated the student appears to be to participate in various activities and tasks in the general education classroom. It is difficult to collect quantifiable data on this aspect but this is best accomplished by listening carefully to the comments a student makes and watching the student's actions to see in what activity he or she is interested and if he or she wants to be in the classroom. Tracking the amount of external reinforcement that needs to be provided (versus intrinsic motivation) for the student to complete a task or activity is a way to monitor progress with this skill as well.

Following Classroom Routines

Many ongoing activities occur throughout every typical day in a general education classroom. Helping the student to understand the purpose of and to follow these routines independently greatly increases his ability to participate in ongoing activities and attend to pertinent stimuli. Following is a list of the common general education activities and routines that students need to learn to perform independently:

- Works quietly on independent tasks
- Keeps personal items in designated space (desk or cubby)
- Locates and uses restrooms
- Locates own preassigned seating location for different activities (circle time, independent work, small group, and so on)
- Sits quietly while teacher is talking to the whole class or to a single student
- Raises hand to ask question
- Raises hand to answer question
- Raises hand to make comment
- Locates and uses needed materials for tasks and activities
- Organizes time and follows routines for completing a task
- Remains on task for a given activity or task for longer periods (fifteen to twenty minutes in lower grades, thirty to forty-five minutes in upper grades)
- Follows instructions to complete two to three steps
- Follows common, simple routines within specific activities (such as arriving at school, lunchtime, and so on)
- Transitions between activities
- Transitions between locations on the school site
- Navigates around the classroom and school site
- Seeks help when appropriate
- Accepts help and correction when appropriate
- Is able to make mistakes, lose a game, or be something other than first in line without disruption to the class
- Volunteers to perform an action

- Follows instructions provided by school staff other than teacher or paraeducator

Many of these skills can also be considered school readiness skills and should be practiced as much as possible prior to entering the general education classroom.

Social Interaction and Communication

Although much information on the social skills of children with ASD is available in the literature, it is still worth mentioning the types of social skills that are important for the student's success within an inclusive education program. Communication skills are included as a part of the social skills category because in order to interact appropriately with one's teacher and peers, the student needs to have functional communication skills. It is important that the student be able to generalize whatever communication system he or she uses (speaking is preferred) to the general education classroom.

> ➔ It is important that whatever communication system the student uses (preferably speaking), he or she be able to generalize it to the general education classroom.

Following is a list (though not an exhaustive list) of important social interaction and communication skills that a student needs to learn and use in the general education classroom:

- Attends to (demonstrates awareness of) peers
- Uses appropriate attention-getting skills (such as taps person on arm, says person's name)
- Shows persistence in initiating interactions if previously ignored
- Tolerates the physical contact of others
- Expresses needs and wants
- Understands basic nonverbal communication (such as nodding or shaking head, shrugging shoulders, furrowing brow or raising eyebrows, lifting hands up)
- Uses basic nonverbal communication
- Shows awareness of effect of own behavior on others
- Shows awareness and understanding of basic emotions displayed by others and responds appropriately (for example, when a peer is crying, the student with ASD does not laugh at him)
- Is able to engage in three to six back-and-forth exchanges in a conversation

- Attempts to engage others in interactions

- Responds to others' initiations to interact

- Is able to engage in appropriate physical interactions with others (is not aggressive or harmful)

- Follows the lead of peers when appropriate

- Shares class materials with peers

- Takes the lead with peers when appropriate

- Shows a preference for playing and interacting with certain peers (for example, appears to like certain peers more than others, showing interest in friendships)

- Demonstrates a sense of humor

Some of the social and communication skills in this list are quite difficult to acquire, but they are skills that will greatly assist the student in being accepted by his or her peers, in participating successfully in activities, and in learning new skills.

Play

A student's ability to play with toys and to play games independently and with his or her peers are important skills that are used throughout each day within the general education classroom. Play activities can be one of the initial routes for facilitating inclusion in the general education classroom because in play the student enjoys a specific activity, toy, or game and acts appropriately while engaging in this activity. After playing in the general education classroom, the student is motivated to return to the classroom because he finds it a fun place to be and that it is fun to be with his peers. Play skills can also be a means for teaching other needed skills, such as attending, remaining on task, and interacting with peers. Acquiring appropriate play skills also facilitates a decrease in inappropriate obsessive and perseverative types of activities in which a student with ASD often engages.

Following is a list of play skills that are important for a student in the general education classroom to acquire and use:

- Plays with toys as they were designed to be played with

- Engages in play with three or more toys, games, or activities over several days

- Remains engaged in independent play with one toy, activity, or game for at least five to ten minutes

- Maintains appropriate proximal play (that is, is not destructive and does not take toys away from other students)
- Chooses from two or more activities or toys
- Follows game-playing rules (that is, takes turns, doesn't cheat)
- Engages in pretend play
- Engages in appropriate talking during play (that is, narrates, pretends conversation)
- Shares toys with peers
- Joins and leaves interactive play activities with appropriate social cues
- Attempts to join or initiate play with peers
- Allows peers to join him during play
- Explores other toys within his environment
- Demonstrates problem-solving skills when a toy or something else does not work

Teaching Strategies

Although it is important for the student with ASD *to learn how to learn* in the general education classroom through typical large- and small-group instruction strategies, it is often unrealistic to expect him or her to learn in that manner when he begins attending the class. By understanding the types of teaching methods that have been used successfully with the student with ASD in the special education classroom, the teacher and paraeducator may be able at first to

> ➜ It is often unrealistic to expect that a student with ASD is able to learn in a large-group setting when he begins attending the class.

adjust their teaching and interaction methods to make them similar to the methods used in the special education classroom (for example, by phrasing the instructions similarly), thus enabling the student to learn and progress more easily. Once the student has become more established in that new environment and is learning and displaying appropriate classroom behavior skills, the teacher and paraeducator can begin fading the teaching accommodations and using the teaching methods that are typically used in that setting, and start to expect the student to attend to and learn within the general education classroom.

In this section of the chapter a variety of teaching strategies are provided for use by the general education teacher and paraeducator as they attempt to teach the student and to facilitate her progress in her inclusive education program. The following list is not exhaustive but it covers many categories and may generate ideas for other strategies that the teacher and paraeducator can create to help a particular student. The teaching strategies are divided into the following categories:

- Implementing goals and objectives
- Facilitating generalization
- Teaching new skills
- Analyzing tasks for completion
- Providing curriculum accommodations and classroom aids
- Using body and verbal language
- Facilitating student independence

Checklists and handouts on these skill and teaching strategies have been created and are provided at the end of this chapter for easy use. Reference is made to each checklist and handout within that category of teaching strategies.

Implementing Goals and Objectives

At the beginning of the inclusion process, the special educator plans, along with the general education teacher and paraeducator, how and when to address the student's goals and objectives. One of the most difficult aspects of educating a student with ASD in the general education classroom is keeping track of his goals and objectives and developing methods for ensuring that teaching addresses those goals and objectives. There are several strategies that can help educators plan for the implementation and timing of working on the goals and objectives.

First, it is helpful to create a matrix (table) that organizes the goals and objectives on the left side and lists the ongoing class activities with a schedule across the top. Within this matrix, an X is placed in each box where a certain goal can be addressed during a specific activity. Referring to this matrix helps the general education teacher and paraeducator know when they need to focus on that particular skill, and ensures the IEP team that all goals and objectives are being addressed. The teacher and paraeducator can be creative in when and how they address specific skills. For example, some social skills can be addressed during lunch time and physical education class and not only during the more obvious activities such as recess and free choice or play time. See the sample matrix in Exhibit 8.1. A blank matrix (Form 8.1) is also provided at the end of the chapter.

> See Exhibit 8.1: IEP Goals and Classroom Schedule Matrix (Sample)

> ✐ Use Form 8.1: IEP Goals and Classroom Schedule Matrix

Student: _____

Teacher: _____

Paraeducator: _____

Exhibit 8.1. IEP Goals and Classroom Schedule Matrix (Sample)

IEP GOALS	8:30–8:40 Arrival Routines	8:40–8:50 Circle Time	8:50–9:45 Reading	9:45–10:00 Snack/Recess	10:00–10:15 Journal Writing	10:15–10:50 Math	10:50–11:30 Social Studies/Science	11:30–12:15 Lunch/Recess	12:15–12:45 Story/Sharing	12:45–1:20 Computers/Music/Art/Library	1:20–1:35 Recess	1:35–2:15 PE/Free Choice
Print name			*		*	*	*		*	*		
Sight word ID		*	*		*	*	*			*		
Phonics		*	*		*	*	*			*		
Number ID	*	*				*				*		*
Addition						*				*		
Get materials		*		*	*	*	*	*		*		*
Cut paper										*		
Ask for help	*	*	*	*	*	*	*	*	*	*	*	*
Initiate play				*					*		*	*
Take-turns play				*					*		*	*
Wait in line	*			*				*		*	*	*
Find locations	*	*		*				*		*	*	*

* Opportunity to work on student's IEP goal

Second, the special educator can create a binder for the student that includes the goals and objectives and a narrative description of teaching procedures for each skill. The special educator can then use these teaching procedures when training the general education teacher and paraeducator on how to work with the student; he or she then models the use of these procedures in the specific activity in the general education classroom. A sample teaching procedure form is provided in Exhibit 8.2.

> See Exhibit 8.2: Teaching Procedure (Sample), and Exhibit 8.3: Time Sample Data: Specific Activity (Sample)

Exhibit 8.2. Teaching Procedure (Sample)

Student: _____   Date introduced: _____

Class or Category of Objects: Generalization

Categorization: Receptive and Expressive Identification

Program Goal

[Student] has acquired receptive and expressive identification of different classes of common objects using isolated pictures on cards. The student will now (1) receptively and (2) expressively identify items in his environment, including books and worksheets, according to each class to which they belong.

Materials and Setup

Materials already present in typical environment of general education classroom.

Procedure

Receptive I: In the context of walking around the class, playing with items, engaging in small-group activity, completing a task, or looking at or reading a book, the instructor slightly isolates a particular object (that is, moves it a little closer to the student than it is to other items or covers up most of the other items on the page, etc.) and asks, "Which one is an animal?" or "Where is the vehicle?" The child should then point to the correct item.

Receptive II: In the context of walking around the class, playing with items, engaging in small-group activity, completing a task, looking at or reading a book, the instructor asks, "Which one is an animal?" or "Where is the piece of food?" The child then points to the correct item (no prompts are provided with positioning, etc.).

Transition to Expressive: Starting with the same receptive teaching procedure of locating the item from the specific class, and then, after the child points to the correct item, the instructor provides a specific praise, such as "That's right; that is an animal," and then says, "What animal is it?" The child responds, "A cat." Then the instructor says, "That's right. What is a cat?" The student responds, "An animal." Alternate between using the name of the item and the class as the first question.

(Continued)

Exhibit 8.2. Teaching Procedure (Sample), *(Continued)*

Expressive: No receptive procedure is used to first locate the item. The instructor and student are not always near the items and may have just finished a task or looking at a book. The instructor asks various questions such as, "What is a cat?" or "Tell me the name of a vehicle."

Prompting and Shaping Target Behaviors

Both of the receptive components may require a position, gestural, or physical prompt to shape the appropriate responses. For the expressive component, a verbal prompt may be necessary to shape the appropriate response. Remember that prompts need to be systematically faded as quickly as possible.

Progress Criterion

Mastery criteria are 80 percent for three sessions, with first trial being the correct answer. Be sure to intersperse acquired classes with new classes to ensure maintenance and generalization.

Data Collection

Provide the child with at least ten opportunities within an hour or session to identify objects receptively, and eventually expressively, according to their class. Use the following general *data/graph* sheet and follow the targets listed.

Targets	Date Introduced		Date Mastered	
	Receptive	Expressive	Receptive	Expressive
Set 1 Animals				
Set 2 Vehicles				
Set 3 Food				
Set 4 Clothing				
Set 5 Furniture				
Set 6 Toys				
Set 7 Body Parts				

Exhibit 8.3. Time Sample Data: Specific Activities (Sample)

Skill: Sit quietly (during group instruction or work activity)

Setting/Time	Length of activity	# Prompts
Circle time: kids sitting on floor, teacher reading book out loud	10 minutes	///

Skill: Participate in choral or group activity

Setting/Time	# Prompts	# Independent
All class singing song with body motions; teacher leading song played on tape	///	//// ///

Skill: Raises hand to ask question or volunteer for something

Setting/Time	# questions	# Opportunities-Volunteer/Independent
Circle time: teacher lecture on math lesson (greater than and less than), thirteen minutes	/	//// //// //

Skill: Interactions with peers

Setting/Time	#Initiations	#Responses	Example Comments/Questions
Completing independent math worksheet that required some group work at student tables (ten minutes)	//	///	Initiations: I think it's not a four (to group in general) Responses: No, I don't know (with eye contact to student)

Third, data collection procedures that correlate to the teaching procedures are created for the measurement of the student's goals and objectives and are also kept in the binder. Because most students with ASD have many goals and objectives, maintaining data can be a time-consuming and difficult process. Creating data sheets that are easy to use and cover work over small increments of time result in obtaining more useful data on the student's progress. Often the most successful way not to overload the person collecting the data is to collect data only two to three times a week (sample data) on each skill or goal. Typically the paraeducator takes the data on the goals and objectives; it is therefore important for her to have input on the structure of the data sheet, so that she understands it, can quickly take notes during an activity, and provides accurate information on the student's responding.

Facilitating Generalization of Skills

Students with ASD often demonstrate a level of difficulty with generalizing their use of acquired skills over different environments, with different instructors, and often with different instructional materials. An initial focus in the student's inclusive education program would be for him to use his *already* acquired skills with his new instructors and peers in the general education classroom. In this way his environment would change but the skill needed would not. This

> ➜ An initial focus in the student's inclusive education program would be for him to use his already acquired skills with his new instructors and with his peers in the general education classroom.

goal can be accomplished by pre-teaching the student part or all of a concept or task before the general education teacher plans to introduce it to the entire class. This approach familiarizes the student with the overall activity or concept and with the steps to complete it, as well as ensuring that the student participates in and completes the activity when it is presented to the whole class. Becoming familiar with a concept and activity prior to its introduction to the whole class also helps the student to attend better to the teacher and to increase his or her motivation to participate and complete the tasks.

Another teaching method used to assist in the development of the skills of generalization is to provide prompting at the appropriate time to encourage the student to use a particular skill and then to provide immediate reinforcement for the successful use of a generalized skill. Afterward, the prompts and immediate reinforcement are slowly faded until the student is using his or her skills more independently and consistently.

Many students with ASD are motivated to be in the general education classroom because they want to be with their typical peers. One strategy that is often successful for generalizing skills is to ask a peer to provide the student with the extra assistance he or she needs to complete a task or participate in an activity. The peer can be told ahead of time which types of instructional phrases and materials the student is familiar with and can then add his or her own words or methods of assistance.

Teaching New Skills

Once a student with ASD generalizes his or her acquired skills to use within the general education classroom and participates more independently

> ✓ Use Checklist 8.1: Facilitating Generalization of Skills

within the classroom, it is important for the student to be able to learn new skills. As noted previously, reinforcement, prompting (and fading), and correction procedures are essential teaching tools for working with students with ASD, and they are also used in teaching new skills. It is always the goal for the student to learn new skills in the same manner in which his typical peers learn them, by using best teaching practices that can easily be embedded within the daily instructional routines. Other strategies that involve more one-to-one involvement between the instructor and student are meant to be faded out as soon as possible. These best teaching practices and procedures of reinforcement, prompting and fading, and correction are discussed in the following pages.

Reinforcement

Because students with ASD are often content to engage in their own perseverative and obsessive activities with certain objects, it can be difficult to motivate them to learn new and appropriate activities that will assist them in functioning within their home, school, and community environments.

The use of reinforcement as a teaching tool provides the means for an instructor to motivate the student to attend and provide correct responses to new instructions. Reinforcement is any consequence that follows a response and increases the like-lihood that the response will occur

> ➡ The use of reinforcement as a teaching tool provides the means for an instructor to motivate the student to attend to and provide correct responses to new instructions.

again in the future under similar circumstances. A reinforcer is anything that the student wants to gain (such as food, a toy, attention, or avoidance of difficult tasks). Any behavior or response—whether inappropriate (incorrect) or appropriate (correct)—can be reinforced. It is therefore important for instructors to monitor closely the type of consequences that follow a student's responses. Following are four examples that demonstrate two ways to use reinforcement appropriately (Examples 1 and 2) and two ways to use reinforcement inappropriately (Examples 3 and 4).

Example 1: Reinforcement of Appropriate Behavior

A: Instructor holds a toy car within view of a student.

B: Student asks instructor, "Have toy car, please?"

C: Instructor gives the student the toy car and says, "Good asking."

Example 2: No Reinforcement of Inappropriate Behavior

A: Instructor holds a toy car within view of a student.

B: Student has a tantrum and tries to take the toy car from the instructor.

C: Instructor ignores the student, walks away, and hides all toy cars.

Example 3: Reinforcement of Inappropriate Behavior

A: Instructor holds a toy car within view of a student.

B: Student has a tantrum and tries to take the toy car from the instructor.

C: Instructor gives the student the toy car.

Example 4: No Reinforcement of Appropriate Behavior

A: Instructor holds a toy car within view of a student.

B: Student asks instructor, "Have toy car, please?"

C: Instructor ignores the student and does not give him the toy car.

The first and second examples present an instructor who is *appropriately reinforcing* a student for a correct response and not reinforcing a student for an incorrect response. This instructor is using reinforcement appropriately to increase appropriate responses and behaviors and decrease inappropriate responses and behaviors. The third and fourth examples present an instructor who is *inappropriately reinforcing* a student for an incorrect response and not reinforcing a student for a correct response. This instructor is inappropriately using reinforcement that increases inappropriate responses and behaviors and decreases appropriate responses and behaviors.

There are two primary reasons for using reinforcement during the instruction process. First, reinforcement is a critical factor in teaching a student new skills. By tying reinforcers directly to the target behavior he wishes to increase, the instructor *teaches* the student the correct response. Second, reinforcers provide the motivation a student needs to learn a skill she may not necessarily care about or consider important. A student needs to see a reason (a "payoff") for providing a response, specifically a correct response, to an instruction. If the instructor makes it clear that she has something the student wants, the student is more likely to be motivated to do what the instructor requests in order to obtain that item or activity (the reinforcer).

It is imperative that the instructor use reinforcers that the *student* prefers and not reinforcers that the *instructor* prefers. Maintaining an up-to-date list of reinforcers (a list of items and activities the student has preferred in the past, and novel, age-appropriate items the student may also prefer) provides the instructor with options he or she can use to figure out what the student wants to gain during a particular work session. Because the strength of a reinforcer (the amount of motivation the reinforcer elicits) can vary from moment to moment, instructors need to implement a quick reinforcement survey at the beginning of each learning session. This continuous reinforcer assessment process ensures that the student stays highly motivated and decreases the likelihood of incorrect responses due to lack of motivation.

> ➜ It is imperative that the instructor use reinforcers that the student prefers and not reinforcers that the instructor prefers.

It is also beneficial to, when possible, allow the student to choose (prior to a learning session) what he would like to earn as a reinforcer for successfully completing a particular learning session—a larger reinforcer than what is earned at intervals during the learning session. In and of itself, choice can be a motivating factor that leads to successful learning because it can make a student feel that he or she has some control over his environment and learning. For example, an instructor knows that a student enjoys looking at books, playing on the computer, and playing with trains. When the instructor and student sit down to work together for the next hour, the instructor shows the student a board with pictures on it. One picture shows the student working appropriately with the instructor, and next to this picture there is an arrow pointing toward a blank spot. At the bottom of the board there are three pictures of the student. In one picture he is reading a book, in another he is playing on the computer, and in the third he is playing with trains. The instructor asks the student to pick which activity he would like to do after "doing good work" with

> ➜ It is beneficial to, when possible, allow the student to choose (prior to a learning session) what he would like to earn as a reinforcer for successfully completing a particular learning session—a larger reinforcer than what is earned at intervals during the learning session).

the instructor. The student chooses a picture and puts it next to the arrow, establishing his choice to play with trains when they are done working. The board remains visible throughout the entire session.

There are three crucial factors in the use of reinforcers that an instructor needs to consider. First, the reinforcers used should be ones that the student has access to *only* during learning sessions and that consequently are not available during the rest of the day, either at home or at school. This limitation ensures that the reinforcers will maintain their

> ➜ Crucial factors regarding reinforcers: 1) Use only ones to which student has no access otherwise; 2) the level of reinforcement needs to match level of difficulty of task; and 3) provide a reinforcer only when it has been earned.

strength and that the student will not become satiated. These items may be kept in special containers in locations the student cannot access. Special reinforcers may also be used for some specific, very difficult learning activities. For example, if a student particularly dislikes writing activities, a teacher may provide the student with one whole M&M'S candy for every word he or she writes without protesting. M&M'S are one of the student's favorite candies and are not used during other learning sessions.

Second, the amount or level of reinforcement provided to the student needs to match the level of difficulty or desirability of the task that the student is being asked to perform. If the student enjoys the task or the task is fairly easy for the student, he requires smaller amounts of reinforcement or reinforcement at less frequent intervals. If the student dislikes the task or the task is difficult, he likely needs a larger amount of reinforcement or to receive reinforcement at more frequent intervals. Instructors need to pay attention to how much motivation to perform various tasks the student displays, and then provide only enough reinforcement to ensure that the student maintains a high level of motivation to perform that task. In other words, high motivation needs low reinforcement, and low motivation needs high reinforcement.

Third, the student should be given access to reinforcers *only* when he has earned them. That is, students must comply with a request or respond correctly to an instruction to receive a reinforcer. Thus, inappropriate behavior, noncompliance, and incorrect responses do not earn reinforcement. For the student to learn this he needs to understand that he must do or give something in exchange for something he wants to gain.

If these instruction-related reinforcement skills are not learned and strictly followed by teachers, their ability to teach students with ASD will be impeded. Thus the process of a student learning a skill is the responsibility not only of the student but of the teacher as well. If a student is not learning a particular skill, the teacher needs to analyze whether reinforcement is being appropriately employed. He or she therefore must ask the following questions:

- Is the student being given access to reinforcers as a reward for making correct responses?

- Does the student want to gain the reinforcer that is being offered?

- Is the student being given reinforcement only when she provides a correct answer?

- Does the amount of reinforcement match the difficulty or preference level of the task?

One final reinforcement option that is especially important in the general education classroom is the use of naturalistic reinforcers provided at naturally occurring times (such as drawing a smiley face on top of the student's worksheet when he has successfully completed it). Most of the student's typical peers work for longer periods of time and receive more naturally occurring reinforcers (praise, high fives, tokens to be saved for larger reinforcer) for their work than students with ASD. The goal is for the student with ASD to gain the ability to be intrinsically motivated about completing tasks and not to need a high level of extrinsic motivation.

Prompting and Fading

An important and somewhat complicated component of helping a student with a task is the use of prompting and fading (getting rid) of prompts to promote independent responding. When assisting the student with an activity or task, the instructor needs to use the least intrusive (that is, most subtle) prompts, accommodations, and modifications necessary (such as the prompt of shifting your gaze toward where the student needs to go) to elicit a correct answer. Doing so will ensure that these prompts, accommodations, and modifications can be faded out as soon as possible. Conversely, the most intrusive prompt, for example, is an obvious one (such as physically taking the student's hand and guiding him to pick up an object). Being aware of the types of prompts one can provide, and understanding the hierarchy (least intrusive to most intrusive) into which these prompts fall, can help an instructor evaluate and use the appropriate prompt to help the student. Following are the main categories of prompts listed in their typically perceived order of intrusiveness:

- *Independent*: no prompts provided to obtain correct answer

- *Gestural prompt*: physical cue to indicate the correct response

- *Imitative prompt*: physical demonstration (model) of the correct response
- *Partial echoic prompts*: partial verbalization of the correct response
- *Full echoic prompts*: full verbalization of the correct response
- *Indirect verbal prompts*: a verbal question that leads the student to determine the correct response
- *Direct verbal prompts*: verbal instruction on how to complete an action, or one step of a multistep task that can be taken to obtain the correct response
- *Position prompts*: placement of materials to increase the likelihood of a correct response
- *Partial physical prompt*: partial manipulation of a student's body to *start* an action to obtain the correct response
- *Full physical prompt*: physical manipulation of the student's body to *complete* an action to obtain the correct response

It is important for an instructor to provide immediate reinforcement for a correct response that has been prompted. Such reinforcement tells the student immediately that this is the response that needs to be provided the next time the same instruction is given. It also ensures that next time the instructor will be able to fade that prompt.

I cannot stress enough the importance of fading prompts. A careful plan for how a student will be prompted and how the prompts will be faded needs to be established. Fading prompts ensures that students do not become dependent on the instructor's assistance to complete a task or provide correct responses. The final goal is for students to be able to provide a correct response independently or complete a task within a naturally occurring situation in a typical environment without a prompt. In the process of fading prompts, the instructor provides higher levels of reinforcement for each correct response given by the student with less prompting; a less-prompted response receives more reinforcement than a more-prompted response. This method increases the student's motivation to provide better and more independent responses and guards against prompt dependency. Another method of decreasing prompt dependency is to use a variety of

> **➔ Prompting Hierarchy**
> - Independent
> - Gestural cue
> - Imitative prompt
> - Partial echoic prompt
> - Full echoic prompt
> - Indirect verbal prompt
> - Direct verbal prompt
> - Positioning prompt
> - Partial physical prompt
> - Full physical prompt

prompt styles (thus decreasing the predictability of certain prompts). This method also makes the learning process more realistic for the student.

It is also essential for instructors to ensure that they are not providing inadvertent prompts when giving instructions to a student with ASD. Many students are able to pick up on subtle actions that an instructor unknowingly performs (for example, his eyes look at something or he performs a slight gesture with his head or body) that indicate to the student what the correct response is. This effect is often discovered when the student cannot correctly perform a task or provide a correct answer when working with other instructors.

Correction

Whereas a prompt is a modification made to the presentation of an instruction to help the student provide the correct response, there are also appropriate correction procedures for ensuring that a student learns the correct response once she has provided an incorrect response. It is important for student and inde-pendent learning that a student not end a task on an incorrect response,

> ➜ Use of appropriate correction procedures ensures that a student learns the correct response once he has provided an incorrect response.

because that response is what remains in the brain and increases the likeli-hood that next time she will provide the same incorrect response because she will thinks it was a correct response. So, the instructor needs to do more than just tell a student her response was incorrect; the instructor needs to help retrain the student's thinking to understand why the response was incorrect and how to arrive at the correct response the next time the same instruction is presented. This help is important for students with ASD because they have difficulty learning from their environment and picking up on the subtle cues that often let a person know she has arrived at an incorrect answer. A correction procedure can be difficult and timely to implement, and sometimes does not need to be implemented if the student catches her own mistake and corrects herself.

Following is a six-step procedure for implementing a correction proce-dure once a student has provided an incorrect response:

1. Present original instruction (with the same level of prompt originally provided).

   - If the response is correct, reinforce appropriately; end the procedure.
   - If the response is incorrect, continue to #2.

- If there is no response, make sure you have the student's attention and that the student is motivated to respond; if she is not, do a reinforcer assessment to gain student motivation. If you believe the student is motivated but still get no response, continue to #2.

2. Adjust the prompt level until the student successfully provides the correct response. (This step may involve several instructional trials with increasing levels of prompts to obtain the correct answer.)

   - Use the least intrusive prompt necessary to obtain success.
   - Repeat the instruction with each level of prompt.
   - Reinforce every correct prompted response with specific praise (but not with a high-level reinforcer).

3. Present the original instruction (with the same level of prompt as provided originally).

   - Depending on the student and the level of prompt that was necessary for a correct response, it may be beneficial to fade the prompts before re-presenting the original, unprompted instruction.
   - If the response is correct, reinforce enthusiastically with a high-level reinforcer (always accompanied by verbal praise).
   - If the response is incorrect or there is no response, attempt a few more corrections by adjusting the prompt level. The teacher needs to end on the most independent response and later reevaluate the overall requirements of the task.

4. Present one or more distracter trials (easy, already mastered skills) once the student has provided the correct response to the most unprompted instruction; these easy instructions and tasks take the student's attention away from the original task and help her remain positive and successful.

5. Present the original instruction to ensure that the student remembers the correct response after being distracted by other tasks for a short time.

6. Move on to a different task and return to the original instruction prior to the end of the teaching session.

Several important reminders for implementing a correction procedure with a student are as follows:

- Before presenting the instruction, always ensure that the student is attending and motivated and that appropriate reinforcers are readily available.

- Always restate the instruction with each prompt so that the correct response is connected to the instruction and not to the prompt (preventing the student from becoming prompt dependent).

- Always reinforce every correct response, regardless of the level of prompt provided, thus acknowledging the correct response to the student and increasing the likelihood that he will respond correctly the next time.

- Save the most powerful reinforcer for the correct, unprompted responses—especially the correct response after the distracter trial.

Handout 8.2 is a user-friendly one-page document that provides helpful reminders related to the appropriate reinforcement, prompt-

☞ Use Handout 8.2: Teaching New Skills: Helpful Reminders

ing and fading, and correction procedures to use when teaching new skills in the general education classroom.

Analyzing Tasks for Task Completion

The planning that needs to take place to facilitate a student's successful participation in and completion of a task or activity significantly affects the student's outcomes. The process includes preparing to deliver the instructions and student requirements (task preparation), presenting the information and materials in a specific manner (task presentation), and helping the student to complete the task in an acceptable manner (task completion).

Task Preparation

First the instructor analyzes the assignment or activity and determines the incremental steps the student needs to take to complete the task. Second, the instructor modifies the instructional materials and creates any extra accommodations to address specific student needs (for example, creating a picture schedule for the steps in the activity). In preparing tasks for students with ASD it is important to decide whether a particular student would understand a concept better if it were presented from part to whole or from whole to part. For example, does the student need to have the big picture in mind in order to understand what steps need to be taken to accomplish that big picture? Or does the student need to learn the parts first in order to grasp the concept of the whole? The following list outlines steps for analyzing and modifying the presentation of a task to a student:

Task Presentation

1. The instructor chooses a specific method for presenting the instructions for carrying out the task (such as shortened or simplified instruction phrases, or modeling).

2. The instructor chooses the prompts the student needs in order to understand the instruction and provide the correct answer.

3. The instructor uses repetition of the task to promote mastery of the concept and of the needed skills.

To facilitate the student's most independent participation in the task, it is important to use the least intrusive accommodations possible, specifically trying not to use physical prompting.

> ➜ To facilitate the student's most independent participation in the task, it is important to use the least intrusive accommodations possible, specifically trying not to use physical prompting.

Task Completion

The instructor first determines the accepted outcome from the student, whether that outcome is the same as the other students' or an alternative outcome, and decides to accept only that response. Then, when the student is working on difficult tasks, the instructor pays attention to his attempts and problem-solving strategies, reinforces these actions, and helps guide the student toward the correct answer without making the student feel as if he or she was incorrect. If the student is not attempting to complete the task or activity, the instructor considers what function the student's behavior might be serving. This means he considers the student's level of ability relative to the level of difficulty and frustration of the task in order to assess the student's reason for noncompliance. It is important when working with students with ASD to note if a particular student consistently displays a need for perfection and thus demonstrates frustration when making mistakes. A teacher would then model sloppy work and making mistakes along with ways to remedy those mistakes

> ✓ Use Checklist 8.2: Task Analysis for Student Task Completion in the General Education Classroom

Providing Curriculum Accommodations and Classroom Aids

Developing appropriate curriculum accommodations and classroom aids requires the most creativity on the part of the educators. Each student with ASD will need different and unique accommodations and modi-

> ✓ Use Checklist 8.3: Curriculum Accommodations and Classroom Aids in the General Education Classroom

fications to help him understand the instructional materials and follow the daily classroom schedule. One guiding principal for making accommodations and modifications for a student with ASD in the general education classroom is to make sure that the accommodations and modifications are socially acceptable and appropriate for implementation within the general education classroom. Peers are often valuable resources for identifying methods and types of accommodating tasks and activities, and they can help with the process of implementation.

The different types of accommodations and modifications that educators can consider when planning for a particular activity or task are as follows:

- *Quantity*: adapt the number of items that the student is expected to learn or complete

- *Time*: adapt the time allotted for learning, task completion, or testing

- *Level of support*: increase the amount of adult or peer assistance provided for the student

- *Input*: adapt the method of instruction that is delivered to the student

- *Level of difficulty*: adapt the skill level, problem type, or rules for how the student may approach the work

- *Output*: adapt how the student may respond to the instruction

- *Participation*: adapt the extent to which a learner is actively or passively involved in the task

- *Alternative goals*: adapt the goals or outcome expectations for using the same materials

- *Curriculum substitution*: adapt the type of activity into an alternative activity that still meets the primary instructional goals of the student

If the general education teacher is going to be grading the student, it is important to note, along with the grade, the type of accommodations or modifications that were made in order for the student to receive that grade.

Many classroom aids have been researched that can be used with students with ASD throughout the daily routines in the general education classroom. Following is a list of such aids (IEP team members can seek further explanations in books and articles written on each of these strategies):

> ➔ Many classroom aids have been researched that can be used with students with ASD throughout the daily routines in the general education classroom.

- Pictures for making visual schedules, warnings for transitions, labels for items and activities, and token economy systems

- Social stories for explaining the purpose of activities and the reasons for the student's appropriate participation

- Video-modeling for demonstrating to students how to behave and interact with other people during various situations

- Role-playing certain activities and types of interactions in order to gain practice before utilizing the skill within a naturally occurring situation

- Lessons on specific social interactions skills to help the student learn to take perspective and gain empathy skills

Obtaining input from the student with ASD, if possible, on the creation or use of these aids will ensure the effectiveness of the strategy and increase the student's motivation to use them.

Body and Verbal Language

Adjusting one's body movements and verbal language when in the vicinity of a student with ASD is important for two seemingly unrelated reasons: (1) the sensory issues of many students with ASD, and (2) the student's lack of understanding of subtle social interaction and communication skills. Both of these elements result in the student having difficulty attending to pertinent stimuli and not understanding instructions.

An instructor needs to pay attention to the types of body movements he or she uses when near the student and not allow them to be unnecessarily large, jerky, or sudden. Such movements can be distracting to both the student with ASD and the typical students, and they draw attention to the adult assisting the student rather than to the task at hand or to the person teaching in front of the class, as well as frightening the student with ASD. During activities an instructor's proximity to the student can help the student to attend better or behave more appropriately. When assisting the student during an activity or having a prolonged conversation, it is appropriate to get down to the level of the student in order to help him with attending, to be as unobtrusive and undistracting as possible, and to not obstruct the student's view of materials or of any other adult who may be teaching or leading the class. Because students with ASD often have difficulty attending to both visual and auditory stimuli at the same time, it can often be helpful to model the correct action while not saying anything (teachers often model and narrate at the same time).

When speaking to the student with ASD, it is important to use words that are descriptive and not vague or general, and to use a calm, even-toned voice that does not indicate frustration or anger or fear. It is also important to use a typical inflection in one's voice and not use a monotone voice or a high-pitched or

> ➡ When speaking to the student with ASD, it is important to use words that are descriptive and not vague or general, and to use a calm, even-toned voice that does not indicate frustration or anger or fear.

low-pitched tone. Because many students with ASD take literally what people say, it is beneficial to provide instructions that are phrased not in the form of a question but instead as a firm statement of fact. For example, saying to a student, "Are you ready to work on your math worksheet?" implies that he has a choice and could say no. Phrasing the instruction instead as "It's time to work on your math sheet" implies that this is the activity on which he will now be working.

It is also beneficial to use phrases that help the student focus on what he or she should be doing and not on what he or she is doing incorrectly at the moment. For example, saying, "Stop playing with your pencil" focuses attention on the inappropriate action that the student is performing and sets an overall negative tone for the activity. Saying instead, while pointing to the student's worksheet, "You need to write your first sentence here" helps the student to focus on exactly what he should be doing and maintains an overall positive tone for the activity. All of these strategies for phrasing sentences and using a calm voice help considerably with preventing noncompliant behaviors on the part of the student, as well as with assisting the student in learning and appropriately participating in activities.

> ✓ Use Checklist 8.4: Body and Verbal Language Intervention Strategies in the General Education Classroom

Facilitating Student Independence

As stated previously, the most important goal for a student with ASD is to become an independent learner and participant within the general education classroom. *Learning to learn* means having the skills to attend to the pertinent stimuli in one's environment, storing that information appropriately within one's mind, and using it appropriately when required to provide a specific response. Many skills are used in the course of this process, including the difficult skill of problem solving. Beginning on the first day that the student with ASD is included in the general education classroom, strategies should slowly be implemented to promote the student's independent learning and participation. This goal of independent learning also needs to be consistently conveyed to the student through the actions and instructions of the educators, who do not want to require a student to do something independently if he or she does not yet have the skills or knowledge to do so. Also, the fading of assistance should be subtle and slow, allowing the student to gain the confidence needed to be motivated to complete the task or activity independently.

There are several strategies that instructors can use to fade extra assistance and promote student independence. Once the student begins to attend the general education classroom, the general education teacher should speak with him or her in the same manner as she speaks with all the other students. This means providing instructions to the student, holding the student to the same standards of appropriate behavior as the rest of the students are held to, and not telling the paraeducator what to tell the student he needs to do or not do. Once the teacher provides instructions to the student, then, if appropriate, the paraeducator can step in and assist the student in following the instructions. Likewise, the paraeducator should not allow himself or herself to be the primary instructor for the student when he is in the general education classroom. If the student has a question or needs help, he should be taught to seek out the teacher and not the paraeducator. Overall, the paraeducator should never be the go-between for the student and another person (teacher, peer, other adult, and so on) who needs to communicate and interact with the student. The paraeducator should also ignore (that is, avoid making eye contact and talking to the student) any efforts on the part of the student to constantly seek confirmation about doing something correctly. Asking once or twice whether he is doing the task correctly and then receiving feedback once the task is completed are important independent learning skills.

The best way for a paraeducator to demonstrate to the student that he or she is not there to be his personal helper is to work with all the students in the class and to act as if the student with ASD is only one of many students who need help. Also, when possible during independent

> ➡ The best way for a paraeducator to demonstrate to the student that he or she is not there to be his personal helper is to work with all the students in the class.

work tasks, the general education teacher can be the one to provide some of the extra assistance to the student while the paraeducator is available to answer the other student's questions. The student's peers can also be a source of support by teaching the student how to ask a peer for help and by teaching the peers how to help the student appropriately.

Another method for promoting independent student learning is to avoid prompt dependency on the part of the student. Typically, prompt dependency becomes a problem because of the consistent close proximity of an instructor (often the paraeducator) to the student during all activities throughout the day. It is essential that the instructors avoid standing or sitting next to the student for prolonged periods (sometimes referred to as the *Velcro phenomenon*). Even though the student may need adult assistance from time to time to complete a task or participate in an activity, it is important for instructors to adjust their proximity to the student consistently. Different students with ASD react differently to the proximity of instructors when they are in the general education classroom; some look for and want someone near them to help with every activity, and some

> ➜ Different students with ASD react differently to the proximity of instructors when they are in the general education classroom.

try to push every adult away from them and do not want help. Thus it is important for the instructors to use careful judgment regarding which activities the student actually needs assistance to complete.

Many students with ASD were in early intervention programs for many years before being included within a general education classroom. This experience can result in the students displaying noncompliant behaviors as the result of the frustration of not having control over their environment or actions. Inclusion in a general education classroom is often appealing to a student with ASD because of the available choices for activities, play, and reinforcers. Allowing the student to choose what he can do within an activity or task can greatly increase his independent participation and motivation skills.

As mentioned earlier, another difficulty that many students with ASD experience is anxieties about winning a game, being first to do something, or being first in line and completing a task with perfection (typically according to their own standards). These anxieties can often cause the student to be disruptive and aggressive within the general education classroom if he does not get his way. Many parents and educators cater to these apparent needs of the student without realizing that they are only increasing the strength of these inappropriate behaviors. Thus it is important for educators not to allow students to always win, to always be first, to

> ➜ Many parents and educators cater to the apparent needs of the student without realizing that they are only increasing the strength of these inappropriate behaviors.

always obtain brand new materials, or to start a task over because of a simple mistake he or she has made. These are important independent learning skills for students with ASD to acquire, because if they are unable to make mistakes and learn how to remedy those mistakes, to be gracious when they do not win a game and learn how to improve his skills to do better next time or to wait for others and be the second, fifth, or the last person to get to do something or go somewhere, they will never be able to function successfully within a typical environment in school, at home, or in the community.

Sometimes educators can make a game out of making mistakes and doing something that looks sloppy; they can make jokes and laugh about it and say, "That's OK, I can do it better next time" or "That's OK, I can fix it by doing _____, and my teacher will still think it is good." Gaining an understanding of turn taking can greatly help a student learn about being first sometimes and not other times. Learning skills for getting a perspective on other students' desire to win games, and learning to say "Good job, you won, maybe I will next time" or "Oh well, I did my best" can help a student learn to lose games and not hurt others' feelings or be overly upset. Also, teaching students how to problem solve ways to fix things or to develop strategies to win a game will help them gain understanding of things they do and do not have control over, and can sometimes help to alleviate their fears and anxieties over being wrong or making mistakes or losing.

It is helpful to discuss not only the methods and strategies used to promote a student's independent learning and participation, but also the strategies that hinder independence

> ✓ Use Checklist 8.5: Facilitating Student Independence in the General Education Classroom

and that have detrimental effects on the student's learning and participation in the general education classroom. Following is a list of the consequences of overuse of adult proximity and assistance:

- *Loss of classroom membership*: general education teacher leaves all program decisions up to paraeducator; general education teacher talks to paraeducator instead of student

- *Separation from classmates*: student is taken out of the middle of an activity to do something else and participates in an activity apart from the class group

- *Prompt dependency*: student waits for individual attention or instruction before starting an activity or work, looks every few seconds toward assistant for cues or instructions, consistently seeks affirmation regarding doing something correctly

- *Hindrance of peer interactions*: adult's presence near student hinders peers from interacting with student (for example, student eating lunch with paraeducator instead of with peers or playing games at recess with adult rather than with peers)

- *Limitations on receiving competent instruction*: student receives primary instruction from paraeducator; quality of education decreases

- *Loss of personal control*: adults make choices for student, adults consistently tell student what is correct and incorrect or give answers for work (do not allow him to make mistakes)

- *Loss of personal or gender identity*: child sitting on paraeducator's lap, or female paraeducator taking male child into women's bathroom with her
- *Interference with instruction of other students*: peers are distracted by the different activity the student is doing, or by the noise and nature of separate instructions being given by paraeducator.

Utilizing Effective Consultation Techniques

As stated previously in Chapter Six, the special educator needs to be a competent leader who is skilled in facilitating collaboration among team members and at providing ongoing support and consultation to the general education teacher and paraeducator who are working directly with the student with ASD on a daily basis. The implementation of these responsibilities significantly affects the process of facilitating the education of a student with ASD in the general education classroom. Although each special educator has unique abilities and talents for collaborating and consulting with the general education teacher and paraeducator, there are several strategies that are helpful in general.

The first strategy is for the special educator to draw on what he already knows from having worked with a particular general education teacher and paraeducator. This prior knowledge determines how much time he or she needs to spend initially to develop a rapport and establishing a trusting work relationship with each of these educators. It is important to listen to their ideas and concerns and to seek feedback from them on the education of the student and on strategies for handling different situations. The special educator should set aside time to communicate regularly and to discuss upcoming events or activities and difficulties that arise. He should never appear to be too busy to provide help. Following through in a timely manner on tasks that one has committed to perform and providing quality products greatly increases the general educators' trust in the special educator's leadership and abilities.

The second strategy is that the special educator needs to facilitate independent problem solving and implementation of various teaching and behavior strategies by the teacher and paraeducator. By explaining the big picture and the thinking process that is used to analyze the function of

> ➡ The special educator needs to facilitate independent problem solving and implementation of various teaching and behavior strategies on the part of the teacher and paraeducator.

a behavior or explaining how to adapt a worksheet or help the student with a difficult activity, the special educator enables the teacher and paraeducator to problem solve in the moment of need and avoid potential problems that could occur from waiting for the special educator to come and help. This also means that the special educator must not portray an attitude of having all the right answers. Providing specific and written feedback to the teacher and paraeducator on questions and concerns or methods of implementation also gives them notes to refer to in the future should a similar situation arise.

The third strategy is that it is beneficial for the special educator to show his or her passion for working with students with ASD and to help the educators recognize and take pride in the small steps of progress that a student makes throughout the school year. Providing constant positive feedback on the successful use and creative implementation of intervention strategies helps the team to maintain a positive attitude and helps to maintain the educators' motivation to continue handling difficult behaviors or teaching situations.

Handout 8.3, which contains these and other minor but effective consultation techniques is provided as a reference for the special educator.

> ☞ Use Handout 8.3:
> Consultation Techniques and Support Strategies: Working with General Education Staff

Summary

Facilitating the education of students with ASD in the general education classroom requires the knowledge, experience, planning, and collaboration of all members of an IEP team (including the special educator, the general education teacher, and the paraeducator). The lists of needed classroom behavior skills, the complicated teaching strategies, and the time-intensive planning and consultation techniques can paint a daunting picture for anyone who is including a particular student with ASD in the general education classroom. But if the team maintains the big picture of assisting the student with ASD to become an independent learner in that environment, these strategies become easier and easier for the general education classroom teacher and, in the end, more and more effective for the student with ASD.

✓ Checklist 8.1. Facilitating Generalization of Skills

✓ Pre-teaching of a particular task or subject matter is performed in a one-to-one manner at home or within other classroom setting before it is introduced in the general education classroom.

✓ All instructors agree on the level and type of responses that will be required and reinforced for the child within each area of instruction.

✓ The special educator, general educator, and paraeducator agree on the appropriate amount and type of prompts that will be provided for the child while performing a given task.

   ✓ A plan is created for fading prompts as soon as possible.

✓ Student is provided with immediate and high-level reinforcement for generalizing acquired skills throughout the day. (Fade this reinforcement.)

✓ Paraeducator and special educator familiarize the general education teacher with how the student initially learned to do a particular task so that the teacher (when appropriate) may restate or simplify the directions for the student.

✓ In the general education classroom and with new instructors the student is required to use acquired skills first before switching the focus to learning new skills.

✓ The paraeducator is consistently working on building the student's attending skills.

✓ Checklist 8.2. Task Analysis for Student Task Completion in General Education Classroom

Instructor Task Preparation

✓ Analyze assignments or activities and determine incremental steps the student will need to take to complete the task.

✓ Modify the instructional materials and create any extra accommodations to address specific student needs.

✓ Decide whether a particular student is better able to understand a concept if it is presented from part to whole or whole to part.

Instructor Task Presentation

✓ Choose a specific method for presenting the instruction for the task.

✓ Choose the prompts needed for the student to understand the instruction and provide the correct answer.

   ✓ Use the least intrusive accommodations possible and prompting, specifically trying not to use physical prompting.

✓ Use repetition of the task to promote mastery of the concept and skills needed.

Student Task Completion

✓ Instructor determines the accepted outcome from the student.

   ✓ This outcome should be the same as the outcome for the other students or an alternative outcome; decide to accept only that response.

✓ Instructor attends to the student's attempts and problem-solving strategies when working on difficult tasks.

   ✓ Instructor reinforces these actions and helps guide the student toward the correct answer without making the student feel as if he or she was incorrect.

✓ Instructor attends to the function of the behavior and to the reasons for noncompletion if the student is not attempting to complete the task or activity.

   ✓ Take into account whether a particular student consistently displays a need for perfection, and incorporate modeling of sloppy work and making mistakes and of ways to remedy those mistakes.

✓ Checklist 8.3. Curriculum Accommodations and Classroom Aids in General Education Classroom

✓ Use the least intrusive accommodations and modifications possible.

✓ Use accommodations and modifications that are socially acceptable among the child's peers.

✓ Use peers as a resource for accommodations and, when appropriate, make them part of implementing the adaptations.

✓ Use different types of curriculum accommodations by varying the following elements:

  ✓ *Quantity*: number of items the student is expected to learn or complete

  ✓ *Time*: time allotted for learning, task completion, or testing

  ✓ *Level of support*: amount of personal assistance provided for the student

  ✓ *Input*: method of instruction that is delivered to the student

  ✓ *Level of difficulty*: skill level, problem type, or the rules for how the student may approach the work

  ✓ *Output*: type or level of responses to the instruction required of the student

  ✓ *Participation*: extent to which a learner is actively or passively involved in the task

  ✓ *Goals*: change in outcome expectations while using the same materials

  ✓ *Curriculum substitution*: type of alternative activity that still meets the primary instructional goals of the student

✓ Use different types of classroom aids:

  ✓ Pictures for visual cues and schedules

  ✓ Social stories

  ✓ Video modeling

  ✓ Role-playing with peers

  ✓ Socials skills lessons

✓ On progress reports and report cards, explanation of grades achieved with modifications and adaptations to curriculum

✓ Checklist 8.4. Body and Verbal Language Intervention Strategies in the General Education Classroom

Body Language

✓ Moderate the amount of movement around the student and the types of movement (large, small, jerking, etc.) so that it is not distracting to the students.

✓ Continually adjust proximity on the basis of the activity and needs of the student (adult is not always sitting next to or hovering near student).

✓ Pay attention to body positioning during a conversation or when providing assistance; adult is at student's level and does not obstruct visibility of teacher or access to materials and peers.

✓ Model appropriate action or behavior as a method of indirect prompting.

Verbal Language

✓ Use specific description words, not general terms.

✓ Use a calm, even-toned, firm voice in all situations.

✓ Use words to praise, redirect, or correct that are not monotone or high-pitched and abnormal.

✓ Use a tone of voice that does not demonstrate anger, frustration, or anxiety.

✓ Use words that help the student focus on the activity or task he or she should be doing, not on what he or she is doing inappropriately:

  ✓ Use statements and instructions that are firm and not in the form of a question: for example, "Let's do—," "Time for everyone to—," and "We need to. . . ."

  ✓ Use statements that give the student choices within the parameters of the activity; for example, "Now we're going to . . . and you may chose . . . or. . . ."

✓ Checklist 8.5. Facilitating Student Independence in the General Education Classroom

Strategies That Best Facilitate Independent Learning and Participation on the Part of the Student

✓ Ensure that the general education teacher interacts directly with the student (not through the paraeducator).

✓ Facilitate appropriate and direct social, play, and appropriate instructional interactions between typical peers and the student.

✓ Help the student be aware of how his or her behavior affects other students.

✓ Allow the student to have some control and make choices within tasks and activities.

✓ Assist the student in attending to the general education teacher for instructions (not to the paraeducator).

✓ Use appropriate prompting and fading procedures and hierarchy.

✓ Use correction procedures that are naturalistic for the activity.

✓ Allow the student to make mistakes and problem solve remedies.

✓ Allow the student time to problem solve a difficult task or activity.

✓ Use least-intrusive adaptations and modifications.

✓ Fade adult presence from being near the student.

✓ Provide naturalistic or functional reinforcement for the student.

Consequences Related to Constant Adult Proximity and Assistance

✓ *Loss of classroom membership*: general education teacher leaves all program decisions up to paraeducator; general education teacher talks to paraeducator instead of student.

✓ *Separation from classmates*: student is taken out of the middle of an activity to do something else; participates in activity apart from class group.

✓ *Prompt dependency*: student waits for individual attention or instructions before starting activity or work, looks toward paraeducator every few seconds for cues or instructions, consistently seeks affirmation for doing something correctly.

✓ *Hindrance of peer interactions*: peers are hindered from interacting with student (for example, student eats lunch with paraeducator instead of with peers, or plays games at recess with adult rather than with peers).

✓ *Limitations on receiving competent instruction*: student receives primary instruction from paraeducator; quality of education decreases.

✓ *Loss of personal control*: adults make choices for student, adults consistently tell student what is correct and incorrect, or provides answers for work (doesn't allow him to make mistakes).

✓ *Loss of personal or gender identity*: sitting on paraeducator's lap or female paraeducator taking male child with her into women's bathroom.

✓ *Interference with instruction of other students*: peers are distracted by the different task or activity the student is doing or by the noise and nature of separate instructions given by the paraeducator.

Student: _____   Paraeducator: _____

Teacher: _____

Form 8.1. IEP Goals and Classroom Schedule Matrix

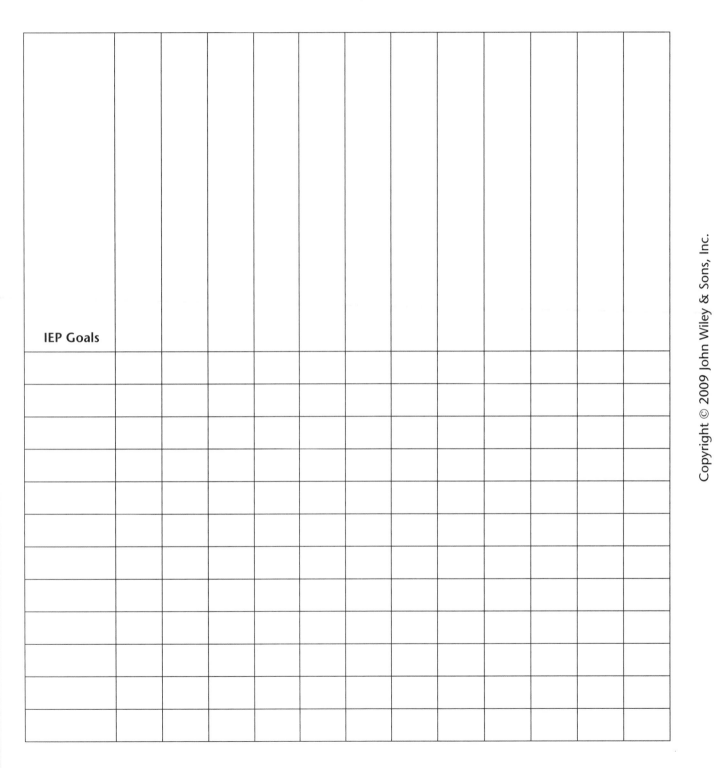

IEP Goals											

☞ Handout 8.1. General Education Classroom Behavior Skills

Attention
- Orients toward person or speaker
- Attends to teacher: one-to-one, small group and large group
- Sits for fifteen to twenty minutes: floor, desk, and table
- Attends to task for ten to fifteen minutes: academic, manipulative, and activity
- Redirects self after interruption
- Imitates behaviors
- Attends jointly to speaker and object or activity

Participation
Increases over time:
- Awareness of environment and peers
- Level and amount of participation in task: one-to-one, small group, student-directed activity, and large group
- Level of motivation to participate
- Internal motivation to maintain appropriate behavior
- Receptive language skills of student
- Expressive language skills of student
- Membership in class: staff and peers enjoy and include student in ongoing activities

Following of Classroom Routines
- Works quietly on independent tasks
- Keeps personal items in designated space
- Locates and uses restrooms
- Locates own preassigned seating location for different activities
- Sits quietly while teacher is talking to class or another student
- Raises hand to ask question
- Raises hand to answer question
- Raises hand to make comment
- Locates and uses needed materials for tasks and activities
- Organizes time and follows routines for completing a task
- Remains on task for a given activity or task for typical amount of time
- Follows instructions to complete two to three steps
- Follows common, simple routines within specific activities
- Transitions between activities
- Transitions between locations on the school site
- Navigates around the classroom and school site
- Seeks help when appropriate
- Accepts help and correction when appropriate
- Is able to make mistakes, lose at a game, and not be first in line
- Volunteers to perform an action
- Follows instructions provided by school staff other than teacher or paraeducator

Social Interaction and Communication
- Attends to (demonstrates awareness of) peers
- Uses appropriate attention-getting skills
- Shows persistence in initiating interactions if previously ignored
- Tolerates the physical contact of others
- Expresses needs and wants
- Understands basic nonverbal communication
- Uses basic nonverbal communication
- Shows awareness of effect of own behavior on others
- Shows awareness and understanding of basic emotions displayed by others and responds appropriately
- Is able to engage in three to six back-and-forth exchanges in a conversation
- Attempts to engage others in interactions
- Responds to others' initiations to interact
- Is able to engage in appropriate physical interaction with others
- Follows the lead of peers when appropriate
- Shares class materials with peers
- Takes the lead with peers when appropriate
- Shows a preference for playing and interacting with certain peers (making friends)
- Demonstrates a sense of humor

Play
- Plays with toys as designed
- Engages in play with three or more toys, games, or activities over several days
- Remains engaged in independent play with one toy, activity, or game for at least five to ten minutes
- Maintains appropriate proximal play
- Chooses from among two or more activities or toys
- Follows game-playing rules
- Engages in pretend play
- Engages in appropriate talking during play
- Shares toys with peers
- Joins and leaves interactive play activities with appropriate social cues
- Attempts to join or initiate play with peers
- Allows peers to join him during play
- Explores other toys within his environment
- Demonstrates problem-solving skills when a toy or something else does not work

☞ Handout 8.2. Teaching New Skills: Helpful Reminders

Reinforcement

Remember to:

- Use as reinforcers items and activities that are highly preferred by the student.

- Provide access to reinforcers only when the student has earned them and only in small amounts (except for new and high-level responses).

- Allow access to specific reinforcers only during work sessions.

- Match amount and level of reinforcement needs to the level of difficulty and desirability of the task.

- Consistently perform reinforcer assessments in order to keep a current record of the student's likes and dislikes.

- Gradually increase expectations for the same level of reinforcement.

Prompting and Fading

Remember to:

- Make a final goal for student to be independent of prompts.

- Use the least intrusive prompt possible.

- Establish a careful plan for prompting and fading.

- Ensure that the type of prompt used depends on the type of response required by the student.

- Begin to fade the prompt as soon as possible after introduction.

- Avoid inadvertent prompts.

- Provide prompt simultaneously or immediately following the instruction.

- Restate the original instruction with the prompt if first response is incorrect.

Correction Procedure

Remember to:

- Use only with skills that the student has acquired.

- Use the six-step process.
  - Restate original instruction and go to Step 2 only if no response or an incorrect response is made.
  - Adjust prompt level until the student provides correct response.
  - Present original unprompted instruction and obtain correct response.
  - Provide distracter trial.
  - Provide the original unprompted instruction again and obtain a correct response.
  - Move to different task and return to original instruction prior to the end of the teaching session.

- Ensure that the student is attending and motivated.

- Restate the instruction before each new prompt.

- Reinforce every correct response as appropriate to level of difficulty or independence.

- Save most powerful reinforcer for correct, unprompted responses.

☞ Handout 8.3. Consultation Techniques and Support Strategies: Working with General Education Staff

- Provide clear expectations for roles and responsibilities for each project, activity, task, and environment.

- Demonstrate respect for each person and for his or her role on the team and acknowledge each person's area of expertise; promotes creativity and individual strengths.

- Build trust and rapport with each general education staff member; be consistent and do everything promised.

- Allow the staff to see the passion and enthusiasm for this work of including students with ASD in the general education; celebrate small steps in progress.

- Provide consistent and specific feedback in both written and verbal form on
  - Appropriate and good actions
  - Inappropriate statements or interactions, and changes needed

- Do not hesitate to demonstrate intervention methods with the student and peers; explain the problem-solving thinking and point out mistakes made and things that worked well.

- By posing leading questions or statements to them, help the staff to initiate answers to their own questions, or to develop their own strategies, interventions, or accommodations.

- Do not pretend to have all the answers; explain the process of using educated guesses based on the student's abilities and characteristics and previous experience.

- Once training and modeling have occurred, wait before stepping into a situation. Allow the staff person to work through the challenge that has arisen as long as it is not interfering with the education of the other students and is not dangerous. Feedback can always be given later.

- Develop signals to use when an educator needs help, a student needs help, or a behavior is interfering with the delivery of instruction.

- Help the general education teacher and the paraeducator establish a good working relationship and ensure that the paraeducator has appropriate authority within the class as a whole.

- Do not promote or participate in gossip-style conversations.

- Occasionally allow extra time in the schedule to be present in the classroom or on-site to "chat."

- Establish consistent meeting and collaboration times; use time efficiently during meetings.

- Facilitate the staff's independence in implementation of strategies, collecting data, and problem solving through difficulties.

- Teach the staff how to analyze situations, activities, and student progress and to look at the overall big picture while still addressing the details.

9

Managing Behavior in the General Education Classroom

ALL students with ASD struggle with behaving appropriately in any environment, and the general education classroom is just one more environment in which they exhibit such difficulties. A crucial component of the inclusive education process for students with ASD is the use of appropriate and effective behavior intervention strategies that are embedded in the student's daily program operations and designed to teach him how to function appropriately in a typical environment and interact appropriately with his peers and adults. The methods employed by applied behavior analysis (ABA) are supported by the largest research base for use with individuals with ASD in the formation of appropriate behaviors.

This chapter presents the basics of ABA, including overviews of the applied behavior analysis process, functional behavior assessment, and developing and implementing a behavioral intervention plan with students with ASD in the general education classroom. Helpful behavior intervention and management strategies are also provided to assist the general education teacher and the paraeducator in the day-to-day process of teaching and interacting with the student.

> ➔ ABA basics: analyze behavior, identify functions of behavior, implement behavior intervention plan

Overview of the Applied Behavior Analysis Process

Applied behavior analysis is the process of systematically applying the principles of behavior in order to "improve socially significant behavior to a meaningful degree and to demonstrate experimentally" that the procedures used were actually responsible for the change (improvement) in the behavior.[1] Accordingly, an instructor *applies* behavior principles in order to change a student's *behavior* and then *analyzes* whether or not the actions taken caused the behavior to change. A crucial component of ABA is the process of *improving the social significance* of the person's behavior. That is, it is important that the change in behavior be observable and meaningful, for example, learning to read or add and subtract, to not hit other people, or to follow a teacher's instructions during class, all of which will improve a student's social acceptance in his or her community.

Studies have demonstrated that the use of ABA intervention methods with children with ASD can produce comprehensive and lasting improvements in many important skill areas, including language, academics, behavior, and social interaction. Because children with ASD do not respond to their environment in the same manner as their typical peers do, they do not readily learn and respond to typical instruction. ABA intervention methods allow instructors to use a systematic process for analyzing behavior and for teaching skills in small units in a way that enables students with ASD to understand and learn.

The ABC paradigm, illustrated in the following diagram, is a fundamental concept within ABA. All ABA procedures involve the manipulation of one or more of the components of this three-term contingency plan.[2]

A →	B →	C
Antecedent	**Behavior**	**Consequence**
Event that occurs immediately before a behavior	Action that occurs in response to an antecedent	Response that follows a behavior that will either increase or decrease that behavior

The ABC paradigm allows a person to analyze behavior that is occurring in *any* environment. By recording a behavior and the events that occurred immediately before and after it, one is able to evaluate its cause (antecedent) and effect (consequence).

Another component that is incorporated into this paradigm is the *setting event* in which a behavior occurs. A setting event is the environment (such as a bus, playground, or bathroom), ecological event (such as lack of food, lack of sleep, or medication), or activity (such as math class or playing with Legos) that sets up the antecedent that triggers a behavior. The setting event provides the context (information) in which a particular antecedent does or does not cause a behavior to occur. For example, a student loves math and dislikes journal time. During math class, when the teacher says, "Take out your notebooks," the student quietly takes out his math notebook and opens it to begin working; but during journal time, when the teacher says, "Take out your notebooks," the student huffs and puffs and throws his pencil on the floor and mutters, "I don't want to do journal writing! I can't write. I hate writing!" The antecedent in both cases is the teacher saying, "Take out your notebooks"; but the setting event for one case is math class and for the other case is journal time. So, the setting event provides valuable information, that it is not the antecedent in particular that causes the noncompliant and disruptive behavior; it is rather the context (the setting event) in which the antecedent occurs. In another example, a student is playing with toys and the teacher says, "Time to put your toys away." The student says, "No, I want to play!" and refuses to put his toys away. At home the same child is again playing with toys and his parent says, "Time to put your toys away." The child says, "No!" and refuses to put his toys away. In the different setting events, the student responds with the same behavior to the same antecedent. This indicates that no matter what the setting event is, the same antecedent, "Time to put your toys away," will cause the same noncompliant behavior.

It is therefore important for instructors to analyze carefully each component of a behavior—the setting event, the antecedent, the behavior itself, and the consequences—in order to track and analyze patterns that occur. This process allows a team to understand the behavior, to more accurately identify the function of that behavior, and to implement teaching strategies to change the problem behavior and increase appropriate behaviors.

The process of analyzing behavior involves the following three steps:

1. Describe the target problem behavior.

2. Determine the function of the target problem behavior.

3. Predict when the target problem behavior will occur.

> ➜ Steps to analyze behavior: describe target problem behavior, determine function of the behavior, predict occurrence of the behavior.

During the analysis process it is important to keep in mind that all behavior that continues to occur is being reinforced in some way. A behavior does not continue if it is not reinforced. Even though it may not be readily evident how or what is reinforcing the behavior, it is still being reinforced.

The first step in analyzing behavior is to *describe the target problem behavior* so that all who work with the and observe the student have an understanding of the behavior and can readily identify and measure it. Using a term such as *tantrum* is vague enough that each person observing a child could list different actions of the student that in the person's mind constitute a tantrum. Using a description, however, such as "When the student does not want to complete a writing task, he displays noncompliant and destructive behaviors in the form of a ten- to fifteen-minute tantrum that consists of at least two or all of the following actions: throwing objects, yelling at people, and kicking his desk and chair," will most likely enable a person observing or working directly with the student to know what to look for, when it will most likely occur, and how long it will probably last. This approach ensures that everyone understands what constitutes a tantrum for this particular student.

There are four guidelines for describing a behavior to making it measurable and observable:

- *Topography:* what it looks like
- *Frequency:* how often it occurs
- *Duration:* how long it occurs
- *Intensity:* how strong it is

Using these four guidelines allows a team to describe and define a target problem behavior accurately so that anyone can observe the behavior and measure its occurrence. This process is an important first step in working toward changing and decreasing an inappropriate behavior. An example of a description using all of these guidelines would be the following:

> He hits the instructor on her arms (upper or lower) with either his left or right hand balled into a fist. He does look at the instructor and hits with all his strength in an up-and-down motion (that is, slamming). The amount of hits in one occurrence happen in quick succession and range from one to five times, until the instructor moves away from the student. The student yells a protest (such as *"No!"* or *"I won't!"*) while he is hitting.

In the second step, the team attempts to *determine the function, or purpose, of the behavior.* Why is the student engaging in this behavior? All behavior is functional, including challenging behavior. There is always a purpose, a function, that each behavior serves; specifically, behavior communicates needs and desires and serves to get those needs and desires met. When attempting to determine the function of a behavior, instructors assess within which of two categories the function of the behavior falls.

> ➜ Functions of behavior: obtaining desirable events or items, avoiding or escaping undesirable events or people

The first category is *obtaining desirable events or items.* A student can engage in a particular behavior in order to experience internal or external stimulation. Internal stimulation is automatic reinforcement resulting from the release of endorphins in the brain. This hormone changes how a person feels and thus can be a desirable internal reinforcer. External stimulation results from a student's attempts to gain attention (whether verbal, physical, visual, or surprise reactions, such as a gasp, yelp, or quick jerk), objects, activity, or events. The attention can be either negative or positive (for example, a teacher may scold a student for disrupting or praise him for working quietly).

The second category is *avoiding or escaping undesirable events or people.* A student can behave in a certain way in order to avoid or escape internal or external stimulation. Undesirable internal stimulation includes headaches, sound, hunger, thirst, internal pain, or tactile irritation. Undesirable external stimulation includes attention from a particular person or group of people; tasks that may be too difficult, too easy, or too repetitive; and events such as changes in routine and transitions to a new location or activity.

All behaviors serve a function that falls into one of these two categories; thus all behaviors serve the purpose of obtaining or escaping something. A particular behavior can also serve more than one function, thus complicating the analysis and intervention procedures. It is important to determine if a behavior is serving more than one function; if it is, then implementing an intervention that targets only one function may decrease the intensity or frequency of the behavior somewhat, but it will not eliminate it, and the behavior will continue to occur. For example, a student may display noncompliant behaviors, such as yelling and throwing things, to escape a difficult writing task, but he may also enjoy the attention he gets from seeing his peers stop their work and look at him when he disrupts the class; so an intervention must target both the attention-getting and the escape behaviors.

> ➔ It is important to determine if a behavior is serving more than one function.

The third and final step of behavior analysis is the process of *predicting when the target behavior will occur*. Once the team has accurately described the behavior and attempted to identify the function of the behavior, they need to predict when and where and with whom the behavior will most likely occur and not occur. This effort entails gathering detailed data in order to identify the other people with whom the student displays the behavior, the settings in which the behavior occurs, and the particular antecedents that consistently trigger it. Data also needs to be collected to identify with whom, in what settings, and as the result of what antecedents the behavior does *not* consistently occur. When the behavior does occur *and* when it does not occur are both crucial pieces of information that help a team predict the occurrence of the behavior.

These three steps of behavior analysis help a team to identify and analyze the function and occurrence of a target problem behavior. This process is called a *functional behavior assessment* (FBA) and it is absolutely necessary in order to identify an appropriate and effective behavior intervention plan (BIP) that will decrease the target behavior and increase appropriate replacement behaviors.

Overview of Functional Behavior Assessment

In order to implement an effective FBA, it is important for the team to meet periodically to collect data on the target problem behavior, to systematically manipulate the test theories, to determine appropriate replacement behaviors, and finally to write a report that summarizes the information that will lead to an effective BIP. The FBA process is described here to assist teams in understanding the steps of the process. The team is encouraged to use other resources as well when they need to implement an FBA with a student with ASD.

First, the team meets to initiate a student problem behavior review. This meeting enables the team to discuss and define the target problem behavior and to identify data collection methods for

- Analyzing the setting event(s), the antecedent(s), and the consequences that cause and maintain the behavior

- Identifying the function(s) of the behavior

- Determining the occurrence of the behavior

Form 9.1 has been designed to help the team summarize the information they currently have and outline their next steps. The team should determine how often they will meet throughout the assessment process, each team member's role and responsibilities throughout the process, the types of data they will need to collect, and their overall timeline for the process.

> Use Form 9.1: Student Problem Behavior Review

If the student is displaying more than one problem behavior, the team needs to determine the primary target behavior and focus on it first. To determine which behavior should be the primary target behavior, the team needs to answer the following questions:

- What behavior is the greatest threat to the student's current placement in the general educa-tion classroom?

> See Exhibit 9.1: Student Problem Behavior Review (Sample)

- Which behavior, if changed, would give the student the greatest access to social reinforcement and positive interactions?

- What behavior, if changed, might effect positive change in other prob-lem behaviors?

In the second step of the FBA, the team begins collecting data on the behavior. Collecting data means identifying the aspects of the behavior that cause it to be a problem behavior and then tracking those aspects. During the data collection process it is important that the special educator continuously evaluate how well the process is going by assessing whether the data sheets are user friendly, whether people are reliable and consistent when they collect data, and whether there are new aspects of the behavior on which data need to be collected. Using the A-B-C Data Analysis form

(Form 9.2) will allow the team to collect qualitative data on the setting event, antecedent, behavior, and consequence. These data, although time consuming to collect and record, are the most valuable pieces of information the team will gather on the student's target problem behavior.

> ✒ Use Form 9.2: A-B-C Data Analysis

> See Exhibit 9.2: A-B-C Data Analysis (Sample)

Data collection sheets and methods also need to be created to collect information on how often the behavior occurs and for how long it occurs each time. If the behavior is aggressive or destructive, the intensity of the behavior also needs to be tracked so that any decrease or increase in its strength can also be noted. Another characteristic that it can be helpful to track is *latency* (how long after an antecedent a behavior occurs). Because data collection can be quite time consuming and because the person collecting the data also has to work with the student at the same time, it can be difficult to maintain accurate records. During this FBA process it may be important to select other qualified educators or administrators to observe the student during certain periods and record data on the target behaviors. Sample behavior data sheets are provided in Exhibits 9.3 and 9.4.

> See Exhibit 9.3: Time Sample: Interval and Exhibit 9.4: Frequency Data (Sample)

An important part of the data collection process is interviewing other relevant persons who work with or provide daily care for the student. These people can provide valuable information on the occurrence or nonoccurrence of the target behavior, and suggest strategies they are currently using to manage the behavior. These people are also sources of information on setting events (such as medication, sleep habits, or interactions with family members) that may be affecting the behavior of the student at school and in the classroom. Other sources of data are student products such as completed homework, completed token economy charts, and previous crisis intervention reports. At the end of this step the team will have fully analyzed the target problem behavior and will have the information they need to describe and define the behavior accurately, to identify the functions of the behavior, and to predict the occurrence of the behavior.

Now the team is ready to begin the third step in the FBA process, which is to implement systematic manipulations to setting events, antecedents, and consequences in order to produce small changes in the causes and effects of the behavior and thus induce relevant changes in the pattern of behavior displayed by the student. The changes that occur in the

Exhibit 9.1. Student Problem Behavior Review
(Sample)

Student: _Timothy_

Review Team: _general education teacher, autism consultant, SLP, OT, mother of student, paraeducator, principal_

Date: _09/25/07_

Setting Events	Antecedents	Problem Behavior(s)	Perceived Function(s)	Actual/Current Consequences
First ten minutes of first classroom activity after any recess. Peers and T are sitting at desks or on the floor.	Teacher giving general instructions about activity.	T talks loudly to peers sitting near him about the game they played at recess or about his favorite football team.	T is having a difficult time transitioning from preferred activity, ending it and settling down to listening quietly to teacher. Wants to continue the fun he was having interacting with peers.	Teacher or paraeducator reminds him that he needs to be listening to the teacher quietly and that recess is over. One of them tells him to go take a quiet time at the isolated desk at the back of the class for about 2–5 minutes.

Exhibit 9.1. Student Problem Behavior Review (Continued) (Sample)

Student: _Timothy_
Review Team: _general education teacher, autism consultant, SLP, OT, mother of student, paraeducator, principal_

Perceived overall functions:

T is having a difficult time transitioning from preferred activity, ending it and settling down to listening quietly to teacher. Wants to continue the fun he was having interacting with peers.

Overall: (1) T really wants to make friends and is learning through social skills instruction how to play games with his peers and how to talk about his favorite things with his friends. He is improving greatly at recess with playing with his peers and they are showing more interest in playing with him. (2) T. has frequently shown difficulty in transitioning from preferred to nonpreferred activities.

Prediction of occurrence:

Talks a lot about his friends. The team believes the poor transitioning behavior will increase unless we can address both his difficulty transitioning to nonprefer

The current consequence of separating T from his peers for a short time and having him sit quietly does work eventually after 2–5 minutes and T is typically able to rejoin the class activity and listen quietly to the teacher. But this consequence is not decreasing the occurrence of the behavior. Upon review of the A-B-C data, it appears that the behavior is increasing and the team thinks this is because he is learning more social interaction skills, and the quality and quantity of his interactions with his peers are increasing and improving. He is very happy and red activities and his wanting to continue interactions with his peers after playing for a while with them.

Next Steps (data collection, systematic manipulations, etc.):

After recesses, T will be given a short (no more than 5 minutes) and easy job to do with a peer that allows him to spend some more time interacting with a peer but in the classroom/school setting, which requires more subdued and quiet behavior. A Social Story will be written and discussed with him by his social skills instruction teacher about transitioning from recess back to class and about getting to do a special job with a peer right when he gets in from recess to help him calm down and get ready for classwork again.

Possible jobs: take something to the office, get out materials to prepare for the next class activity, clean up an area from a previous activity

A-B-C data will continue to be collected on how this strategy works—specifically duration and frequency.

Exhibit 9.2. A-B-C Data Analysis (Sample)

Student: Kenny

Date/Time	Setting Event	Antecedent	Behavior	Consequence	Comments	Initials
02/20/08 1:36 pm	Math lesson lecture by teacher. Students looking at worksheet while teacher doing examples on whiteboard. Some examples had the number 5 in the equations.	Teacher walked by K's desk and said quietly to K, "You need to look up at the board."	K. yelled, "I don't like fives!!!" and slumped in his chair.	Teacher ignored K. Paraeducator (without saying anything or looking at K) put a check mark next to Need to listen quietly on his behavior monitoring sheet.	After a minute or two, teacher asked K, "What is 2 + 6, K.?" from front of class and he answered, "Eight." Teacher said, "That's right, good job, K." K. smiled.	S.A.
02/21/08 10:20 am	Reading groups of 4 kids working at different stations throughout rooms. 2 groups have a teacher and two groups work independently. Change every 20 minutes. K is with group doing independent worksheets. K is drawing on his paper.	Paraeducator (helping another child at another table) said to K, "K, you need to finish your worksheet; when you're done you can draw."	K. slammed pencil down on top of paper and looked at paraeducator.	Paraeducator said to K in monotone voice, "Go for 1 minute to the quiet square." K walked to square and sat down. Paraeducator set timer for 1 minute.	After timer went off, K went back to his desk and started working on his worksheet. After a couple of minutes, paraeducator praised him for "good working" and put a check mark next to Good job working quietly on his behavior sheet.	S.A.

Exhibit 9.3. Time Sample: Interval
(Sample)

Student: _Andy_   **Activity:** _Free Choice Play Time_

Target Behavior(s): _Engaged in play with toys as designed—building blocks,_
rolling cars, and banging on drums

Problem Behavior(s): _Engaged in self-stimulatory behaviors—flicking fingers in front_
of eyes, rocking body back and forth and humming, rubbing palms on thighs

Time Sample: _10:00–10:30 am_   **Date:** _10/23/08_

Target Behavior		Problem Behavior	
Time Interval	Comments	Time Interval	Comments
10:02–10:04 (2 min.)	Rolled cars and banged them into blocks (no pretend noises)	10:00–10:02 (2 min.)	Flicking fingers in front of eyes with head titled sideways
10:08–10:12 (4 min.)	Lined up four long blocks and then put short blocks on top (three stories high)	10:04–10:08 (4 min.)	Flicking fingers in front of eyes and then rocking and humming
10:17–10:23 (6 min.)	Knocked down block tower and lined up a long row of blocks, then drove car on the row of blocks	10:12–10:17 (5 min.)	Rubbing palms on thighs and then flicking fingers in front of eyes
10:25–10:30 (5 min.)	Rolled cars around between the scattered blocks	10:23–10:25 (2 min.)	Rocking and humming

Exhibit 9.4. Frequency Data (Sample)

Student: Karen

Date/Initials	Behavior	Period	# Of Incidents	Comments
03.14.08 D.S.	Flapping left hand (nondominant hand) next to side of head during independent work periods.	10:05–10:20 am	//// //// ////	Working on reading worksheet. Each incident is about 4–6 flaps. Then she goes back to work.
0.3.14.08 D.S.	Flapping both hands at sides of head during instruction period.	10:30–10:50 am	//// ///	Teacher providing instruction regarding art activity. Kids sitting at desks. Each incident is about 3–5 flaps.

pattern of the problem behavior provide information on the effects that the manipulations have on decreasing or increasing the problem behavior.

It is through these manipulations that the team is able to determine what intervention strategies will prove to be the most effective in decreasing and then eliminating the problem behavior. The following variables can be manipulated in the setting events, antecedents, and consequences:

> ➡ It is through these manipulations that the team is able to determine what intervention strategies will prove to be the most effective in decreasing and then eliminating the problem behavior.

Setting Events

- Home events and schedules
- School and classroom routines
- Classroom arrangement
- Time of day (morning or afternoon, class period) of event, task, or activity
- Time in schedule (prior to or after certain activities) of event, task, or activity
- Number of students or adults in the room with the student
- Sensory distractions and irritants (light, heat, noise, and so on)

Antecedents

- Instruction (prerequisite skills, quantity, abstractness, developmental level)
- Functionality of task
- Interest in task
- Tone of voice used in presentation of the lesson
- Length of time before reinforcement after the display of appropriate behavior
- Length of time spent on a task
- Participation in group versus individual instruction
- Type and level of prompting provided during tasks and activities
- Availability of choice and control
- Variety and availability of reinforcers

Consequences

- Type of reinforcer

- Quantity of reinforcer

- Degree of repetitiveness of reinforcer

- Manner of provision of reinforcer

- How long after occurrence of behavior the reinforcement or punishment is given

- Type of punisher

In the fourth step of the FBA process the team uses the information and data they have gathered on the function of the behavior and the systematic manipulations they have implemented to test the causes and effects of the behavior to decide what replacement behaviors they will attempt to increase or teach to the student in order to replace the problem behavior. It is important for the team to understand that eliminating the target behavior does not eliminate the function of the behavior. This means that a new, appropriate behavior needs to take the place of the problem behavior, and the replacement behavior needs to serve the same function the problem behavior served. If a problem behavior is only eliminated and not replaced with an appropriate behavior, the student will find a new problem behavior to serve the function of the old behavior. A replacement behavior that will increase the chances of a student adopting the appropriate behavior and no longer displaying the inappropriate behavior must

> ➡ It is through these manipulations that the team is able to determine which intervention strategies will be most effective in decreasing and then eliminating the problem behavior.

- Be incompatible with the problem behavior

- Currently occur at a low rate due to low reinforcement

- Prove to be more functional than the problem behavior

- Provide more desirable social reinforcement than the problem behavior

- Have been demonstrated previously by the student

- Enable the student to participate more (or with better quality) in the LRE

In the fifth and final step the team meets to provide and discuss a summary of all their findings and to propose a plan for behavior intervention. A thorough FBA includes the following information:

- Reason for the student's referral

- Student's current appropriate and inappropriate behavior patterns

- Method and summary of behavior analyses

- Description of target problem behavior

- Setting events in which target problem behavior potentially occurs

- Antecedent events that causing target problem behavior to occur

- History of consequences and interventions implemented

- Hypothesized function of the target behavior

- Potential functional alternative and replacement behaviors

- Recommendations for BIP

All people working with the student need to contribute to the FBA and agree to the types of strategies that have been recommended and to how they will be implemented, including who is responsible for implementing the different components of the plan. The plan will not be effective if even one person disagrees with an intervention strategy and therefore does not implement it.

Overview of Developing and Implementing a Behavior Intervention Plan

Once a thorough FBA has been completed, a comprehensive BIP needs to be developed that incorporates all of the information and recommendations from the FBA. The purpose of the BIP is to describe the three main intervention strategies that everyone working with the student will be implementing. The first intervention strategies described in the BIP are the setting event and the antecedent strategies for preventing the target behavior and promoting appropriate behaviors. Using data from the FBA on the occurrence of the target behavior and on the systematic setting event and antecedent manipulations that have been tried, and taking into account the information from the interviews and the hypothesized function of the behavior, a BIP explains strategies for the following goals:

> ➡ Once a thorough FBA has been completed, a comprehensive behavior intervention plan needs to be developed that incorporates all the information and recommendations from the FBA.

- Changing setting events so that some antecedents no longer occur

- Inserting other stimuli with or right before or after specific antecedents in order to change their effect

- Creating new antecedents or the ways in which the antecedents occur

The second intervention strategy described in the BIP is the consequence intervention strategy for decreasing the occurrence of the target behavior. Using data from the A-B-C data analysis sheets and the systematic manipulations that have been implemented, and using information from interviews, the strategies describe the following elements:

- Least-restrictive to most-restrictive consequences for the target behavior (when, who, how, where, and so on)

- Methods for promoting the safety of other students and staff

- Procedures for handling behavior outbursts and crisis situations

The third intervention strategy described in the BIP is the replacement behaviors along with reinforcement methods for increasing their occurrence. Using data from systematic manipulations already implemented and information from hypothesized functions, the BIP provides and describes alternative appropriate behaviors that

- Serve the same function as the target behavior (access or avoid)

- Are age appropriate and acceptable

- Do not interfere with the academic environment or with other BIPs

The BIP describes replacement behavior intervention methods that use the following three approaches:

- Teaching new appropriate replacement behaviors

- Reinforcing appropriate behaviors

- Increasing opportunities for appropriate behaviors to occur by changing the setting events and antecedents or by manipulating situations

The BIP also needs to include a description of the data collection methods that will be used to track the implementation of the behavior interventions—specifically how the target problem behavior and replacement behaviors will be displayed. The team will also need to discuss any training that the teachers and paraeducators and any other relevant school personnel will need to implement the BIP effectively and safely. Most important, the BIP itself will need to be evaluated, the performance of the behavior intervention strategies will need to be reviewed, and the plan's progress or lack of progress will have to be discussed. A BIP needs to be a flexible and changing plan that at all times accurately reflects the current status of the student's behavior patterns and the intervention strategies that have been implemented. The team members need to share implementation responsibilities and to support the general education teacher and paraeducator, specifically during the beginning stages, when implementation can be particularly difficult. The

☞ Use Handout 9.1: Ongoing BIP Implementation Considerations and Evaluations

user-friendly Implementing the Behavior Implementation Plan checklist (Checklist 9.1) and the Ongoing BIP Implementation Considerations and Evaluation handout (Handout 9.1)

> ✓ Use Checklist 9.1:
> Implementing the Behavior
> Implementation Plan (BIP)

have been created to help IEP teams remember the important implementation and evaluation components of a BIP.

If a particular student with ASD already has a BIP that is already being implemented when the IEP team decides to change his placement to the general education classroom, it is important to ensure that the plan is adjusted for implementation in the new environment. Prior to including the student in the general education classroom, the team needs to evaluate whether setting events and antecedents are occurring that have been known to cause the target problem behavior to occur and to cause consequences that would increase the occurrence of the problem behavior. Also, the team needs to ensure that the reinforcement procedures for appropriate behaviors are right for the new classroom and can be effectively implemented. Because the general education teacher and paraeducator would not have been a part of the FBA, it is important to explain how the assessment occurred so that they can understand the history behind the current BIP. It is also important that they be able to give input on changes that need to be made to the BIP in order for effective implementation to take place in the general education classroom.

> ➡ The team needs to ensure
> that the reinforcement
> procedures for appropriate
> behaviors are right for the new
> classroom and can be effectively
> implemented.

Behavior Intervention Strategies

There are many different day-to-day behavior intervention strategies that appear to be simple but can make a significant difference when implemented together on a consistent basis with students with ASD. As previously discussed, students with ASD have difficulty learning by observing others; thus it is important that appropriate behaviors be taught and reinforced while inappropriate behaviors are being specifically targeted to decrease. The higher the student's functioning, the more important it is to explain the intervention (including reinforcement) methods fully to the student. If possible, seeking the student's input on the intervention strategies and subsequent rewards and consequences for his behavior can be an integral part of the BIP and can motivate the student to cooperate with the implementation process.

Although it is impossible to discuss all of the possible behavior intervention strategies that can be used with students with ASD, general education teachers and paraeducators have found a variety of strategies to be effective and helpful. These strategies fall into three main categories that appear to be crucial for students with ASD and their successful inclusion within the general education classroom:

- Prevention
- Reinforcement
- Transitions and Routines

Prevention

One of the most powerful tools that the general education teacher and paraeducator have available to increase proactively the likelihood that a student will display a target appropriate behavior and decrease the occurrence of a target problem behavior is the use of strategies that prevent the target problem behavior from ever occurring. The less a student performs a behavior, the less likely it is that he will display that behavior again in the future. Prevention strategies also help decrease the occurrence of other problem behaviors.

> ➡ The less a student performs a behavior, the less likely it is that he will display that behavior again in the future.

Students with ASD often seek the easiest method (the path of least resistance) of achieving a goal: to access or avoid something. Instructors therefore need to invest time and energy in setting up an environment that promotes appropriate behavior and prevents inappropriate behavior. Essentially instructors are showing the student a specific path (appropriate behaviors) to travel down that has fences (limitations) alongside it to keep the student on that path so he does not stray from it and perform inappropriate behaviors that will lead him away from learning specific skills, interacting and playing with peers, and receiving his education in the general education classroom.

Following is a list of some of the many prevention strategies that instructors can use to help the student perform appropriate behaviors and decrease the occurrence of inappropriate problem behaviors:

- Use antecedent and setting event intervention strategies to distract the student from engaging in problem behavior.
- Allow natural and logical consequences (while also maintaining the safety of the student and others) for inappropriate behavior to enable the student to understand better the reasons for not performing the problem behavior.

- Provide the student with frequent opportunities and the choice to take breaks during or after specific activities.

- Provide a specific place or space in the class for the student to take a break to calm down or regain composure when needed.

- Decide in advance which occurrences of problem behavior (such as those with high levels of intensity) will result in the removal of the student from the general education classroom (to an inclusion classroom or other location) in order to implement consequences for the behavior.

- Plan ahead when there are specific tasks and activities that the student needs to perform within the inclusion classroom that may be more difficult and therefore might cause problem behavior. Special procedures may be needed to prevent the problem behavior.

- Provide the student with choices and options (such as order of tasks to be completed, which items to use, and so on) within given activities in order to increase the student's motivation and perceived control.

- Ensure that the student understands the consequences for inappropriate and target problem behaviors.

- Praise peers around the student when they display an appropriate behavior that is being targeted for the student.

- Prevent the student from having access to activities and items that promote his engagement in self-stimulatory behaviors.

- Allow extra time for the student to complete tasks.

- Decrease the level of difficulty of tasks initially so that they are easier for the student to complete in order to increase the student's motivation to continue doing the task in the future.

- Do not raise your voice or allow the student to see you get upset with him.

- Implement consequences for peers who bully, antagonize, or tease the student.

- Stand near the student and make comments out loud about desired appropriate behaviors to the group of students working with or near him.

- Provide a minimum of attention (such as eye contact, comments, body orientation) to the student when preventing or handling an inappropriate behavior and instead act as if you are doing something as a natural matter of course.

- Be consistent, specifically when
  - Implementing consequences for inappropriate behavior
  - Implementing classwide rules and behavior management system
  - Following through with actions stated; if not possible, nothing should be said

- Start with the least intrusive consequences and interventions so as not to promote the student's dependence on prompts or external reinforcements to perform appropriate behaviors.

- Provide the student with special "jobs" to perform in the classroom (such as turning the computers on and off or taking notes to the office for the teacher) to help him feel important and in charge.

- Ask the student to answer questions about topics that are his strengths, to help peers see him as interesting and intelligent and to increase the student's motivation to participate in class activities.

- Provide visual and auditory explanations as well as models for completing specific tasks.

Another effective prevention strategy is to develop a daily classroom behavior data sheet for the student. The instructors and the student work together to decide what are the target appropriate behaviors that the student needs to display throughout the day and during specific activities. These behaviors are written out on a form, and a contract or token economy system that rewards appropriate behaviors and delivers consequences for inappropriate behaviors is established between the student and the instructors. The data sheet is a visual reminder to the student of this contract, and it keeps track of his performance throughout the day. It is important that as much as possible instructors avoid taking reinforcers away from the student. Earning reinforces for appropriate behavior and not earning them for inappropriate behavior is a most effective strategy for students. Three examples of forms for monitoring the daily classroom behavior of students with ASD are provided here.

> See Behavior Data Sheets: Exhibit 9.5: Daily Classroom Behavior 1 (Sample); Exhibit 9.6: Daily Classroom Behavior 2 (Sample); and Exhibit 9.7: Daily Classroom Behavior 3 (Sample)

It is also beneficial for a general education teacher and paraeducator to have a predetermined or standard BIP for noncompliant and disruptive behavior. This plan addresses the most common problem behaviors that students in general and, students with ASD in particular demonstrate during class. If a student with ASD is included in a general education classroom and does not already have a BIP, then having available a generic plan of intervention strategies for prevention and consequence for the teacher and paraeducator to use may prevent the need for developing a specific intervention plan for the student in the future. All of the strategies can

Exhibit 9.5. Daily Classroom Behavior 1
(Sample)

	Safe	Good Voice	Asks for Help	Follows Directions	Flexible	Comments
Warm-up	+	−	+	P	−	Did not want to do activity; did not talk nicely to teacher
Reading	+	+	+	+	+	Worked hard
Math	+	+	+	+	+	
Recess (rest)	−	−	+	P	+	Pushed peer out of line for swings
Language group time	+	P	P	+	+	
Kindergarten class	+	+	+	+	+	Had fun during center time
Independent work tracking (record minutes student works independently during allocated time, i.e. writing: 10m/15m	Reading: 10m/15m	Math: 10m/10m				
Daily points	5	3.5	5.5	5	5	24
I need __25__ points to earn __10__ minutes of computer game by __12:00__ .						
+ I did a great job following instructions (1 point); P I needed help following instructions (1/2 points); − I did not do a good job following instructions (0 points)						

apply to typical students as well, and the general education teacher can present the plan to the parents of all her students with the explanation that these are strategies she uses to prevent inappropriate behaviors, and consequences she uses to decrease problem behaviors. A sample behavior plan is provided in Exhibit 9.8.

See Behavior Plan in Exhibit 9.8: Standard Behavior Plan for Noncompliance and Disruptive Behavior Within the General Education Classroom (Sample)

Exhibit 9.6. Daily Classroom Behavior 2
(Sample)

Behaviors	Class: Warm-Up	Class: Reading	Class: PE/Music/Comp	Class: Math	Class: Sci/Soc	Class: Centers	Daily Points
Follow instructions first time	P	+	+	+	−	+	4.5
Stay on task	P	+	P	+	P	+	4.5
Listen to others and respond to them	+	+	+	+	+	+	6
Wait my turn	+	+	P	+	+	P	5
Appropriate talking (positive and good words)	+	+	+	+	−	+	5
Good personal space	+	+	P	+	+	+	5.5
Tell my feelings (I messages)	+	+	+	+	+	+	6
Stay at my desk/stay on topic	+	+	+	+	P	+	5.5
Safe behavior	+	+	+	+	+	+	6
							48
Comments		Really liked the topic	Whole class was rowdy		Activity was more difficult today	Played well with two peers	

I need __45__ points to earn __10 min.__ of drawing by __2:30pm__ .

+ I did a great job following instructions (1 point);   P I needed help following instructions (1/2 points);
− I did not do a good job following instructions (0 points)

Students with ASD always struggle to behave appropriately in their classroom, home, and community. It is important that the expectations placed on a particular student do not exceed what is reasonable for him at his current level of understanding and abilities. The higher functioning the

Exhibit 9.7. Daily Classroom Behavior 3 (Sample)

How are you doing in class today, [student's name]?   Date: _____

GOOD JOB—KEEP IT UP!

Nothing in mouth or nose	☺	☺	☺	☺					
Looking at teacher	☺	☺	☺	☺					
Doing work	☺	☺	☺						
Following instructions	☺	☺	☺	☺					
Using words	☺	☺	☺						

I need <u>15</u> ☺ to get <u>5</u> minutes of <u>free choice during center time</u>

NEED TO CHANGE NOW

Put eyes on teacher	☹								
Get back to work	☹								
Take hands and things out of mouth and nose	☹	☹	☹						
Follow teacher's instructions	☹								
Stop arguing									

Every <u>3</u> ☹ <u>I pick up trash for 2 minutes during recess</u>

---

student is, the more stress and anxiety he often experiences because he feels different; he does not understand how he is different and thus struggles to "hold things together" when he is around peers at school. Parents need to expect new problem behaviors to appear at home as the student progresses and becomes more successful with behaving appropriately at school. This happens because the student needs a break, needs to let go, to be himself or herself and let out frustrations when he is at home, in a safe place with people who love and accept him unconditionally. The IEP team needs to prepare the parents for this phenomenon and to help them develop intervention strategies to help themselves and the student at home. This preparation can prevent much confusion on the part of the parents as well as prevent the problem behaviors from getting out of control and detrimentally affecting the progress the student is making at school.

> ➡ It is important that the expectations placed on a particular student do not exceed what is reasonable for him at his current level of understanding and abilities.

Exhibit 9.8. Standard Behavior Plan for Noncompliance and Disruptive Behavior in the General Education Classroom (Sample)

Target Problem Behavior

Noncompliance and disruptive behavior: refusing to comply with an instruction given a second time to a student or group of students

Definition of Behavior

Noncompliance and disruptive behavior: behavior may consist of (but is not limited to) one or more of the following: saying no or shaking head; walking or running away from activity, instructor, or location of task; making loud noises; turning away from task or instructor; laying on floor.

Antecedents

Precursors to problem behavior: (a) presentation of an instruction to complete a task or participate in an activity; (b) presentation of an instruction to transition to the next activity or task

Function of Behavior

Possible reasons for problem behavior: (a) to escape from activity or task; (b) to resist change; (c) to move from a reinforcing task or activity to a nonreinforcing task or activity; (d) to get attention; (e) unknown

Antecedent Interventions

Interventions to implement before the behavior occurs in an attempt to prevent the behavior:

a. Develop a reinforcement or token economy system in which the rate of reinforcement is high in the beginning and gradually decreases as appropriate behaviors (on-task behavior) increase. Allow reinforcer to be visible in order to provide a constant reminder of what the student is working for. This system should be planned out and followed through by everyone working with the student. Just before the instruction for the task, activity, or transition occurs, the student should be reminded of the reinforcement for doing the task or activity. Praise and attention should always be paired with the tangible reinforcement, with the eventual goal of praise and attention serving as the reinforcement.

b. Decrease amount or difficulty of task (or both), as well as interspersing easy and difficult tasks, so that successful completion is more easily obtained. Gradually increase amount and difficulty to typical length and level of difficulty as appropriate behaviors increase.

c. Before presenting instruction, make sure the student is paying attention or that you know he can see or hear the instruction, and present the instruction only one time before prompting him.

d. Do not present an instruction when you are not prepared to make the student follow through.

e. Present instruction in a statement format, not as a question. Keep voice even-toned and do not display frustration in your voice.

f. Make sure that reinforcers are not delivered unless the student complies with the instruction.

(Continued)

g. When appropriate (there are definitely times when it is not appropriate) give the student an opportunity to make choices about reinforcers and about the task or activity he will do. All choices should be equally appropriate.

h. Begin each period in the new location (special education classroom or general education classroom) with a reinforcing activity or task with the teacher (if possible) to establish a reinforcing environment and thus improved instructional control.

i. Provide warning of upcoming transitions with verbal, sound, or picture cues while also using the plan mentioned in item a of this list.

j. Activities (or the length of an activity) that are causing overstimulation (because of lack of structure or being allowed to engage in self-stimulation or running around) and thus are resulting in the display of problem behavior should be decreased or eliminated whenever possible.

k. Any time an appropriate behavior is displayed, the student should be reinforced with praise and, if appropriate, be given reinforcement sooner than planned.

Replacement Behaviors to be Taught or Reinforced

a. Follows instructions immediately

b. Displays on-task behavior

c. Transitions to next activity or task immediately

Consequential Intervention Strategies (Secondary Emphasis)

It is important that whoever presents the initial instruction is the same person who follows through with the task or activity and with handling the behaviors. The person should follow through with the task or activity while ignoring the target behavior. This approach includes maintaining an even-toned voice (not displaying frustration), not saying anything about the behavior ("don't do _____"), using sentences that focus the student on the appropriate behavior he should be displaying ("we need to write _____"), praising peers around him who are displaying the appropriate behavior, not giving eye contact until appropriate behavior is displayed, and positioning oneself (as much as possible) so as to be the least physically intrusive and to avoid being kicked, hit, or bumped by the student.

Interventions to Occur upon Display of Target Behavior

a. Ensure that the reinforcer is inaccessible to the student but visible and that it remains that way even if the student runs away from the instructor or runs toward the reinforcer.

b. Restate to whole group instructions that includes what they need to be doing.

c. Praise one or two peers near the student for the specific appropriate behavior.

d. Provide the least intrusive prompt to obtain compliance. These prompts (not in a particular order) could involve (1) a gestural prompt (pointing), (2) a verbal prompt ("pick up your pencil"), or (3) a slight physical prompt (putting the pencil in the student's hand, nudge his elbow, physically guiding his body gently toward the desired destination with two hands on his back).

(Continued)

Exhibit 9.8. Standard Behavior Plan for Noncompliance and Disruptive Behavior in the General Education Classroom (Sample), *(Continued)*

e. Continue to present the task while increasing the prompt level. This could involve (these are not in a particular order): (1) hand-over-hand prompting to do a task or activity (prompting the student to pick up toys and put them in a box, or to pick up a pencil and begin writing); (2) holding in place the chair that the student is sitting in so he cannot push himself away from the desired location (a table) or knock himself over; (3) if possible, position your body so the student cannot leave his present location.

f. Attempt to obtain compliance on an alternative simple task, such as a simple physical imitation task, as in saying "do this" followed by a physical movement (such as touching the nose). Then return to the original task and instruction.

g. Do not allow the student to have a reinforcer or to proceed to any further activity or task *until he has complied with the original instruction.*

If Child Is Disrupting Class

h. If the child is making noises or yelling for a significant period and disrupting class (to be determined by staff in the situation), the instructor should say, "We need to go outside and be quiet" and point to the door. He should use an even-toned voice and give the student a chance to walk out by himself. If he refuses, the teacher should stand behind the student, put his hands under the student's armpits, and gently guide him out. He must be taken to a location that has previously been agreed upon by the team.

i. Either agree on an amount of time (such as thirty seconds) he needs to remain calm and quiet before going back to class, or use an egg timer to display the time and say, "We need to go back into the class in _____ minutes," and then go back when the timer rings, even if he is still upset. If the child continues with disruptive behavior, reset the timer and go through the cycle again. (This plan is set up to keep the child from thinking he can just stay out there forever and not have to do tasks.)

j. The student then goes back into class and resumes the task or activity he left, even if the class has moved on, and then allow him to go on after successful completion.

Reinforcement

Previously, in Chapter Eight, I explained the process of using reinforcement to teach students with ASD. The same principles apply to teaching new behaviors and decreasing inappropriate behaviors. Specifically, reinforcement is a teaching tool to be used when helping the student learn how and when to perform specific appropriate behaviors. Instructors cannot expect a student with ASD to understand automatically what is expected of him in certain environments and during specific activities. Strategies for improving and increasing appropriate behavior and decreasing inappropriate behavior do the following:

- Use natural and logical reinforcers for different behaviors in order to help the student appear more typical and learn what is naturally reinforcing.

- Allow the student to choose reinforcers in order to increase and maintain a high level of motivation to perform appropriate behaviors.

- Provide reinforcement for only appropriate behaviors and withhold all reinforcement upon display of inappropriate behavior; ensure that inappropriate behaviors are not inadvertently reinforced.

- Engage with the student in fun and preferred activities on a consistent basis to maintain a positive and reinforcing relationship.

- Provide reinforcement and continually adjust the appropriate amount and level of reinforcement for the type and level of difficulty of the appropriate behavior.

- Provide intermittent reinforcement for acquired appropriate behaviors in order to maintain higher frequency of appropriate behavior.

- Use reinforcers that match the function of the appropriate behavior.

- Provide immediate reinforcement when new and appropriate behaviors are displayed in order to acknowledge the occurrence and increase the frequency of those behaviors.

- Fade external reinforcement and amount of reinforcement for appropriate behaviors so that the student learns to be intrinsically motivated so he can appear more typical.

- Maintain consistent data on the level, amount, and type of reinforcement provided to the student for various appropriate behaviors.

- Ensure that all instructors are consistent with their delivery of reinforcement in order to improve the student's performance and generalization of behavior.

Using a token economy system with a students with ASD can be an effective method for reminding the student of the appropriate behavior he needs to display, and it can maintain his motivation to do so because he wants to earn a specific reinforcer. It is also the best way to help a student learn to function in a more typical environment with peers who do not receive a reinforcer for every appropriate behavior they display. In the beginning it can be difficult for a student with ASD to understand how a token represents the reinforcer, and earning a token may not hold any

> ➜ It is important to pair the token immediately with the delivery of the reinforcer and to increase gradually the number of tokens earned before receiving reinforcement.

meaning. It is therefore important to pair the token immediately with the delivery of the reinforcer and gradually increase the number of tokens earned before receiving reinforcement.

Transitions and Routines

Transitioning between environments and activities and changing routines can often cause intense difficulties for many students with ASD. Because students with ASD do not typically learn from the subtle social cues (auditory and visual) that people provide about actions and events that will occur in the future, a transition to something new can come as a complete surprise to that student. Many students with ASD also seek sameness and therefore want to continue doing the same thing, to stay in the same environment, or to do a specific activity the same way every time. If a person attempts to make a change or make the student change something, the student often displays intense noncompliant and disruptive behaviors (such as yelling, screaming, kicking, hitting, running away, and throwing objects). To stop these behaviors, instructors or parents unfortunately often alter their plans and allow the student to continue to gain that sameness.

In order for students with ASD to learn to function in typical environments, such as the general education classroom, it is important for them to learn to perform many different activities and to participate in different events within different environments, with different people and different materials. It is important to start teaching these students at the earliest age possible to transition appropriately to new activities and environments and to handle changes in routines throughout the day. This approach ensures that by the time the student enters a general education classroom he has the ability to participate successfully in the various daily activities and events. Following are several strategies that instructors can use to help students with ASD handle change and make successful transitions throughout the day:

> ➡ It is important to start teaching the student at the earliest age possible in order to help him transition appropriately to new activities and environments and to handle changes in routines throughout the day.

- Provide the student with his own visual schedule (words and pictures) that shows him what time and what kind of activities and events he will be participating in, along with the locations and other people who will be there.

- Describe and discuss the activities within the student's schedule for the day.

- Discuss upcoming nonpreferred activities many hours before they occur and while the student is calm; discuss rewards the student will gain for behaving appropriately.

- Provide auditory or visual warnings prior to the end of an activity.

- Provide auditory or visual warnings about upcoming changes in the routines for specific activities or in the schedule for the day.

- Provide a high level of reinforcement for appropriate behaviors displayed during transitions and changes; may also need to provide high frequency of reinforcement during the transition or change process.

- Provide assistance or prompts to the student during transition or routine changes (such as having a peer help him clean up, or having an adult help the student to get materials for new activity).

- Provide extra time for the student to make transitions.

- Do not discuss an upcoming nonpreferred activity while the student is currently engaged in preferred activity.

- Follow through with transitions and changes in routines once the student has been told they will occur; do not alter plans on the basis of noncompliant behavior.

- Follow through with appropriate reinforcers and consequences for the student for appropriately or inappropriately transitioning and handling changes in routines.

- Build in small changes to routines consistently before adding larger changes.

One strategy that has significantly improved the ability of students with ASD to participate appropriately in transitions or in difficult or nonpreferred activities and to display appropriate behaviors during changes in routines is Social Stories, created by Carol Gray. Social Stories describe to a student what an activity is, why and when it occurs, what the appropriate behaviors are that the student needs to display, why it is important to display those behaviors, and the benefits of engaging in the activity or change. Descriptive, perspective, directive, and control statements are utilized to write social stories. The first three statements are written by the teacher for the student. *Descriptive*

> ➔ Social stories describe to a student what an activity is, why and when it occurs, what the appropriate behaviors are that the student needs to display, why it is important to display those activities, and the benefits of engaging in the activity or change.

statements tell the student the where, what, who, when, and why information on a specific activity or situation. *Perspective statements* describe how other people feel or what they are thinking about the activity or situation. *Directive statements* tell a student what is expected of him and what appropriate behaviors he needs to display during the activity or situation. Finally, *control statements* are written in first-person language and, if possible, by the student. He states what strategies he will use to help himself perform the appropriate behaviors. It is important to use enough descriptive and perspective sentences so that the student fully understands the situation and the thoughts and feelings of others.

The goal of a social story is to provide a concrete object that the student may grasp in order to understand something that is difficult for him to understand, and to help him behave appropriately during that situation. The story helps to dissolve a student's anxiety about the situation. Having the story written down with accompanying pictures helps to take away the stress of the social interactions that are involved when a teacher discusses the situation with the student. It also helps the student take the story into his control and read and use it whenever he needs it and not have to be continually reminded what is happening and what to do, and so on. Carol Gray has written many books and has a helpful Web site for people to use to write social stories. Following is an example of a social story that has been adapted from a Carol Gray book titled *Lunch at School* and originally written by Mike Johnson (Gray, 1994, pp. 100–101):

> When the bell rings at 11:40 am, it is time for lunch. I walk to the cafeteria and I get in line behind the other students. We are all hungry and we all want to eat soon. I wait my turn to get my lunch.
>
> While I wait I need to think about what I want to eat so I can tell the lunch person right away when it is my turn. She is busy and can't wait very long for me to decide.
>
> Next, I take a tray and get a fork and a spoon. I give my tray to the lunch person and tell her what I want for lunch. She puts it on a plate and onto my tray.
>
> Next, I pick up a fruit that I want to eat. Then I pick up my milk. I give my money to the lunch lady. Sometimes she will give me some money back.
>
> Now I find a place to sit and eat. I carry my tray to the table. I sit next to a friend. It is good to talk to my friends while we are eating lunch. We can talk about recess or funny games we like to play.
>
> After I finish eating, I bring my tray to the lady that washes the dishes.

All of these behavior intervention strategies are provided in easy-to-use Checklist 9.2.

> ✓ Use Checklist 9.2: Behavior Management Techniques for the General Education Classroom

Summary

Understanding and analyzing behavior and implementing behavior intervention strategies is a challenging and daunting process and can be even more so when performed within a general education classroom. Because a student's problem behaviors can be the one factor that prevents him from receiving his education in the general education classroom, it is crucial that an IEP team invest the time and resources that are necessary to prevent and intervene appropriately with problem behaviors. It is important for the team to recognize the feasibility of implementing some behavior intervention strategies over others. It is also important that the general education teacher and paraeducator receive needed training to help them effectively implement a BIP. The ultimate goal is always to fade the BIP that has been implemented specifically for the student. If the team is unable to fade these behavioral supports, it would be appropriate to reevaluate the strategies they are using and the appropriateness of the student's placement in the general education classroom.

✓ Checklist 9.1. Implementing the Behavior Intervention Plan (BIP)

Getting Started

✓ Train relevant staff about intervention for problem behavior(s).

✓ Explain the relevant components of the BIP to the student.

✓ Make necessary changes to the student's daily schedules and routines.

✓ Prepare data collection sheets (along with explanations and data procedure sheets).

✓ Prepare intervention procedure sheets:

  ✓ Implementing and changing setting events and antecedents

  ✓ Teaching and reinforcing replacement behavior(s)

  ✓ Implementing and changing consequences

Implementing and Changing Setting Event and Antecedent Interventions

✓ Make separate lists of interventions for different environments and staff.

✓ Explain and model procedures for interventions.

✓ Help develop new materials (such as picture schedule, social story, choice board, etc.).

Teaching Replacement Behaviors

✓ Explain and model (across environments and staff):

  ✓ Procedures for teaching new behaviors

  ✓ Reinforcement procedures for

    ✓ Behaviors to increase

    ✓ New behaviors to develop

    ✓ Data collection procedures

✓ Help develop new materials (such as visual cues, social story, etc.)

✓ Develop and implement an observation schedule (fidelity of implementation)

✓ Checklist 9.2. Behavior Management Techniques

Prevention

✓ Use setting event and antecedent strategies to redirect or distract the student from engaging in self-stimulatory or other inappropriate displays of behavior.

✓ Use logical and natural consequences rather than arbitrary consequences for inappropriate behaviors.

✓ Praise peers (within earshot of the student) for engaging in appropriate behavior.

✓ Be consistent:

  ✓ Implement consequences for inappropriate behaviors.
  ✓ Implement classwide rules and a behavior management system.
  ✓ Follow through with actions stated (do not threaten over a consequence); if not possible to follow through, nothing should be said.

✓ Ignore inconsequential inappropriate behaviors.

✓ Do not reinforce or provide attention to the student while he is engaged in inappropriate behavior.

✓ Prevent the student from gaining access to ''problem'' items (that is, self-stimulatory behaviors, obsessions).

✓ Prevent the student from engaging in inappropriate behavior without appearing to intervene.

✓ Allow extra time to complete difficult tasks.

✓ Allow extra time for transitions.

✓ Allow the student to have some control or choice with certain activities or events.

✓ Make the student feel important by allowing him to perform ''special'' jobs.

✓ Comment out loud about what appropriate behaviors are desired (without providing eye contact).

✓ Decrease the difficulty level of a task.

✓ Allow the student to take breaks during a difficult task.

✓ Make sure the student is paying attention when instructions are provided.

✓ Minimize distractions for the student.

✓ Watch for peers who bully or antagonize the student.

✓ Do not allow the student to see an adult become visibly upset over problem behaviors.

✓ Use data to continually adjust behavior interventions.

Reinforcement

✓ Use natural and logical reinforcers whenever possible.

✓ Provide immediate reinforcement for display of new appropriate behaviors.

✓ Provide the level and amount of reinforcement that are appropriate for the particular type of behavior.

✓ Provide intermittent reinforcement for acquired behaviors.

✓ Provide reinforcement that matches the function of the behavior.

✓ Provide specific reinforcement praise for appropriate behaviors (use what works for the student).

✓ Engage in preferred activities with the student on a regular basis.

✓ Withhold reinforcement when inappropriate behavior is displayed.

(Continued)

✓ **Checklist 9.2. Behavior Management Techniques,** *(Continued)*

✓ Fade the amount and level of reinforcement.

✓ Allow student to choose reinforcers.

✓ Provide consistent implementation of reinforcement.

✓ Maintain consistent data.

Transitions and Routines

✓ Provide the student with his own visual schedule (in words and pictures) that shows him what kind of activities and events he will be participating in and when, along with the locations and people.

✓ Describe and discuss the activities in the student's schedule for the day.

✓ Discuss upcoming nonpreferred activities many hours before they occur and while the student is calm; discuss rewards that the student will gain for behaving appropriately.

✓ Use incentives and prompts (motivation) to assist the student with transitions from one place to another—such as from home to school—from one activity to another—for example, provide a job the student needs to complete in order for class to start—or from activity to activity—there is a natural reinforcer in the next activity.

✓ Provide visual and auditory warnings before transition to new activity.

✓ Provide visual and auditory warnings before ending preferred activity.

✓ Provide visual and auditory warnings about change in the routine of an activity or day.

✓ Do not describe upcoming nonpreferred activity while still engaged in preferred activity.

✓ Use data to assist in analyzing transitions; difficulties may not always lie in going from preferred to nonpreferred activity.

✓ Provide small changes in routines before implementing larger ones.

✓ Consistently follow through on predetermined routines.

Student: _____

Review Team: _____

Date: _____

✏ Form 9.1. Student Problem Behavior Review

Setting Events	Antecedents	Problem Behavior(s)	Perceived Function(s)	Actual/Current Consequences

(Continued)

✎ Form 9.1. Student Problem Behavior Review (Continued)

Perceived functions:

Prediction of occurrence:

Next steps (data collection, systematic manipulations, etc.):

Student: _____

Location: _____

✐ Form 9.2. A-B-C Data Analysis

Date/Time	Setting Event	Antecedent	Behavior	Consequence	Comments	Initials

☞ Handout 9.1. Ongoing Behavior Intervention Plan (BIP) Considerations and Evaluations

Data Collection

- Evaluate and adjust data collection procedures by
  - Type
  - Level of difficulty
- Measure occurrence of replacement behavior(s) (increase)
- Measure occurrence of target problem behavior(s) (decrease)
- Graph and evaluate behavior change and report back continually to the team and instructors

Fidelity of Implementation of Procedures

- Observe and meet regularly and collect data on implementation
- Help instructors to
  - Implement with accuracy and efficiency
  - Be consistent with themselves across activities and environments
  - Be consistent with one another across activities and environments
  - Adjust procedures for interventions as needed, according to data collection

Evaluating and Adjusting the BIP

- Is the replacement behavior increasing?
  - What do the data indicate about pattern of behavior?
  - Are instructors able to teach and appropriately reinforce replacement behaviors?
  - Does the replacement behavior match the function of the target problem behavior?
  - Are appropriate antecedent interventions and reinforcement procedures being used?
  - Are appropriate data collection procedures being used?
- Is the target problem behavior decreasing?
  - What do the data indicate about the patterns of behavior?
  - Has the correct function of the problem behavior been identified?
  - Were correct setting events, antecedents, and reinforcers for problem behavior identified?
  - Are instructors able to implement consequences for target problem behavior appropriately?
  - Are the correct data collection procedures being used?
- Is the student's quality of participation in activities increasing?
  - Does the student spend more time in the least restrictive environment (LRE)?
  - Does the student spend more time engaged in activities or with peers?
  - Does the student appear to be happier?
- Is external reinforcement decreasing?
  - Is the staff appropriately fading out reinforcement?
  - Does the student appear not to want or need as much reinforcement to perform appropriate behavior?

Maintenance of BIP

- Staff has appropriate training to handle problem (such as aggressive or destructive) behaviors
- Reinforcement of staff for efforts and appropriate implementation of BIP
- Ongoing meetings about current status of and major changes needed to BIP
- Attention to any legal issues related to student's BIP

Facilitating Social and Communication Skills in the General Education Classroom

10

ONE of the most challenging deficits of children with ASD is in social interaction skills. Social interaction deficits stem from the child's inability to use effective communication skills to understand what others are thinking and to use those same skills to know what he needs to say or do to respond or to initiate a successful interaction with another person. All children on the spectrum of autism disorders exhibit some degree of deficit in the nonverbal and verbal communication skills needed to function successfully in a general education classroom. This means that all educators working with a student with ASD can expect this to be a skill area in which they will need to develop goals and objectives for the student and, consequently, teaching strategies for themselves to use to address those skills. Because of the wide range of these skill deficits, however, and how they manifest themselves in different students, and because of their abstract nature, educators need to be prepared for significant challenges in teaching social and communication skills.

Many books, articles, and other resources (videos, visual aids and worksheets, and so on) specifically address social and communication skill deficits in children and youth with ASD. Extensive research has also been conducted on the nature of social skill deficits and on how to teach social and communication skills. To date, this research remains quite controversial. Some strategies for teaching social skills have been reported to be effective (for example, social stories, role-playing, and modeling), although a recent meta-analysis study shows that overall social skills training has yet to be proved effective as an intervention method because of the students' continued difficulty using the skills they have been taught.[1] Even so, children with ASD continue to need assistance in learning and using appropriate social and communication skills with adults and peers. Educators need to do the best they can with the resources currently available to develop a social and communication skills training intervention for each student with ASD with whom they are working. Developing such interventions is primarily the responsibility of the special educator, although when a student is being included in a general education classroom, the general education teacher and, if applicable, the paraeducator also need to be involved in the implementation of the intervention.

This chapter focuses on the necessary components of a social and communication skills training program for students with ASD within the general education environment. The details of specific social skills assessments and teaching lessons are not included, but a list of resources that provide all this information and more is offered at the end of the chapter.

The chapter discusses the following five components of developing an effective social skills training program for a student with ASD:

- Social skills assessment
- Determination of social skills teaching strategies
- Location and modality of social skills training,
- Implementation of social skills training
- Ongoing evaluation and adjustment of social skills training

Social Skills Assessment

The development of an effective social skills training program for a student with ASD begins with a thorough assessment of the student's social skills. This assessment helps the instructors first to understand what skills the student has already learned and then to establish realistic

> ➜ The development of an effective social skills training program for a student with ASD begins with a thorough assessment of the student's social skills.

and attainable goals for the student. It is recommended that the instructors use a social skills assessment questionnaire or checklist that covers the following skill areas:

- Play behaviors
- Emotional and self-regulation
- Problem solving
- Conversations
- Asking questions
- Participation in groups

Social skills questionnaires are most useful when they are completed by both the parents and the primary teacher of the student with ASD. The perspectives of both parties are valuable sources of information on the student's understanding and use of social and communication skills in different environments.

It is important to discover which social and communication skills the student never or almost never displays and which skills she sometimes or often displays. The skills she never or almost never uses need to be developed in the student's repertoire.

> → It is important to discover which social and communication skills the student never or almost never displays and which skills she sometimes or often displays.

There are a variety of reasons that a student does not often use a certain skill. Usually it is because the student has not yet acquired the skill or does not understand when to use the skill (or cannot use it). The skills that are sometimes or often displayed are those that the student has acquired and typically understands when to use but for some reason chooses not to use or is not motivated to or won't use. Once this information has been gathered in a social skills assessment, the skill deficit areas can be categorized as "Can't do" and "Won't do," which will help the intervention team get the big picture of what skills still need to be *taught* and what skills need to be *reinforced*. This classification does not of course apply to all skill deficits; thus an instructor (the person leading the social skills group) needs to verify in more detail the reasons for the skill deficits.

It is also important for the same instructor to work with the student's parents and teachers to prioritize the social skill deficits in order to clarify which are the most important for the student to learn first, second, and so on. At the end of this assessment process, the instructor should have a good idea which skills to target with a particular student. He or she can then decide what type of teaching strategies will work best.

Determination of Social Skills Teaching Strategies

An important consideration in selecting the appropriate social skill intervention and teaching strategies is the concept of "accommodation versus assimilation."[2] Accommodation, as it relates to social skills training, is the process of modifying the physical or social environment to promote opportunities for social interaction. Assimilation is instruction that facilitates the development of social skills the student needs in order to engage in successful interactions in his environment. A successful social skills training program incorporates both accommodation and assimilation. Focusing on one and not the other only sets the student up to fail. Providing a student with many opportunities to interact with his peers without giving him the skills necessary to interact

> → Providing a student with many opportunities to interact with his peers without giving him the skills necessary to interact with them leads to failure.

with them leads to failure. Likewise, providing skill instruction without modifying the environment to be more accepting of the student with ASD also sets him up for failure. The key is both to teach the skills *and* to modify the environment. This approach ensures that the student will have both the tools and the opportunities he needs to interact successfully with his peers.

The instructor therefore needs first to determine what kind of teaching strategies are needed to facilitate the learning of a particular social skill, and then to determine how to modify aspects of the student's environment to provide opportunities for the student to practice this skill. To decide what type of strategies will be most effective with the student, the instructor needs to understand the student's receptive language abilities.[3] Receptive language abilities demonstrate how well the student comprehends language. In other words, they demonstrate at what level the student understands verbal language and follows directions, and whether he understands the meaning of words and at what level of abstractness. A verbal IQ score helps to identify a student's receptive language skills. A student who has poor receptive language skills will need an intervention that provides training in grasping the meaning of words (semantics) and incorporate visual aides and break skills down into smaller increments. Students with stronger receptive language skills are able to participate in an intervention that uses verbal language to explain how and why certain things are done.

Examples of teaching strategies that help teach social skills include the following:

- *Discrete trial teaching*: an ABA-based teaching method that helps students learn basic words that are used in verbal instructions and questions, and helps improve attending skills

- *Incidental teaching*: using a naturally occurring moment during an ongoing activity and in an ongoing environment to help teach the student to use a specific social skill

- *Peer mentoring, tutoring, or modeling*: training typical peers in the student's class to use specific strategies to initiate and respond to the student in a way that promotes and increases the quality and quantity of the social interaction during ongoing activities

- *Social Stories and Social Skill Picture Stories*: stories presented to the student in written or picture form that explain the correct way to act in a specific situation and that depict what other people are feeling and thinking and what positive things happen if the student behaves appropriately[4]

- *Video modeling*: student observes himself/or other people performing the desired behavior and then discusses it with his instructor and peers

- *Role-playing*: student practices performing the desired behavior with peers and adults, typically first in an isolated setting and then in the context of the environment in which the behavior naturally occurs

- *Games*: uses the structure of a preferred game (for example, *Candyland, Jeopardy, Wheel of Fortune*) to help the student learn and practice using specific social skills

- *Structured learning*: teaches skills through a series of steps that explain the skill steps, model the skill steps, role-play the skill steps with feedback, and practice the skill steps in and outside of the teaching setting[5]

Location and Modality of Social Skills Training

Deciding whether the student will learn new social skills best in a one-to-one, small-group, or large-group setting, and deciding where the teaching of these skills should occur, is the beginning of the development of an effective social skills program. To make these determinations, the instructor must assess the student's ability to attend to and focus on a topic that an instructor is discussing or modeling. If the student struggles to attend to the instructor, it is important to determine whether his inattentiveness is due to his inability to sustain attention to one thing or to constantly perseverating on something else either related or unrelated to the topic. A student who struggles with perseveration is able to keep his attention on one thing, just not on what is relevant. If such a student's attention can be redirected to the relevant topic by the use of verbal prompts and reinforcers (a token economy), he may then be able to participate in small-group social skills training. If a student has poor receptive language skills or poor attending skills, or both, he is not ready to participate in a small group and would benefit instead from individual intervention or possibly from being paired with one other student with similar skill levels.

> ➜ A student who struggles with perseveration is able to keep his attention on one thing, just not on what is relevant.

Developing small groups can be a difficult process. The instructor or team must determine whether the student with ASD would benefit from having typical peers in the group and whether those typical peers are available. On the basis of my personal experience and through discussions with colleagues, it appears to me that if the social skills group consists of high-functioning students with autism or Asperger's syndrome, it is often better not to have typical peers in the group as well because without them the students with autism or Asperger's are often more relaxed and honest about their struggles and less worried about making mistakes when they role-play new skills and so on. There are times when having typical peers in a social skills group adds to the motivation of students with ASD and inspires them to attend and perform better in order to please their typical peers. If typical peers are part of the group, it is best for the students with ASD to be a homogeneous group so that the instruction can proceed appropriately for their common levels of ability.

The best size for a small group is from four to six students, and if possible it can be quite helpful to have a paraeducator assist the group with modeling, role-playing, prompting, reinforcing, and handling inappropriate behaviors. There is no prescription for how long to work with a particular group of children or for how many skills to target, but common practice among most professionals is to have social skills groups meet weekly for ten to twelve weeks for forty to sixty minutes per week, and to work on and practice one new social skill each week. Practice activities are homework with classroom

> ➜ Common practice among most professionals is to have social skills groups meet weekly for ten to twelve weeks for forty to sixty minutes per week, and to work on and practice one new social skill each week.

teacher follow-up. Although students need social skills training throughout the year, breaking up and reorganizing the social skill groups periodically to create different group dynamics can help both the students and the instructors. Of course, if an individual student or group of two or three students has poor receptive language and attending abilities, it is possible that a new social skill would be introduced only every three weeks and that the work with that student or group could span a year. Social skills groups typically meet in the special educator's (inclusion facilitator's) classroom or in another small room that has been provided for their use. Often, however, the group moves to a different and more relevant location for role-play and practice for a portion of the social skills group time.

There are occasions when a school site or general education class implements social skills training for all of its students. This means that a social skills curriculum and a specific instruction time are built into the daily and weekly class schedules. The general education teachers may be trained in the delivery of the curriculum, or the special educator at the school may work with different classrooms at different times throughout the day to provide instruction (in music or PE, for example). This approach can be both beneficial and difficult for a student with ASD. Although the student is learning the new skills along with his peers, the typical students often do not need as much explanation and practice in order to understand other people's perspectives or how to perform the skill appropriately. The student with ASD can feel confused and may not feel comfortable asking questions or role-playing because he has not yet fully grasped the concept. In some schools that have schoolwide social skills instruction, the students with ASD receive instruction in their own small social skills group and then join the large-group social skills lessons in the general education classroom for further practice and for generalization and maintenance.

It is often difficult to determine when to have the social skills group meet. Sometimes, the students are pulled out of their general education classroom once a week or during lunch or before or after school. The choice of meeting time depends on the availability of staff, students, and transportation. Of course the more students there are in the group, the more difficult it is to coordinate their schedules.

Implementation of Social Skills Training

The instructor needs to provide the appropriate amount of structure and fun for the social skills group in order to facilitate learning while maintaining the students' interest and their motivation to learn. Putting effort into preparation before the social skills group starts and establishing guidelines during the first social skills session greatly increases the probability of success overall.

> ➜ The instructor needs to provide the appropriate amount of structure and fun for the social skills group in order to facilitate learning while maintaining the students' interest and their motivation to learn.

Preparing for the social skills group involves assembling the needed materials and deciding on the rules and schedule. Depending on the age group and academic abilities of the students, the instructor makes posters of the rules and schedules that match the student's abilities (using words, sentences, pictures, or some combination) If the students can read, it is also beneficial to have handouts of the main explanation points for the skill with one or two pictures of people demonstrating that skill. Having a snack time in the schedule is greatly appreciated by the students, who are often hungry and find food a motivating aspect of any activity.

During the first session the instructor reviews the purpose of the social skills group (that is, to make friends, to learn to play with others, and so on) and informs the students of the rules, which typically include the following:

- Keep your hands and feet to yourself (do not touch or hurt others).

- Use nice words and tone of voice when talking to each other (no teasing, yelling, insulting, or using swear words).

- Listen to others when they are talking (no interrupting and no talking for an excessive amount of time).

The instructor tells the students how they can earn tokens (reinforcers) for following the rules, and what the consequences will be for not following the rules. If applicable, it helps to seek the students' input into the rules and to ask them what they want to earn for following the rules. This participation increases their motivation for behaving appropriately. The instructor reviews the schedule for the group and goes over how their time together each week will be structured. It is also beneficial to discuss at this time that they will have homework, which will consist of specific tasks that they will practice at home and in their daily school routines. The remainder of the first session should be spent getting the students acquainted with one another and having them practice following the rules while they talk. The instructor needs to provide more structure for the discussion topics during the first couple of sessions to help the students attend, participate, and stay on topic. This approach helps to establish a predictable routine and to familiarize the students with the instructor's expectations. Snack time also can be part of an ongoing activity or occur as a break.

Each of the remaining sessions focuses on a new skill. The instructor uses the teaching strategies he has determined will best meet the needs of the students in the group. At the beginning of each session the instructor spends a short time reviewing the rules and the schedule, as well as reviewing the previous week's skill lesson and the practice homework. It is important that the instructor emphasize the need for generalizing the use of the skill at home and with the students' peers in his class.

> ➔ It is important that the instructor emphasize the need for generalizing the use of the skill at home and with the students' peers in class.

Ongoing Evaluation and Adjustment of Social Skills Training

The instructor of the social skills group needs to maintain a data collection system, beginning with baseline data, that will allow him to measure skill progress or lack of progress over time. Data need to be collected on both the quality and quantity of the skill performance and in both the social skills group setting and the naturalistic setting (home and classroom). Determining how well a particular student is doing helps the instructor to know whether the current teaching strategies are effective and whether the modality and location of the instruction continue to be appropriate for the student. It is also important that one student not be significantly ahead or behind the other students. Making adjustments to instruction on the basis of student skill acquisition and performance is important, but if only one student in the group is struggling and the rest are progressing, the discrepancy can result in the display of inappropriate behaviors by all of the students due to frustration, boredom, or failure. The struggling student possibly needs to be removed from the group for more individual instruction (or put into a two-student group) before participating in a small group again.

Summary

Teaching social skills to students with ASD is one of the most challenging aspects of a special educator's work. In any culture, social skills have such a multitude of unwritten rules and nonverbal components that it can be difficult to explain these skills even to a typical person, and much more so to a student with ASD. It is important to remember that one of the biggest detriments to the understanding and learning of social skills for any individual with ASD is the lack of ability to take another person's perspective. Students with ASD can appear self-centered and egotistical because they view all interactions from only their point of view. An instructor needs to remain objective about the fact that the disability actually prevents students with ASD from knowing that other people have thought processes separate and different from their own and that they have their own reasons for desiring certain items or for doing certain activities. With careful planning, with the right strategies, and with the right amount of time, many of these perspective-taking skills can be learned and used by individuals with ASD. Having a sense of humor, great patience, and objectivity can make teaching social skills to students with ASD great fun!

> ➡ Having a sense of humor, great patience, and objectivity can make teaching social skills to students with ASD great fun!

Resources for Social Skills Lessons and Activities

Atwood, T., Callesen, K., & Nielsen, A. M. (2008). *The CAT-kit: Cognitive Affective Training*. Arlngton, TX: Future Horizons, Inc.

Autism Society of America: http://www.autism-society.org

Baker, J. E. (2003a). *Social skill picture books.* Arlington, TX: Future Horizons.

Baker, J. E. (2003b). *Social skills training: For children and adolescents with Asperger syndrome and social-communication problems.* Shawnee Mission, KS: Autism Asperger Publishing.

Council for Exceptional Children: http://www.cec.sped.org

Gray, C. (2000). *New social story book.* (Illustrated ed.) Kentwood, MI: Gray Center.

McGinnis, E., & Goldstein, A. (2003). *Skillstreaming in early childhood: New strategies and perspectives for teaching prosocial skills.* (Rev. Ed.) Champaign, IL: Research Press. (Books, cards, CD-ROM, DVD)

McGinnis E., & Goldstein, A. (2003). *Skillstreaming the elementary school child: New Strategies and perspectives for teaching prosocial skills.* (Revised Ed.) Research Press, Champaign, IL. (Books, cards, CD-ROM, DVD)

Quill, K. (2000). *Do-watch-say-listen: Social and communication intervention for children with autism.* Baltimore, MD: Paul H. Brooks.

Winner, M. G. (2000). *Inside out: What makes a person with social cognitive deficits tick?* San Jose, CA: Michelle Garcia Winner.

PART **IV**

Program Maintenance and Evaluation of Inclusion Program

Evaluating the Inclusion Program and Student Progress

11

THROUGHOUT and at the end of each school year the IEP team is monitoring the progress of each student with ASD who is being included in the general education classroom, and it is evaluating the effectiveness of the inclusive education program that has been created to meet the students' needs. Because inclusive education programs, the various components of a student's educational program, and the unique and multiple needs of students with ASD are so complex, the evaluation and monitoring process needs to be both multilayered and ongoing.

It is important for all members of an IEP team, especially the parents of the student with ASD, to understand that although placement in the general education classroom for the entire day was appropriate for a particular student during a particular school year, it is not necessarily the appropriate placement for the following year, or at least placement in the general education classroom may not be appropriate for the whole day. It is hoped that this will not be the case, because the goal would be for the student to be in the general education classroom all day every day. But a few students with ASD who have been in inclusion programs that I have facilitated have eventually needed more specialized instruction in the resource classroom, for example, or in the inclusion classroom when they enter grades three, four and five. In these grades the subject matter becomes more difficult, more abstract, and less directly related to the student, so sometimes the student with ASD becomes unable to grasp the concepts at the same grade level as his peers. An IEP team may also decide that it is appropriate for a student to repeat a particular grade in order to continue working on the same academic subject matter with the same classroom behavior expectations using the same social and play interaction skills.

> ☞ Use Handout 3.1: Legal Guidelines for Appropriate Placement of Students with ASD in the General Education Classroom (in Chapter Three).

The multilayered inclusive education and student progress evaluation process is implemented by using specific measurement and assessment tools to analyze the following four parameters, outlined in Chapter Three as the guidelines for appropriate placement of students with ASD in the general education classroom:

- Appropriate instructional methods and supports
- Student readiness

- Appropriate student participation

- Student benefits from participation

  These guidelines are used to

- Help prepare the student for inclusion in the general education classroom

- Determine if the student's primary needs can be met in the general education classroom

- Ensure that the student's behaviors do not hinder the education of his classmates

- Determine the appropriate services the student needs in order to benefit socially and academically in the classroom

Once a student has been receiving his education in the general education classroom for several months, the IEP team uses the same four parameters as guidelines to determine whether the student is progressing toward the goals and objectives that address his primary needs, and to assess whether the inclusive education program provides an accepting environment that includes the services and instructional methods the student needs in order to succeed.

This chapter describes a multilayered evaluation process that uses these four parameters. Several ideas on how the team is to proceed in response to favorable and unfavorable evaluation results are included.

Appropriate Instructional Methods and Supports for General Education Classrooms

The instructional methods, services, and accommodations provided need to be both individualized to meet the student's needs and appropriate for ongoing use and implementation within the general education classroom. This means that what the student needs in order to learn in the general education classroom must be balanced with what

> ➔ The instructional methods, services, and accommodations provided need to be both individualized to meet the student's needs and appropriate for ongoing use and implementation within the general education classroom.

the general education teacher, paraeducator, and special educator can reasonably be expected to implement while still educating and attending to the needs of all the students in the classroom. It is important to ensure that the needs of the student with ASD do not come before the needs of the typical students and inhibit their learning.

This chapter provides a tool to guide the special educator through evaluating the following strategies of an inclusive general education classroom to determine whether that classroom provides appropriate accommodations, services, and aids for the student with ASD.

Individualized Instructional Strategies

- Offers a range of materials appropriate for the age group, ability level, and learning tasks of the student with ASD

- Offers activities appropriate for the student's IEP or IFSP goals and objectives

- Varies the IEP or IFSP objectives addressed throughout the day and across the week

- Preplans individualization within groups

- Arranges activities to allow for choice making

- Uses "helpers" to accomplish routine activities

- Uses materials and activities within the setting to meet the student's needs

- Uses partial participation during activities when appropriate

- Uses incidental or functional teaching when appropriate

- Embeds IEP or IFSP goals into functional, naturally occurring activities

- Accommodates and modifies materials and curricula when appropriate

- Uses teaching strategies appropriate for the student and the setting

- Uses material cues, contingencies, and fading as appropriate

- Uses appropriate rate of presentation

- Uses prompts effective for age group, ability level, and learning tasks

- Capitalizes on the student's strengths

This list is included in the first section of Form 11.1, the Evaluation of Inclusion, Instruction, and Management Strategies in the General Education Classroom form.

> ✒ Use Form 11.1 (first section): Evaluation of Inclusion, Instruction, and Management Strategies in the General Education Classroom

The following forms and checklists from Chapter Eight can be used for more detailed evaluation of specific instructional strategies:

- Form 8.1: IEP Goals and Classroom Schedule Matrix

- Checklist 8.1: Facilitating Generalization of Skills

- Handout 8.2: Teaching New Skills: Helpful Reminders

- Checklist 8.2: Task Analysis for Student Task Completion in the General Education Classroom

- Checklist 8.3: Curriculum Accommodations and Classroom Aids in the General Education Classroom

- Checklist 8.4: Body and Verbal Language Intervention Strategies in the General Education Classroom

- Checklist 8.5: Facilitating Student Independence in the General Education Classroom

To evaluate the ongoing training and support that have been provided to the general education teacher and paraeducator, the special educator or administrator must first maintain a record of the types and amounts of training and support that have been provided to the general education teachers and paraeducators throughout the year. The following types of training and support, which have been discussed in previous chapters, could be provided to the general education teacher and paraeducator depending on the characteristics and needs of the student being included:

Training

- General information: characteristics and types of ASD, current research

- Inclusion intervention methods

- Specific teaching and intervention methods: applied behavior analysis, including discrete trial teaching and communication systems

- Behavior management techniques: functional behavior assessment (FBA), behavior intervention plans (BIP), reinforcement

- Curriculum accommodations and modifications

- Communication and language intervention methods

- Social interaction and play skills intervention methods

Support

- Information and materials on relevant topics

- Ongoing consultation and collaboration with special education personnel

- Assistance in modifying and accommodating curricula and environment

- Release time for meetings (team and collaboration, IEP)

- Paraeducator assistance in classroom

Next the special educator needs to use an evaluation questionnaire (such as the one provided for IEP teams in Form 11.2 at the end of this chapter) to seek feedback from the general education teacher and paraeducator about the training and support that were provided to them. If the team is able to and comfortable doing so, they should meet to review the feedback and discuss the most and least

> 🖉 Use Form 11.2: Inclusion of Students with ASD: Training and Support for General Education Teachers and Paraeducators Evaluation Questionnaire

helpful training and support provided, and the most significant challenges of including the particular student with ASD. This information can be summarized and given to the teacher who will work with that student the next year, as well as to the paraeducator and special educator.

If the evaluation reveals that the appropriate instructional strategies, services, and accommodations are not being provided to the student with ASD in his current placement in the general education classroom, the team needs to determine whether

- It is reasonable to expect the teacher and the paraeducator to implement the needed strategies and accommodations within the general education classroom

- The teacher and paraeducator lack the ability to implement the needed strategies and accommodations

- The teacher and the paraeducator have the appropriate support from the special education personnel to implement the needed strategies and accommodations

- The general education teacher and paraeducator have had the training and time they need to learn and develop the necessary skills

- The amount of one-to-one time needed to teach the student new skills and the amount of time needed to develop and implement accommodations and modifications take too much time away from the typical students and inhibit their learning

Student Readiness for the General Education Classroom

An important aspect of deciding to include a student with ASD in the general education classroom is to determine if he has the skills he needs to function appropriately in and benefit from education in that setting. (This does not mean he must always be perfectly quiet or calm or that he already has all the skills needed to be in the general education classroom.)

> ➡ An important aspect of deciding to include a student with ASD in the general education classroom is to determine if he has the skills he needs to function appropriately in and benefit from education in that setting.

This aspect was discussed in detail in Chapters Three and Four. The behavior skills needed for the general education classroom were also discussed in Chapter Eight. It is important to note that no child with ASD, as well as no typical child, enters kindergarten with all the behavior skills that he or she will need to function appropriately over the coming years in the general education classroom. Kindergarten is the perfect setting in which to learn these skills. That is why I so highly recommend keeping a student with ASD in kindergarten for two years. Following is a list of general education classroom behavior skills that the student needs to acquire:

- Attention
- Participation
- Social interaction and communication
- Following of classroom routines
- Play

These skills are essential for every student to develop as he or she progresses in school. In assessing a student's readiness for inclusion in the general education classroom, the IEP team evaluates whether over time the student is acquiring and using more of these skills independently. The evaluation grid presented in Form 11.3 lists the desired general education classroom behavior skills. While observing the student periodically, the evaluator records the date

> ✎ Use Form 11.3: General Education Classroom Behavior Skills Evaluation

of the observation and the level of ability the student demonstrates on that date. The information provided on this grid allows the team to determine if the student is gaining skills and independently demonstrating them over time.

If unfavorable results are obtained from the evaluation of the student's acquisition and independent use of general education classroom behaviors over time, the team needs to determine whether

- The appropriate goals and objectives have been established
- The appropriate teaching and intervention strategies are being utilized to address the student's needs, goals, and objectives
- The student is unable to learn and use his skills in the general education classroom

First, the team analyzes the current goals and objectives to ensure that they appropriately address the student's needs and abilities, which means they are attainable in and measureable over the time that has been allocated to them. Any adjustments necessary are then made to the skills or to the time allocation.

Second, the team analyzes the teaching and intervention strategies used by the general education teacher and paraeducator to determine whether they are indeed implementing the appropriate strategies to ensure success, and whether it is reasonable to implement these strategies in the general education classroom. Any necessary changes are then made to the teaching strategies utilized with the student.

Third, the team analyzes whether prior to inclusion in the general education program the student had an appropriate individualized and intensive special education program that addressed his primary needs and helped the student learn to learn skills. An intensive early intervention program focuses not only on teaching the specific skills that a student is lacking, but also on teaching the student how to attend to people in his environment, how to learn from interactions with these people, and how to problem solving in the various situations he encounters throughout the day. These learning-to-learn skills will directly affect the student's ability to develop the general education classroom behavior skills necessary to function and learn in that environment and eventually to function and learn in his community.

It is the duty of the team to balance the student's need to acquire the skills he must have in order to learn to learn with his need to develop the appropriate classroom behavior. This balance is delicate and critical because many of these skills can be developed only through an intensive

> ➜ It is the duty of the team to balance the student's need to acquire the skills he must have in order to learn to learn with his need to develop the appropriate classroom behavior.

special education program, and some skills are gained only through participation in the general education classroom. Thus, if a student is not progressing toward his goals and objectives and not gaining the general education classroom behavior skills he needs, the team may have to move him to an appropriate special education classroom that provides the intensity and lower teacher-to-student ratio that the student will need in order to progress in his learning.

Appropriate Student Participation in the General Education Classroom

Evaluating the student's participation in the general education classroom means that the IEP team determines not only whether the student is contributing to a safe learning environment and is not hindering the education of his classmates, but also whether the team itself has implemented the correct behavior intervention strategies to increase appropriate behaviors and decrease inappropriate behaviors.

First, the team determines if the student is consistently and over time demonstrating aggressive, destructive, and disruptive behaviors that are impeding his and his classmates' ability to learn in the general education classroom. The team analyzes any data that have been collected on these behaviors to assess whether they have increased or decreased.

Second, the team evaluates the overall classroom behavior management strategies used to support the student's needs within the general education classroom. The second section of Form 11.1, The Evaluation of Inclusion, Instruction, and Management Strategies in the General Education Classroom, lists as relevant the following classroom management strategies implemented by the general education teacher and paraeducator:

> ✎ Use the second section of Form 11.1: Evaluation of Inclusion, Instruction, and Management Strategies in the General Education Classroom.

Basic Classroom Management

- Provides appropriate amount of structure for classroom routines and activities.
- Provides clear behavior expectations and consistent follow-through with all students.
- Uses strategies to prevent inappropriate behaviors and increase appropriate behaviors.
- Provides appropriate amount of attention to all students in class.
- Implements individual student behavior management plans.
- Provides adequate amount of appropriate reinforcement for student.
- Uses functional and naturalistic reinforcement when possible.
- Separates emotion from behavior management.
- Offers adequate amount of appropriate encouragement to all students.
- Facilitates transitions that flow smoothly without disruptions.
- Elicits feedback from students and parents that is enthusiastic, specific, and positive.

For further detailed evaluation of the implementation of specific behavior management intervention techniques, the team can review the FBA and BIP strategies described in Chapter Nine, including Checklist 9.2, Behavior Management Techniques for the General Education Classroom.

If the evaluation obtains unfavorable results, determining that the student consistently displays behaviors that are aggressive, destructive, or disruptive and that inhibit the learning of his classmates, the team needs to take one of the following steps:

- Implement an FBA to analyze the purpose of the behaviors and determine methods of appropriate behavior intervention to be incorporated into a comprehensive BIP

- Review the behavior data collected during the FBA and BIP to determine why the behavior continues and if there has been a general decrease or increase in the display of the behavior.

Overall, the team needs to determine if the behavior intervention strategies that are necessary to decrease the inappropriate behaviors and increase the appropriate behaviors can be reasonably implemented within the general education classroom. If the behaviors are so severe or the intervention strategies necessary to change the student's behaviors require such specialized skills that keeping the student in the classroom during the behavior intervention process would be significantly detrimental to the learning of the typical students, then the team needs to remove the student to an appropriate special education classroom. The student would be educated there for as long as is appropriate to decrease the inappropriate behaviors to such a level that the student's time in the general education classroom can be gradually increased again.

Student Benefit from Participation and Education in the General Education Classroom

At the beginning of the inclusion process, the team identified the student's primary needs and determined whether they could be met in the general education classroom. Those needs that the team decided could be met in the general education classroom fall into either the social or the academic category. The team now needs to determine if the student is making appropriate progress toward his goals and objectives in the general education classroom, and thus to assess whether the student is benefiting socially or academically from being included and educated in that setting. This part of the evaluation has two layers. First, the team needs to evaluate continually the data on the student's progress or lack of progress toward his goals and objectives, and then to immediately adjust the teaching and intervention strategies accordingly. Second, at the annual IEP review the team must evaluate the student's progress toward the goals and objectives, or lack thereof, alongside the individualized teaching strategies, accommodations, and aides and services that have been implemented for the student throughout the year. The team must then determine whether the student's social or academic progress or lack of progress is due to the student's abilities or inabilities or to the appropriateness or inappropriateness of the program implementation. Again, the team must then balance the reasonable expectations for implementation of an individualized education pro-

> ➔ The team must determine whether the student's social or academic progress or lack of progress is due to the student abilities or inabilities or to the appropriateness or inappropriateness of the program implementation.

gram within the general education classroom with the needs of the student.

Although the primary benefits the student with ASD receives from participating and being educated in the general education classroom are social and academic, another important component that needs to be evaluated is *inclusive benefit*. That is, the team needs to evaluate the overall attitude and strategies of the general education teacher and paraeducator as they include and work with the student in the general education classroom. Sometimes the student may not be able to benefit either academically or socially from being included because the overall attitude of the instructors creates a classroom environment that is hostile to the student and does not promote a positive and tolerant atmosphere of acceptance of all students, specifically students with disabilities. The following strategies that need to be evaluated are also listed in the last section of Form 11.1, Evaluation of Inclusion, Instruction, and Management Strategies in the General Education Classroom:

> 🖉 Use third section of Form 11.1: Evaluation of Inclusion, Instruction, and Management Strategies in the General Education Classroom

Inclusive Interaction Strategies

- Conveys respect for all students
- Demonstrates own receptiveness and initiates collaboration with special education personnel
- Encourages interactions among students
- Emphasizes similarities among students
- Teaches peers to work with student with ASD
- Demonstrates own willingness and initiates working with student with ASD during various activities
- Answers questions about student honestly and straightforwardly

- Appropriately integrates student's form of communication within class and activities

- Facilitates methods for peers to work with the student with ASD

- Includes student in ongoing conversations

- Prompts peers to interpret nonverbal communication

- Facilitates direct communication with student

- Teaches peers to include student in decision making and choosing activities

- Provides assistance without interrupting peer interactions

- Appropriately fades from student's interactions

- Invites peers to work with the student

Information gained from the evaluation questionnaire will help the general education teacher and paraeducator to better understand their attitudes toward inclusion and toward working with students with ASD.

If the team's evaluation of the student's academic and social benefit from being included in the general education classroom produces unfavorable results, the team then uses Form 1.1, the ASD Characteristics: Student Profile, and Form 4.1, the LRE Services and Placement Determination form, to reevaluate the student's primary needs and whether those needs truly can be met in the general education classroom, or whether the child's primary needs possibly have changed. The team also uses the various teaching strategies checklists provided in Chapter Eight to determine what teaching techniques and intervention methods need to be adjusted in order to meet the student's needs more appropriately.

If the team's evaluation of the student's benefit from being included in the general education classroom produces unfavorable results, the team also needs to evaluate the school staff's overall attitude toward inclusion and acceptance to determine whether the attitude of a particular teacher is unique or the entire school struggles with accepting and educating students with disabilities, specifically the student with ASD in the general education classroom. If the entire school is still struggling, then the special educator and administrator (principal) need to develop strategies for the following:

- Improving the staff's understanding of disabilities (specifically ASD)

- Appreciating the benefits of inclusion of students with ASD

- Making training and support available to help with including students with ASD in the classroom

If it is only one general education teacher who struggles with working with the student with ASD, then the staff needs to determine why she struggles and whether her attitude extends to inclusion of all students with disabilities (and ASD) or applies only to that one student. The team must also discuss the possibility of moving the student to a different general education classroom with a teacher who demonstrates a more receptive, inclusive attitude and a willingness to work with the student and receive support from the special education personnel. The principal should also initiate a plan with the current teacher for improving her attitude and teaching techniques.

Summary

Periodically evaluating the student's overall educational program, specifically his progress toward his goals and objectives, is an important and integral component of implementing a successful inclusive education program. It is thus important that the team not only consistently evaluate the inclusive education program and the student's progress, but also engage in the actions necessary to solve any problems that arise from the evaluation.

The team evaluates the following components:

- Whether the appropriate instructional strategies and individualized services and accommodations have been implemented in the general education classroom to meet the student's needs

- Whether the general education teacher and paraeducator are receiving the training and supports they need to implement the strategies

- Whether the student continues to gain the skills he needs to function appropriately in the general education classroom and consistently demonstrates appropriate behaviors that contribute to a safe learning environment

- Whether he continues to benefit academically and socially from his education while also being accepted and treated as a full member of the general education class

If any of these elements is found lacking, the team must determine whether it is a result of the team's own challenges and problems with the implementation of the appropriate individualized strategies and accommodations, or the result of the student's inability to learn and acquire the appropriate skills needed to continue to be included in the general education classroom.

✎ Form 11.1. Evaluation of Inclusion, Instruction, and Management Strategies in the General Education Classroom

Student: _____   General Education Teacher: _____

Paraeducator: _____   Special Educator: _____

Evaluator: _____   Dates of Observation: _____

Strategies	Comments
Individualized Instructional Strategies	
Offers a range of appropriate materials for age group, ability level, and learning tasks	
Offers activities appropriate for the student's IEP/IFSP goals and objectives	
Varies the IEP/IFSP objectives addressed throughout the day	
Preplans individualization within groups	
Arranges activities to allow for choice making	
Uses "helpers" to accomplish routine activities	
Uses materials and activities within the setting to meet the student's needs	
Uses partial participation during activities when appropriate	
Utilizes incidental or functional teaching when appropriate	
Embeds IEP/IFSP goals into functional, naturally occurring activities	
Accommodates and modifies materials and curriculum when appropriate	
Uses teaching strategies appropriate for the student and the setting	

(Continued)

✎ Form 11.1. Evaluation of Inclusion, Instruction, and Management Strategies in the General Education Classroom *(Continued)*

Student: _____   General Education Teacher: _____

Paraeducator: _____   Special Educator: _____

Evaluator: _____   Dates of Observation: _____

Uses material cues, contingencies, and fading as appropriate	
Uses appropriate rate of presentation	
Uses prompts effective for age group, ability level, and learning tasks	
Capitalizes on the student's strengths	
Basic Classroom Management Strategies	**Comments**
Provides appropriate amount of structure to classroom routines and activities	
Provides clear behavior expectations and consistent follow-through with all students	
Provides appropriate amount of attention to all students	
Utilizes strategies to prevent inappropriate behaviors and increase appropriate behaviors	
Implements individual behavior management plans	
Provides an adequate amount of and appropriate reinforcement for the student	
Utilizes functional and naturalistic reinforcement when possible	
Separates emotion from behavior management	
Offers an adequate amount of appropriate encouragement	

(Continued)

Form 11.1. Evaluation of Inclusion, Instruction, and Management Strategies in the General Education Classroom (*Continued*)

Student: _____   General Education Teacher: _____

Paraeducator: _____   Special Educator: _____

Evaluator: _____   Dates of Observation: _____

Enables transitions to flow smoothly without disruptions	
Elicits feedback from students and parents that is enthusiastic, specific, and positive	
Inclusive Interaction Strategies	**Comments**
Conveys respect for all students	
Demonstrates own receptiveness and initiates collaborations with special education personnel	
Encourages interactions among students	
Emphasizes similarities among students	
Teaches peers to work with student	
Demonstrates own willingness and initiates working with the student during activities	
Answers questions about the student honestly and straightforwardly	
Appropriately integrates the student's form of communication into class and activities	
Facilitates methods for peers to work with the student	
Includes the student in ongoing conversations	
Facilitates direct communication with the student	
Teaches peers to include the student in decision making and choosing activities	
Prompts peers to interpret nonverbal communication	
Provides assistance without interrupting peer interactions	
Appropriately fades from the student's interactions	

Student: _____   Paraeducator: _____

General Education Teacher: _____

✎ Form 11.2. Inclusion of Students with ASD
Training and Support for General Education Teachers and Paraeducators
Evaluation Questionnaire

Throughout the past year you have been working with special education and administrative personnel as a part of an IEP team that placed a student with ASD in your classroom. Please answer the following questions about the training and support you received. This feedback will help the special education and administrative personnel improve the services for students with ASD who are included in the general education classroom, and support the general education personnel who work daily with these students.

1. **For *only* those types of training you received, please indicate how much you felt you *needed the training* and how *useful the information* was to you.**

   a. General information: overview of ASD, characteristics, interventions

	Low				High
Perceived need:	1	2	3	4	5
Perceived usefulness:	1	2	3	4	5

   b. Specific intervention method: ABA, TEACCH, PECS, etc.

	Low				High
Perceived need:	1	2	3	4	5
Perceived usefulness:	1	2	3	4	5

   c. Behavior management techniques

	Low				High
Perceived need:	1	2	3	4	5
Perceived usefulness:	1	2	3	4	5

   d. Communication and language intervention methods

	Low				High
Perceived need:	1	2	3	4	5
Perceived usefulness:	1	2	3	4	5

   e. Curriculum and environmental accommodations and modifications

	Low				High
Perceived need:	1	2	3	4	5
Perceived usefulness:	1	2	3	4	5

   f. Social interaction and play skills intervention methods

	Low				High
Perceived need:	1	2	3	4	5
Perceived usefulness:	1	2	3	4	5

   g. Inclusion methods

	Low				High
Perceived need:	1	2	3	4	5
Perceived usefulness:	1	2	3	4	5

(Continued)

Student: _____   Paraeducator: _____

General Education Teacher: _____

✎ Form 11.2. Inclusion of Students with ASD
Training and Support for General Education Teachers and Paraeducators
Evaluation Questionnaire (Continued)

h. Other type of training: _____

	Low				High
Perceived need:	1	2	3	4	5
Perceived usefulness:	1	2	3	4	5

2. For *only* those types of support you received, please indicate how much you felt you *needed the training* and how *useful the information* was to you.

a. Information and materials on relevant topics

	Low				High
Perceived need:	1	2	3	4	5
Perceived usefulness:	1	2	3	4	5

b. Ongoing consultation and collaboration with special education personnel

	Low				High
Perceived need:	1	2	3	4	5
Perceived usefulness:	1	2	3	4	5

c. Assistance in modifying and accommodating curriculum and environment

	Low				High
Perceived need:	1	2	3	4	5
Perceived usefulness:	1	2	3	4	5

d. Release time for meetings (team meetings, consultation meetings, IEP meetings, etc.)

	Low				High
Perceived need:	1	2	3	4	5
Perceived usefulness:	1	2	3	4	5

e. Paraeducator assistance within the classroom

	Low				High
Perceived need:	1	2	3	4	5
Perceived usefulness:	1	2	3	4	5

f. Other source of support _____

	Low				High
Perceived need:	1	2	3	4	5
Perceived usefulness:	1	2	3	4	5

3. Which sources of training and support do you believe best met your needs while teaching students with ASD within the general education classroom? (Please check all that apply.)

- ❏ Formalized training (teacher certification program, graduate school)
- ❏ Professional development (workshops, seminars, trainings)
- ❏ Online courses

(Continued)

Student: _____   Paraeducator: _____

General Education Teacher: _____

🖎 Form 11.2. Inclusion of Students with ASD Training and Support for General Education Teachers and Paraeducators
Evaluation Questionnaire (Continued)

❑ Information and materials on relevant topics
❑ Ongoing consultation and collaboration with special education personnel
❑ Assistance in modifying and accommodating curriculum
❑ Team meetings
❑ Paraeducator assistance within classroom (instructional assistant)
❑ Other sources: _____
❑ I have not received any training or support that was helpful to me.

4. **Please indicate the degree of challenge you have experienced with the following situations and issues while teaching students with ASD in the general education classroom.**

	Degree of Challenge				
	Greatest				**None**
a. Sufficient time to address the needs of students with ASD (attention, behavior, modifications)	5	4	3	2	1
b. Sufficient time to address needs of typical students	5	4	3	2	1
c. Preparation of students with ASD to meet academic demands and standards	5	4	3	2	1
d. Dealing effectively with the behavior of the students with ASD	5	4	3	2	1
e. Getting the support needed to teach students with ASD effectively	5	4	3	2	1
f. Working with the parents of students with ASD	5	4	3	2	1
g. Working with the parents of typical students	5	4	3	2	1
h. Preparation and implementation of curriculum modifications needed for students with ASD	5	4	3	2	1
i. Other source of challenge: _____	5	4	3	2	1

5. **What other types of training and sources of support would you like to receive the next time you include a student with ASD in your class?**

_____

_____

_____

Comments:

_____

_____

_____

_____

✎ Form 11.3. General Education Classroom Behavior Skills
Evaluation

Student: _____

Key: I = Independent; P = Prompted; N/D = Not demonstrated; N/A = Not applicable						
Skill	*Date*	*Level of Ability*		*Skill*	*Date*	*Level of Ability*
Attention				*Social Interaction and Communication*		
Orients toward person or speaker				Attends to (demonstrates awareness of) peers		
Attends to teacher: 1:1, small group, large group				Uses appropriate attention-getting skills		
Sits for 15–20 minutes: on floor, at desk, at table				Shows persistence in initiating interactions, if previously ignored		
Attends to task for 10–15 minutes: academic, manipulative, activity				Tolerates the physical contact of others		
Redirects self after interruption				Expresses needs and wants		
Imitates behaviors				Understands basic nonverbal communication		
Attends jointly to speaker and object or activity				Uses basic nonverbal communication		
Participation: increases over time				Shows awareness of effect of own behavior on others		
Shows awareness of environment and peers				Shows awareness and understanding of basic emotions displayed by others and responds appropriately		
Level and amount of participation in task: 1:1 small group, student-directed, large group				Is able to engage in 3–6 back and forth exchanges in a conversation		
Level of motivation to participate				Attempts to engage others in interactions		
Internal motivation to maintain appropriate behavior				Responds to others' initiations to interact		
Receptive language skills of student				Is able to engage in appropriate physical interaction with others		
Expressive language skills of student				Follows the lead of peers when appropriate		
Membership in class: staff and peers enjoy and include student in ongoing activities				Shares class materials with peers		
				Takes the lead with peers when appropriate		
				Shows preference for playing and interacting with certain peers (making friends)		
				Demonstrates a sense of humor		

(*Continued*)

✐ Form 11.3. General Education Classroom Behavior Skills
Evaluation (Continued)

Student: _____

Key: I = Independent; P = Prompted; N/D = Not demonstrated; N/A = Not applicable						
Skill	*Date*	*Level of Ability*		*Skill*	*Date*	*Level of Ability*
Following of classroom routines				*Play*		
Works quietly on independent tasks				Plays with toys as designed		
Keeps personal items in designated space				Engages in play with three or more different toys, games, or activities over several days		
Locates and uses restrooms				Remains engaged in independent play with one toy, activity, or game for at least 5–10 minutes		
Locates own preassigned seating location for different activities				Maintains appropriate proximal play		
Sits quietly while teacher is talking to class or other student				Chooses from two or more activities or toys		
Raises hand to ask question				Follows game-playing rules		
Raises hand to answer questions				Engages in pretend play		
Raises hand to comment				Engages in appropriate talking during play		
Locates and uses needed materials for tasks and activities				Shares toys with peers		
Organizes time and follows routines for completing a task				Joins and leaves interactive play activities with appropriate social cues		
Remains on task for a given activity or task for typical amount of time				Attempts to join or initiate play with peers		
Follows instructions to complete 2–3 steps				Allows peers to join him during play		
Follows common, simple routines within specific activities				Explores other toys within environment		
Transitions between activities				Demonstrates problem-solving skills when a toy or something else does not work		
Transitions between locations on the school site						
Navigates the classroom and school site						
Seeks help when appropriate						
Accepts help and correction when appropriate						
Is able to make mistakes, lose at a game, and not be first in line						
Volunteers to perform an action						
Follows instructions provided by school staff other than teacher or paraeducator						

Facilitating Successful Transitions to a New Classroom

12

HELPING a student with ASD to transition to a new grade and new classroom each year can be a stressful process for the instructors, the student, and the student's family. It can feel like starting over again and again. The goal is that the more years a student with ASD has been included in the general education classroom, the more smoothly the transitions will be because everyone involved will be familiar with the changes that occur. The key aspect of helping a student with ASD to transition to a new class is adequate planning and concise preparation. The IEP team must consider all of the successes and all of the challenges the student (and instructors) experienced that year, and then armed with that information the team can make the necessary changes to enable the transition to be as smooth as possible and thus allow the beginning of the new school year to be as free of stress and anxiety as possible for everyone and establish the grounds for a successful coming year.

Several important preparation tasks enable the IEP team to implement an organized and successful transition. As previously mentioned, the special educator facilitates the student's transition and thus leads the team through these preparatory tasks. To begin, the IEP team meets at least two months prior to the end of the school year to discuss appropriate placement options for the following school year. This meeting might coincide with the annual IEP meeting, when the goals and objectives and classroom placement are discussed. Because each year the placement options that will meet a student's needs may change, it is important for the IEP team to engage in a comprehensive evaluation of the inclusive education program and of the student's progress before engaging in the development of a transition plan for the next school year. These evaluation strategies are discussed in Chapter Eleven.

If the IEP team decides that for the following year it is appropriate for the student to continue to be included in the general education classroom for the majority or part of his day and to proceed to the next grade level, the team then needs to discuss what classroom and teacher will be the best fit for the student and his needs. This may be an easy decision if the team's members are familiar with all of the teachers and classrooms for the next grade, but in case they are not, they need to plan times to observe the classrooms and meet with the prospective teachers. All of the strategies for initiating the inclusion process that are described in Chapter Seven are used during this transition process. The preliminary meeting ends with establishing the next meeting time (about a month later), when the new general education teacher will be included. After this meeting and prior to the observations of the prospective general education classroom, it is helpful for the principal to talk to the prospective teachers and explain the purpose of the observations and the possibility of this student with ASD being included in their class the next year.

While the relevant members of the IEP team are observing prospective classes and meeting the general education teachers, the student's current general education teacher and paraeducator and the special educator can be assembling a portfolio of the following materials:

- Work samples

- Visual aid samples

- Behavior intervention materials

- Form 7.5: Summary of Abilities and Interests

- Form 7.6: Student Interest Survey

- Form 1.1: ASD Characteristics: Student Profile

- Form 12:1: General Education Teacher Overview

- Form 12.2: Paraeducator Overview

> ✎ Use Form 12.1: General Education Teacher Overview, and Form 12.2: Paraeducator Overview

The last two forms were created to gather the teacher's and the paraeducator's thoughts and ideas about working with the student with ASD throughout the past year. This portfolio is provided to the next year's general education teacher and, if applicable, to the paraeducator who may be working with the student in the classroom.

Once all of the classrooms have been observed, the team meets again briefly to discuss and decide which teacher and classroom will best fit the student. Then the principal talks to the teacher who is the team's top choice to ensure that he or she is willing and has a positive attitude toward the student and the inclusion process. Once the decision about the appropriate classroom and teacher has been made, the teacher is provided with the student's portfolio, a time is set up for her to observe the student in his current classroom, and a second transition meeting is scheduled.

The second transition meeting is held, primarily for the benefit of the new general education teacher, and to make final plans for the strategies that are going to be used to help the student's transition to the next year go as smoothly as possible. All of the student's current pull-out and push-in supplementary services (SLP, OT, PT, and so on) are reviewed and an appropriate schedule for these services is determined for the next year. The team discusses the aids, accommodations, and modifications that are currently being used with the student and seeks the new teacher's input on whether to use the same or similar services the next year. The team also decides whether an ability awareness lesson is appropriate for the new classroom and, if so, plans when this will take place.

A plan is also established for specific transition activities to be implemented at the end of the present school year and at the beginning of the next school year. Following are some of the most helpful transition activities for the student:

- Visit the new classroom.
- Meet the new teacher before the end of the school year.
- Acquire several pictures of the classroom and the teacher to look at and talk about over the summer.
- Review a Social Story about transitioning to new classrooms each year.
- Visit the classroom a few days before the new school year begins.

These strategies help the student to prepare for the transition during the summer, to understand why he needs to move to a new class, and to have a picture in his mind of what his new class and new teacher look like. Coming back to visit again just before the school year starts, without other students around, helps the student understand what his classroom will look like (because when he visited at the end of the previous school year another class was in session and teachers often change things at the beginning of the year), where his desk is, and if he has not attended a classroom during the summer, how it feels to be in one again. If the student does attend summer school, similar transition strategies can be used for that class and teacher as well.

Finally, before the end of the school year it is helpful to hold one additional meeting that includes the current general education teacher, the current paraeducator, the special educator, and the new general education teacher. This small, more informal team meeting enables the staff who are working directly with the student with ASD to discuss in more detail the day-to-day academic and behavior intervention strategies that are presently being used. It also gives the new teacher an opportunity to ask more detailed questions and gain a clearer understanding of what it might be like to work with the student. The special educator, the new teacher, and the paraeducator also set a time and date for the student to visit the new classroom, and a time that the team will meet one week after the new school year has started. A checklist of all these transition activities is provided for the special educator's benefit in Checklist 12.1.

> ✓ Use Checklist 12.1: Transition to New Classroom Checklist

It is also possible that a student might change to a new classroom during the school year if his family moves to a new school district. The same planning and preparation strategies need to be implemented in that situation. This will likely be a more difficult transition because the policies and special education program at the receiving school district may be different from those at the current school, so the sending IEP team will need to be as helpful as possible in providing comprehensive information on the student's IEP and inclusion program.

Summary

It is extremely important that an IEP team attend to the unique needs of each student with ASD when a major transition is about to occur in the student's education program. It is almost a given that any problem behaviors the student is prone to display when he is anxious or afraid will appear at a heightened rate and intensity during these major transition times. The school staff and parents will need to prepare explicitly for these behaviors and know how to intervene appropriately (in both antecedent and consequence interventions) when it happens. Thus, in order to implement a successful transition plan, the IEP team should not hesitate to invest a lot of time and energy in the preparations. All of the tasks listed in Checklist 12.1, Transition to a New Classroom, are necessary and none should be omitted. Carrying out these tasks provides the student with the information and tools he will need to understand and therefore make the major transitions he needs to make. The skill of being able to transition successfully will be needed by the student throughout the remainder of his life.

Student: _____

✓ Checklist 12.1. Transition to a New Classroom

✓ Initial transition meeting is held at least two months prior to the end of the present school year to discuss appropriate classroom placement for next year. Date and time: _____

  ✓ Discuss the results of the evaluation of the inclusive education program and student progress.

  ✓ Discuss prospective teachers and classrooms to receive student for the next year.

    ✓ Plan for observations:

      Teacher/class: _____ date: _____ time: _____

      Teacher/Class: _____ date: _____ time: _____

      Teacher/Class: _____ date: _____ time: _____

  ✓ Set tentative time for next team meeting, to be held with next year's teacher.
    Date and time: _____

✓ Principal talks to prospective teachers about the student with ASD and upcoming observations.

✓ Portfolio is assembled to reflect the student's current academic and behavior status:

  List of contents: _____

_____

✓ Decision is made about next year's classroom teacher and the teacher is informed by the principal:
Teacher/class: _____

✓ Next year's classroom teacher receives student's portfolio and observes him in current classroom.
Date and time: _____

✓ Second transition meeting is held with previous team members *and* next year's general education teacher. Date and time: _____

  ✓ Introduce all team members and allow parents to make their own statement if desired.

  ✓ Discuss current supplementary services and discuss times for implementation next year:

    Service: _____ Day/time: _____

    Service: _____ Day/time: _____

    Service: _____ Day/time: _____

  ✓ Discuss current aids, accommodations, and necessary modifications.

  ✓ Decide whether ability awareness lesson is needed, and if so, when.
    Date and time: _____

  ✓ Discuss any pertinent changes in services for the next year.

  ✓ Address any questions or concerns from the team and the new teacher.

  ✓ Discuss and plan arrangements for transition at the end of the current school year and the beginning of the new school year: Transition activities to occur: _____

_____

✓ Arrange for final, small planning meeting with the current teacher and paraeducator, the special educator, and next year's teacher. Date and time: _____

✓ Arrange for student's visits to the new classroom.
  Before end of school year: Date and time: _____
  Beginning of next school year: Date and time: _____

✓ Arrange for meeting one week after new school year begins.
  Date and time: _____

Student: _____   Date: _____

Teacher: _____   Paraeducator: _____

✐ Form 12.1. General Education Teacher Overview

My initial fears about working with _____ in my class were _____

_____

_____

I was able to deal with those fears by _____

_____

_____

I felt that the training and support provided for me and the student were _____

_____

_____

A few of the most important things I learned throughout this year in my work with this student were _____

_____

_____

_____

Some things that worked well with this student were _____

_____

_____

_____

Some of the most difficult aspects of working with this student were _____

_____

_____

_____

Something I would have done differently was _____

_____

_____

_____

Additional comments _____

_____

_____

_____

Student: _____   Date: _____

Teacher: _____   Paraeducator: _____

🖉 **Form 12.2. Paraeducator Overview**

My initial fears about working with _____ in the general education

class were _____

_____

_____

_____

I was able to deal with these fears by _____

_____

_____

_____

I felt that the training and support provided for me and for the student were _____

_____

_____

_____

_____

A few of the most important things I learned throughout this year in my work with this student were _____

_____

_____

_____

_____

_____

Some things that worked well with this student were _____

_____

_____

_____

_____

Some of the most difficult aspects of working with this student were _____

_____

_____

_____

_____

Additional comments: _____

_____

_____

_____

_____

_____

_____

Conclusion

AS you conclude the reading of this book, you are also concluding the development of a big picture of an appropriate and effective inclusion program for students with ASD. It is my hope that you have come to understand the individual components of the program that assists administrators, special and general educators, parents, and paraeducators to successfully include a student with ASD in a general education classroom. The checklists, handouts, and forms provided here are the guides to initiating the inclusion program for students with ASD, following through on the process, and maintaining the day-to-day implementation, evaluation, and intervention strategies with the student and the IEP team.

I encourage you to look ahead at the task that may at first appear quite daunting and in which you will encounter many obstacles. In all my work with students with ASD, creating an inclusion program has often been difficult, but it has almost always been rewarding. It takes great energy and hard work to make even small steps forward, but when these successes occur, the difference made in many lives—not just the life of the student with ASD—is truly rewarding. Including this student is the ultimate test in educating this child; it is essentially a make-it-or-break-it scenario. The pressure on the teachers and the paraeducators to enable such a student to succeed in the general education classroom can be great. This is why it is most important to coordinate an IEP team whose members collaborate consistently, trust one another, rely on each other for support and ideas when times are difficult, and celebrate together when things go well. An IEP team is built for each individual student with ASD in the school and district. Establishing a cooperative and competent team is what makes the difference in the success of a student with ASD in a general education class.

It is crucial for educators and administrators to take one step at a time when establishing effective inclusion programs for students with ASD. Using the information presented in Chapter Five, develop an action plan with goals and objectives that can be handled realistically in a reasonable amount of time. *Reasonable* is the key word, because it cannot be done all at once. It is more important to be proactive with good leadership and to spend the necessary time and energy from the beginning to get everything in place for starting the inclusion of students with ASD. Too much is at stake and there is too much to lose when initially including a student with ASD in the general education program. The most important element is the positive attitudes of the general education staff and parents. Funding, training, and staff preparation are also crucial.

It is important to remember that there will be difficult times even when everyone has worked hard to proactively create an effective program and implement all the correct strategies. There are students with ASD who initially do well and then for some reason encounter great difficulties, or students who disrupt a general education classroom or need so much one-to-one attention that the general education teacher is unable to teach her class effectively because the student's classmates are hindered from receiving the attention they need. Any of these situations can be discouraging, and they require a team to reevaluate the student's overall program. It is also very important, however, not to underestimate the *potential* of a given student with ASD and the power of being educated along with one's typical peers. Many times I have worked with a team who initially thought it would be a while before a student's time in the general education classroom could be increased because they thought his behavior would be too disruptive. But once the student was included in the general education classroom and was aware of the environment and his typical peers, his behavior and his on-task skills greatly improved. It was evident that he wanted to stay in that classroom and wanted to be with his peers. It is therefore not uncommon for students who are included in the general education classroom to demonstrate academic, communication, and social skills that they had not demonstrated previously. This is evidence that they have learned from the appropriate models of their typical peers and have been given opportunities to interact with these peers and use skills they had never used before. It is very encouraging to see this and it is the exact direction desired in the education of children with ASD. The team should be sure to increase the student's classroom time accordingly. To summarize, I offer a statement that many people have heard me use when I am encouraging teams to be positive while also being realistic: *Hope for the best, but prepare for the worst.*

Another factor to be remembered is that when mistakes have been made with a particular student, teacher, paraeducator, or principal, it is best to be open and honest with the team about the mistake, to apologize, and to ask for assistance in getting back on track. Such a situation can be very difficult to remedy, but typically it builds the team members' trust in one another and helps everyone to be vulnerable about their weaknesses and to seek support from one another. An example of a difficult situation caused by one of my mistakes came when I was initiating placement of a student in the general education classroom and realized too late that the IEP team had not spent enough time investigating his academic abilities before including him at his neighborhood public school. The private school he had attended assured us that he was on grade level, but in fact his math skills were several grade levels below the level of the class in which he was now being included. If we had known this we would have proactively modified his math work to accommodate his needs and ability level so he could be successful and would not have come to hate math time and exhibit tantrums when he knew math work was next on the schedule. He disrupted the class so much so that he had to be removed from math time, which caused the need to implement a behavior plan and transfer his math class to the special education classroom. Later we were able to transition him back into the general education class for math, and we finally got him back on track with appropriate classroom behavior and modified math work. We also added instructional time in the special education class later in the day to work toward bringing him up to grade level with his math skills. It was discouraging to feel that I had caused this student and the teachers unnecessary hardship and wasted much valuable time. Fortunately this IEP team worked collaboratively throughout the process, communicating and meeting consistently about strategies and changes, and reliably implementing the behavior plan. They also insisted on collectively taking the "blame" for the mistake, saying that they all should have thought about retesting him prior to his entry into the general education classroom, and that they had learned a lot about handling behaviors and about the student in particular that would be helpful in working with him in the years to come. This situation ended positively, but if it had not been for the wonderful collaborative IEP team, this student might well not have been successful in the general education classroom.

Another important consideration is the attitudes and feelings of the parents of the student with ASD. The parents of one such student with whom I worked were adamant about him being included in the general education classroom all day starting the first day of school. They felt that the general education classroom (and their child's being with typical peers) was the only appropriate placement. The student was therefore placed in the general education classroom, but it soon became apparent that he was not making progress with his social, independence, or crucial classroom behavior skills and consistently needed much one-to-one attention in order to participate in the ongoing activities. Although the IEP team continued to work hard to adjust strategies and accommodate the classroom for him, and although they took copious notes and collected many data on his performance, it was soon evident that his needs truly were not being met in the general education environment. It was advantageous that we had known this student before he was included in the general education classroom and had anticipated this as a possibility. The team began working with the parents to prepare them for the likelihood that the general education classroom possibly was not the educational or social environment that would meet their child's needs. They explained how ongoing assessments were being made to review the overall program and the student's progress in particular. We remained open with the parents about our concerns, constantly communicating the changes being implemented, and the parents regularly observed the classroom while we continually sought their input. Finally the team felt it was time to meet about a possible change of placement, even though such a change would initially be difficult and possibly saddening for the parents as well as for the staff. There was no question that this student with ASD needed more than could be offered in the general education classroom.

The staff was prepared for the parents to be upset and adamant about keeping their child in the general education classroom. Because the staff had been so open with the parents and the parents had been so involved in the general education placement, nothing that was discussed at the meeting was new to the parents. The staff openly shared their compassion and love for the student. It was obvious that the parents had prepared themselves for the meeting and were surprisingly agreeable to the proposed changes in their child's program. As the meeting concluded, the mother left and the father stayed to finish the paperwork. He looked at us with tears in his eyes and told us about the struggle this past year had been for them as they watched the IEP team work hard with their son. He said it was obvious they cared about him, yet it was also obvious they were not able to help him learn the skills he needed within the general education classroom. He stated that their struggle was due to, on the one side, feeling strongly, that their son needed to be in the general education environment with typical children and, on the other side, seeing a team of competent, caring staff working to include their child and yet not succeeding in making the placement work. They had finally recognized that nothing more could be done and had therefore came to the conclusion that they needed to listen to the advice of the staff about what program would work for their son. This father thanked us for being open and honest with them throughout the process. As he concluded, there was not a dry eye in the room. We knew that those parents had come to a very difficult realization about their child and his future, and although it was so hard to see their sadness, we knew we had helped them come to this point at an early stage in his life rather than later, when he would have been a teenager or an adult who had lost valuable time and not acquired critical functional-living skills.

These examples from my experience are told here to encourage other teams as they work together to develop inclusion programs for the many students with ASD who will grace the general education classrooms with their presence in the coming years. This work will never be easy, but each experience will make the person working with these students both humble and more competent. Children with ASD are amazing individuals who are an incredible mystery, some coming with more clues than others. Successfully including a student with ASD in the general education classroom is the ultimate goal and it requires meticulous preparation in order to be proactive and prepared for the worst and best possible scenarios. I wish for you that you would enjoy both the journey and the unique and amazing students with ASD who are entrusted to your care.

Glossary

Abstract Reasoning: the ability to understand the overall context of a given situation, to recognize the contributing factors and other people's thoughts and feelings, and adjust one's behavior accordingly.

Auditory Processing: the ability to analyze or make sense of information received through the ears.

Auditory Stimuli: the information that is presented to a person through a means that makes sound.

Continuum of Service and Placement Options: the varying amounts and types of intervention services (i.e. academic, behavior, social, speech and language) provided for students with disabilities in different types of classrooms.

Delayed Echolalia: repeated speech utterances heard in the past.

Echolalic Speech: previously heard speech utterances repeated continually.

Executive Functioning: the ability to retrieve and use previously learned concepts and apply them to the present situation, including planning, organizing, strategizing and paying attention to details.

Full Inclusion: the educating of students fully with disabilities in the general education classrooms, regardless of disability or severity of disability.

Generalization: the application of knowledge gained about one thing to other environments and stimuli.

Immediate Echolalia: speech utterances repeated instantly after they were heard.

Inservice: training and education given while a person is working as a teacher.

Joint Attention: one's ability to share and maintain attention between other people and objects or activities at the same time.

Locomotion: the ability to move one's body from place to place.

Matching Tasks: visually identifying items that are the same.

Manual Dexterity: the ability to perform actions with both hands.

Metarepresentation: the capacity to understand the thoughts and feeling of other people and to interpret their behavior based on what they may be thinking.

Motivation: a person's reason for engaging in a given behavior.

Nonverbal Communication: intentional, non-symbolic communication in which a child typically uses few isolated and non-sophisticated gestures while often also exhibiting aggressive and self-injurious behaviors.

Overgeneralization: applying one learned concept to all items or activities in that category.

Overselective Responding: attention to only certain [few] features/cues rather than all the features/cues available.

Perceptual Tasks: those tasks that assess nonverbal concept formation, visual perception and organization, simultaneous processing, visual-motor coordination and learning, and include the ability to separate figure and background in visual stimuli.

Perseverative (Perseverate): repetitive and unending actions performed with certain objects.

Preservice: training and education gained prior to becoming a teacher.

Primary Consideration of Placement: the first location that is considered for the child's delivery of the child's educational intervention services.

Proprioception: a person's ability to sense where one's body is in space.

Regular Education Initiative (REI) Movement: the goal of educating typical children together with children with disabilities in the same "regular" education classes.

Self-stimulatory Behaviors: highly preferred actions a person continually performs and/or attempts to perform.

Spatial Tasks: the action of attending to and locating things in relationship to oneself.

Supplemental Supports and Services: those additional supports and services that are not typically provided by the general education teacher or special education teacher in the classroom, i.e. occupational therapy, paraeducator assistance outside of special education classroom, speech and language therapy, adaptive physical education, behavior intervention plan, etc.

Tactile Stimuli: information that the body gains through touching items or people.

Verbal Delays: the use of some speech by a student while also displaying significant delays in the use of typical sentences, i.e. phonology, syntax and semantics.

Vestibular Processing (Stimuli): a person's ability to interpret the body's movement, maintain balance, and remain steady.

Visual Processing: the act of analyzing or making sense of information taken in through the eyes.

Visual Stimuli: the information that is presented to a person through materials that can be seen.

Notes

Introduction

1. Burack, Root, & Zigler, 1997; Harrower & Dunlap, 2001.
2. Harrower & Dunlap, 2001.
3. Mesibov & Shea, 1996.
4. Harrower & Dunlap, 2001.
5. Burack et al., 1997.
6. Mesibov & Shea, 1996; Simpson & Myles, 1993.
7. Kauffman & Hallahan, 2005; Simpson, 2004.
8. Burack et al., 1997; Helps, Newson-Davis, & Callais, 1999; McGregor & Campbell, 2001; Simpson, de Boer-Ott, & Myles, 2003.
9. Miller, 1990.
10. Burack et al., 1997.
11. Du Paul & Henningston, 1993; Koegel, Koegel, Hurley, & Frea, 1992; Locke & Fuchs, 1995; Odom, Hoyson, Jamieson, & Strain, 1985; Odom & Watts, 1991; Strain, Kohler, Storey, & Danko, 1994.
12. Dugan, Kamps, Leonard, Watkins, Rheinberger, & Stackhaus, 1995; Harris, Handlemann, Kristoff, Bass, & Gordon, 1990; Kamps, Barbetta, Leonard, & Delquadri, 1994; Quill, 1990; Simpson et al., 2003; Simpson & Myles, 1993.
13. Cook, Tankersley, Cook, & Landrum, 2000; Werts, Wolery, Snyder, & Caldwell, 1996.
14. Burack et al., 1997.
15. Scruggs & Mastropieri, 1996.
16. McNally, Cole, & Waugh, 2001; Soodak, Podell, & Lehman, 1998.
17. Buell, Hallman, & Gamel-McCormick, 1999; Salend & Duhaney, 1999.
18. Cook, et al., 2000; Kavale & Forness, 2000; Lindsay, 2003; McNally et al., 2001; Pivik, McComas, & LaFlamme, 2002; Snyder, Garriott, & Aylor, 2001.
19. McGregor & Campbell, 2001.
20. Helps et al., 1999.

Chapter One

1. American Psychiatric Association (APA), 2000, p. 64.
2. APA, 2000.
3. Schuler, 1995; Sullivan, 1994; Van Meter, Fein, Morris, Waterhouse, & Allen, 1997; Burack & Volkmar, 1992; Committee on Educational Interventions for Children with Autism, 2001.
4. Sullivan, 1994; Committee on Educational Interventions for Children with Autism, 2001.

5. APA, 2000; Koegel, Koegel, Frea & Smith, 1995; Grandin, 1995; Schuler, 1995; Committee on Educational Interventions for Children with Autism, 2001; Myles & Simpson, 2003; Atwood, 1998; Simpson & Myles, 1998; Mauk, Reber, & Batshaw, 1997.
6. Meyer and Minshew (2002).
7. Meyer & Minshew, 2002, p. 154.
8. Meyer & Minshew, 2002, p. 155
9. Meyer & Minshew, 2002, p. 156.
10. Committee on Educational Interventions for Children with Autism, 2001.
11. Atwood, 2006; Myles & Simpson, 2002.
12. Myles & Simpson, 2002.
13. Grandin, 1995, Koegel, Koegel & Parks, 1995; Rosenblat, Bloom, Koegel, 1995, Simpson & Myles, 1998.
14. Myles & Simpson, 2003, Rourke & Tsatsanis, 2000.
15. Quill, 2000.
16. Grandin, 1995; Atwood, 2006.
17. Rourke & Tsatsanis, 2000; Myles & Simpson, 2003; Atwood, 2006; Myles & Simpson, 2002.
18. Rourke & Tsatsanis, 2000; Myles & Simpson, 2003; Atwood, 2006.
19. Atwood, 2006; Myles & Simpson, 2003; Grandin, 1995.
20. Myles & Simpson, 2003; Atwood, 2006.
21. Wolfberg, 1999.
22. Atwood, 1995; Myles & Simpson, 2003.
23. Wolfberg, 1999.
24. Schuler, 1995, p. 17.
25. Koegel, 1995
26. Ogletree, 1998, p. 143
27. Schuler, 1995; Koegel, 1995.
28. Tsai, 1998
29. Atwood, 2006, Myles & Simpson, 2003; Landa, 2000; Rourke & Tsatsanis, 2000.
30. Atwood, 2006; Landa, 2000.
31. Atwood, 1998; Committee on Educational Interventions for Children with Autism, 2001.
32. Committee on Educational Interventions for Children with Autism, 2001, p. 115.
33. Simpson & Myles, 1998; Committee on Educational Interventions for Children with Autism, 2001; Schuler, 1995; Koegel, Koegel Frea & Smith, 1995; Mauk et al, 1997.
34. Atwood, 2006; Myles & Simpson, 2003.
35. Atwood, 2006; Myles & Simpson, 2003; Smith, 2000.
36. Kilburn & Rosen-Lieberman, 1998; Grandin, 1995; Atwood, 2006; Myles & Simpson, 2003; Cook & Dunn, 1998; Autism Society of America, 2002.

Chapter Two

1. Kavale & Forness, 2000.
2. Reynolds, Wang & Walberg, 1987.
3. Pugach & Lily, 1984; Reynolds & Wang, 1983.
4. Lipsky & Gartner, 1989; Stainback & Stainback, 1984.

5. Lipsky & Gartner, 1989.
6. Dorn, Fuchs, & Fuchs, 1996; Kauffman, 1993; Meredith & Underwood, 1995.
7. Kavale & Forness, 2000; Pivik et al., 2002.
8. Kavale & Forness, 2000; Pivik et al., 2002.
9. Buell et al., 1999; Kavale & Forness, 2000; Pivik et al., 2002.
10. Kavale & Forness, 2000.
11. Antonak & Livneh, 1988; Shaw & Wright, 1967.
12. Antonak & Livneh, 1988.
13. Cook et al., 2000.
14. Good & Brophy, 1972.
15. Silberman, 1971.
16. Brophy & Good, 1974.
17. Willis & Brophy, 1974; Cook et al., 2000.
18. Cook et al., 2000.
19. Cook et al., 2000.
20. Fisher, Sax, Rodifer, and Pumpian, 1999.
21. Livneh, 1982.
22. Brownlee & Carrington, 2000; Fisher, Pumpian, & Sax, 1998; Kishi & Meyer, 1994; Peltier, 1997; Rimmerman, Hozmi, & Duvdevany, 2000.
23. Salend and Duhaney, 1999.
24. Buell et al., 1999.
25. McNally et al., 2001; Scruggs & Mastropieri, 1996; Soodak et al., 1998; Winzer, 1998.
26. McNally et al., 2001.
27. Scruggs and Mastropieri, 1996.
28. McGregor and Campbell, 2001.
29. Helps, S. et al., 1999, p. 294.
30. Volkmar, Klin, & Cohen, 1997.
31. Winzer, 1998.
32. McGregor and Campbell, 2001.
33. Cook et al., 2000; Fox & Yssledyke, 1997.
34. Cook, Semmel, Gerber, 1999.
35. Fox and Yssledyke, 1997.
36. Scruggs & Mastropieri, 1996.
37. Cook et al., 1999.
38. Fisher, Pumpian, & Sax, 1998; Fisher, Sax, Rodifer, & Pumpian, 1999
39. Staub and Peck, 1994/1995.
40. Brownlee & Carrington, 2000; Rimmerman et al., 2000.
41. Brownlee & Carrington, 2000.
42. Brownlee & Carrington, 2000; Rimmerman et al, 2000.
43. Cook, 2002; Lombardi & Hunka, 2001.
44. Cook, 2002; Lombardi & Hunka, 2001; Shade & Stewart, 2001; Stanovich & Jordan, 2002; Wolfe, Boone, Filbert, & Atanasoff, 2000.
45. Coombs-Richardson & Mead, 2001; Lombardi & Hunka, 2001; Simpson et al., 2003; Stanovich & Jordan, 2002; Villa, Thousand, & Chapple, 1996.
46. Villa et al., 1996, p. 43.
47. Coombs-Richardson & Mead, 2001; McLeskey & Waldron, 2002; Pugach & Johnson, 1996.

48. Stanovich and Jordan, 2002.
49. Cook, 2002; Hobbs & Westling, 2002; Shade & Stewart, 2001; Stanovich & Jordan, 2002; Wolfe et al., 2000.
50. Cook, 2002; Coombs-Richardson & Mead, 2001; Lombardi & Hunka, 2001; Stanovich & Jordan, 2002; Villa, et al., 1996.
51. Wolfe et al., 2000.
52. de Boer, 2005.
53. Klinger, Ahwee, Pilonieta, & Menendez, 2003; McLeskey & Waldron, 2002; Weiner, 2003.
54. McLeskey & Waldron, 2002; Villa et al., 1996.
55. Coombs-Richardson & Mead, 2001; Werts et al., 1996.
56. Klinger et al., 2003 McLeskey and Waldron, 2002.
57. McLeskey and Waldron, 2002.
58. McLeskey & Waldron, 2002.
59. Weiner, 2003.
60. Hobbs & Westling, 2002.
61. Gallagher, 1997; Buell et al., 1999; Shade & Stewart, 2001.
62. Werts et al., 1996.
63. Salend and Duhaney, 1999.
64. Friend & Cook, 1992; Graden & Bauer, 1994; Heron & Harris, 2001; Pugach & Johnson, 1995, 1996; Reeve & Hallahan, 1996; Simpson & Myles, 1996; Whelan, 1996.
65. Friend & Cook, 1992; Graden & Bauer, 1994; Heron & Harris, 2001; Pugach & Johnson, 1996, 1995.
66. Buell et al., 1999; Cross & Villa, 1992; Soodak et al., 1998; Villa et al., 1996.
67. Hobbs, 1997.
68. Hobbs, 1997.
69. de Boer, 2005.
70. Mesibov & Shea, 1996.
71. Autism Society of America, 1994, p. 2.
72. Simpson and Myles, 1998, p. 18.
73. Treatment and Education of Autistic and Related Communication-Handicapped Children (TEACCH), 1996, p. 2.
74. Burack et al., 1997; Harrower & Dunlap, 2001; Simpson et al., 2003.
75. Davis, Brady, Hamilton, McEvoy, & Williams, 1994; Hall, McClannahan, & Krantz, 1995; Sainato, Strain, Lefebvre, & Rapp, 1987; Taylor & Levin, 1998; Zanolli, Daggett, & Adams, 1996.
76. Dunlap, Koegel, Johnson, & O'Neill, 1987.
77. Callahan & Rademacher, 1999; Koegel et al., 1992; Sainato, Strain, Lefebvre & Rapp, 1990; Strain et al., 1994.
78. Dugan et al., 1995; Hunt, Staub, Alwell, & Goetz, 1994; Goldstein, Kaczmareck, Pennington, & Shafer, 1992; Kamps et al., 1994.
79. Hunt, Farron-Davis, Wrenn, Hirose-Hatae, & Goetz, 1997.
80. Koegel, Koegel, Harrower, & Carter, 1999; McGee, Almeida, Sulzer-Azaraoff, & Feldman, 1992; Pierce & Schreibman, 1995, 1997; Smith & Camarata, 1999.
81. Autism Society of America, 1994; Burack et al., 1997; Koegel & Koegel, 1995; Harrower & Dunlap; 2001; Simpson et al., 2003; Simpson & Myles, 1998; Smith, Polloway, Patton, & Dowdy, 1995; TEACCH, 1996.

82. Simpson et al., 2003.
83. Simpson et al., 2003, p. 2.
84. Scruggs & Mastropieri, 1996
85. Antonak & Livneh, 1988.
86. Cook, 2002; Lombardi & Hunka, 2001; Stanovich & Jordan, 2002.
87. Helps et al., 1999; McGregor & Campbell, 2001.

Chapter Three

1. U.S. Department of Education, 2004, Section 612(a)(5)(A).
2. Yell & Drasgrow, 1999.
3. Etscheidt, 2006; Yell & Drasgow, 1999; Yell, 1998.
4. Etscheidt, 2006; Yell & Drasgrow, 1999; Yell, 1998.
5. Yell & Drasgrow, 1999; Yell, 1998.
6. Etscheidt, 2006; Dramer, 2001; Yell, 1999
7. Etscheidt, 2006; Yell & Drasgow, 1999.
8. Yell & Drasgow, 1999.
9. Etscheidt, 2006; Dramer, 2001.
10. Yell & Drasgow, 1999.
11. Simpson, de Boer-Ott, Griswold, Myles, Byrd, Ganz, Cook, Otten, Ben-Arieh, Kline, Adams, 2005.
12. Mandlowitz, 2002: Zirkel, 2002.
13. Etscheidt, 2006; Mandlowitz, 2002; Nelson & Huefner, 2003; Yell & Drasgrow, 2000; Zirkel, 2002.
14. Cajon Valley Union School District, 2004.
15. Pleasant Valley School District, 2001.
16. Ramsey Board of Education, 2003.
17. Douglas County School District RE-1, 2001.
18. Board of Education of the Oceanside Union Free School District, 2004.
19. Redlands Unified School District, 1998.
20. Youngstown City School District, (2003).
21. Caldwell-West Caldwell Board of Education, 2002; Neptune Township Board of Education, 2002.
22. Lancaster-Lebanon Intermediate Unit 13, 2003.
23. *Blount* v. *Lancaster-Lebanon Intermediate Unit 13*, 2003.
24. Raab & Dunst, 2004.
25. Etscheidt, 2006.
26. Odom, 2000.
27. U.S. Department of Education, IDEA 34 C.F.R. pts. 300, 303, p.12480.
28. Soodak, Erwin, Winton, Brotherson, Turnbull, Hansen, 2002.
29. Etscheidt, 2006.
30. Fowler, Donegan, Lueke, Hadden, & Phillips, 2000.

Chapter Five

1. National Center on Educational Restructuring and Inclusion (NCERI), 1995.
2. Special Education Expenditure Project, 2004.
3. Koegel, Rincover, & Egel, 1982.
4. Young, Simpson, Myles & Kamps, 1997; Jones & Bender, 1993; Simpson & Myles, 1990.

5. Young et al., 1997; French & Cabell, 1993.
6. Boomer, 1994.
7. Lewis & Doorlag, 1999; Zionts, 1997.
8. Vaughn, Schumm, Jallad, Slusher, Saumell, 1996.
9. Simpson & Myles, 1996.
10. Frea and Hepburn, 1999; Simpson and Fiedler, 1999.
11. Simpson and Fielder, 1999.
12. Webber, Simpson, & Bentley, 2000.

Chapter Nine

1. Cooper, Heron, & Heward, 1987, p. 14.
2. Cooper et al., 1987.

Chapter Ten

1. Bellini, Peters, Benner, & Hopf, 2007.
2. Bellini, 2003.
3. Baker, 2003b.
4. Gray, 2000; Baker, 2003a.
5. Baker, 2003b; McGinnis & Goldstein, 2003.

References

American Psychiatric Association. (2000). *Diagnostic and statistical manual of mental disorders,* Fourth Edition, *Text Revision.* Washington, DC: American Psychiatric Association.

Antonak, R. F., & Livneh, H. (1988). *The measurement of attitudes toward people with disabilities.* Springfield, IL: Thomas Books.

Atwood, T. (1998). *Asperger's syndrome: A guide for parents and professionals.* Philadelphia: Jessica Kingsley.

Atwood, T. (2006). *The complete guide to asperger's syndrome* (2nd ed). Philadelphia: Jessica Kingsley.

Atwood, T., Callesen, K., & Nielsen, A. M. (2008). *The CAT-kit: Congnitive Affective Training.* Arlngton, TX: Future Horizons, Inc.

Autism Society of America. (1994). *Educating children with autism.* Bethesda, MD: Autism Society of America.

Autism Society of America. (2002). What is autism? Retrieved April 16, 2002, from http://www.autism-society.org/packages/packages.html

Baker, J. E. (2003a). *Social skill picture books.* Arlington, TX: Future Horizons.

Baker, J. E. (2003b). *Social skills training: For children and adolescents with Asperger syndrome and social-communication problems.* Shawnee Mission, KS: Autism Asperger Publishing.

Bellini, S. (2003). Making (and keeping) friends: A model for social skills interaction. *The Reporter, 8,* 1–10.

Bellini, S., Peters, J., Benner, L., & Hopf, A. (2007). A meta-analysis of school-based social skills interventions for children with autism spectrum disorders. *Remedial and Special Education, 28,* 153–162.

Blount v. *Lancaster-Lebanon Intermediate Unit,* 40 IDELR 62 (ED PA 2003).

Board of Education of the Oceanside Union Free School District, 4 ECLPR 568 (SEA NY 2004).

Boomer, L. (1994). The utilization of paraprofessionals in programs for students with autism. *Focus on Autistic Behavior, 9,* 1–9.

Brophy, J. M., & Good, T. L. (1974). *Teacher-student relationships: Causes and consequences.* New York: Holt, Rinehart and Winston.

Brownlee, J., & Carrington, S. (2000). Opportunities for authentic experience and reflection: A teaching programme designed to change attitudes towards disability for pre-service teachers. *Support for Learning, 15,* 99–105.

Buell, M. J., Hallman, R., & Gamel-McCormick, M. (1999). A survey of general and special education teachers' perceptions and inservice needs concerning inclusion. *International Journal of Disability, Development, and Education, 46,* 143–156.

Burack, J. A., Root, R., & Zigler, E. (1997). Inclusive education for students with autism: Reviewing ideological, empirical, and community considerations. In

D. Cohen & F. Volkmar (Eds.), *Handbook of autism and pervasive developmental disorders* (2nd ed., pp. 5–40). New York: Wiley.

Burack, J. A., & Volkmar, F. R. (1992). Developmental of low- and high-functioning autistic children. *Journal of Child Psychology and Psychiatry, 33,* 607–616.

Cajon Valley Union School District, 4 ECLPR 561 (SEA CA 2004).

Caldwell-West Caldwell Board of Education, 36 IDELR 118 (SEA NY 2002).

Callahan, K., & Rademacher, J. A. (1999). Using self-management strategies to increase the on-task behavior of a student with autism. *Journal of Positive Behvaior Interventions, 1,* 117–122.

Committee on Educational Interventions for Children with Autism: Division of Behavioral and Social Sciences and Education, National Research Council. (2001). *Educating children with autism.* Washington, DC: National Academy Press.

Cook, B. G. (2002). Inclusive attitudes, strengths, and weaknesses of pre-service general educators enrolled in a curriculum infusion teacher preparation program. *Teacher Education and Special Education, 25,* 262–277.

Cook, B. G. & Dunn, W. (1998). Sensory integration for students with autism. In Simpson, R. L. & Myles, B. S. (Eds.), *Educating children and youth with autism: Strategies for effective practice.* Austin, TX: Pro-Ed.

Cook, B. G., Semmel, M. I., & Gerber, M. M. (1999). Attitudes of principals and special education teachers toward the inclusion of students with mild disabilities: Critical differences of opinion. *Remedial and Special Education, 20,* 199–207.

Cook, B. G., Tankersley, M., Cook, L., & Landrum, T.J. (2000). Teachers' attitudes toward their included students with disabilities. *The Council for Exceptional Children, 67,* 115–135.

Coombs-Richardson, R., & Mead, J. (2001). Supporting general educators' inclusive practices. *Teacher Education and Special Education, 24,* 383–390.

Cooper, J., Heron, T., & Heward, W. (1987). Applied behavior analysis. Upper Saddle River, NJ: Prentice-Hall.

Cross, A., Traub, E., Hutter-Pishgahi, L., & Shelton, G. (2004). Elements of successful inclusion for children with significant disabilities. *Trends in Early Childhood Special Education, 24,* 169–183.

Cross, G., & Villa, R. (1992). The Winooski school system: An evolutionary perspective of a school restructuring for diversity. In R. Villa, J. Thousand, W. Stainback, & S. Stainback (Eds.), *Restructuring for caring and effective education: An administrative guide to creating heterogeneous schools* (pp. 219–237). Baltimore: Brookes.

Daniel R. R. v. State Board of Education, 874 F.2D 1036 (5th Cir. 1989).

de Boer, S. (2005). *Pro-Ed series on autism spectrum disorders: How to do discrete trial training.* Austin, TX: Pro-Ed.

Dramer, L. K. (2001). Inclusion and the law. *Music Educators Journal, 87,* 19–22.

Davis, C. A., Brady, M. P., Hamilton, R., McEvoy, M. A., & Williams, R. E. (1994). Effects of high-probability requests on the social interactions of young children with severe disabilities. *Journal of Applied Behavior Analysis, 27,* 619–637.

Dorn, S., Fuchs, D., & Fuchs, L. S. (1996). A historical perspective on special education reform. *Theory into Practice, 35,* 5–22.

Douglas County School District RE-1, 35 IDELR 295 (SEA CO 2001).

Dugan, E., Kamps, D., Leonard, B., Watkins, N., Rheinberger, A., & Stackhaus, J. (1995). Effects of cooperative learning groups during social studies for students with autism and fourth grade peers. *Journal of Applied Behavior Analysis, 28,* 175–188.

Dunlap, G., Koegel, R. L., Johnson, J., & O'Neill, R. E. (1987). Maintaining performance of autistic clients in community settings with delayed contingencies. *Journal of Applied Behavior Analysis, 20,* 185–191.

Du Paul, G. J., & Henningston, P. N. (1993). Peer tutoring effects on the classroom performance of children with attention deficit hyperactivity disorder. *School Psychology Review, 22,* 134–143.

Etscheidt, S. (2006). Least restrictive and natural environments for young children with disabilities: A legal analysis of issues. *Topics in Early Childhood Special Education, 26,* 167–178.

Fisher, D., Pumpian, I., & Sax, C. (1998). High school students' attitudes about the recommendations for their peers with significant disabilities. *Journal of the Association for Persons with Severe Handicaps, 23,* 272–282.

Fisher, D., Sax, D., Rodifer, K., & Pumpian, I. (1999). Teachers' perspectives on curriculum and climate changes. *Journal for a Just and Caring Education, 5,* 256–68.

Fowler, S., Donegan, M., Lueke, B., Hadden, D., & Phillips, B. (2000). Evaluating community collaboration in writing interagency agreements on the age three transition. *Exceptional Children, 67,* 35–50.

Fox, N. E., & Ysseldyke, J. E. (1997). Implementing inclusion at the middle school level: Lessons for a negative example. *Exceptional Children, 64,* 81–94.

Frea, W. D., & Hepburn, S. L. (1999). Teaching parents of children with autism to perform functional assessments to plan interventions for extremely disruptive behaviors. *Journal of Positive Behavior Interventions, 1,* 112–116.

French, N., & Cabell, E. (1993). Are community college training programs for paraeducators feasible? *Community College Journal of Research and Practice, 17,* 131–140.

Friend, M., & Cook, L. (1992). The fundamentals of collaboration. In *Interactions: Collaboration skills for school professionals* (pp. 1–14). White Plains, NY: Longman.

Gallagher, P. A. (1997). Teachers and inclusion: Perspectives on changing roles. *Topics in Early Childhood Special Education, 17,* 363–386.

Goldstein, H., Kaczmareck, L., Pennington, R., & Shafer, K. (1992). Peer-mediated intervention: Attending to, commenting on, and acknowledging the behavior of preschoolers with autism. *Journal of Applied Behavior Analysis, 25,* 289–305.

Good, T. L., & Brophy, J. E. (1972). Behavioral expression of teacher attitudes. *Journal of Educational Psychology, 63,* 617–624.

Graden, J. L., & Bauer, A. M. (1994). Using a collaborative approach to support students and teachers in inclusive classrooms. In L. Idol, A. Nevin, & P. Paolucci-Whitcomb (Eds.), *Collaborative consultation* (pp. 85–100). Austin, TX: Pro-Ed.

Grandin, T. (1995). The learning style of people with autism: An autobiography. In Quill, K.A. (Ed.), *Teaching children with autism: Strategies to enhance communication and socialization* (pp. 11–32.). Albany: Delmar.

Gray, C. (2000). *New social story book* (illustrated ed.). Kentwood, MI: The Gray Center.

Hall, L. J., McClannahan, L. F., & Krantz, P. J. (1995). Promoting independence in integrated classrooms by teaching aides to use activity schedules and decreased prompts. *Education and Training in Mental Retardation, 30,* 23–31.

Harris, S. L., Handlemann, J. S., Kristoff, B., Bass, L., & Gordon, R. (1990). Changes in language development among autistic and peer children in segregated and integrated preschool settings. *Journal of Autism and Developmental Disorders, 20,* 23–31.

Harrower, J. K., & Dunlap, G. (2001). Including children with autism in general education classrooms: A review of effective strategies. *Behavior Modification, 25,* 762–784.

Hartmann v. *Loudoun County Board of Education,* 118 F. 3D 996 (1997).

Helps, S., Newson-Davis, I. C., & Callais, M. (1999). Autism: The teacher's view. *Autism, 3,* 287–298.

Heron, T. E., & Harris, K. C. (2001). *The educational consultant* (4th ed). Austin, TX: Pro-Ed.

Hobbs, T. (1997). Planning for inclusion: A comparison of individual and cooperative procedures. *Unpublished doctoral dissertation,* Florida State University, Tallahassee.

Hobbs, T., & Westling, D. (2002). Mentoring for inclusion: A model class for special and general educators. *The Teacher Educator, 37,* 186–201.

Hunt, P., Staub, D., Alwell, M., & Goetz, L. (1994). Achievement by all students within the context of cooperative learning groups. *Journal of the Association for Persons with Severe Handicaps, 19,* 290–301.

Hunt, P., Farron-Davis, F., Wrenn, M., Hirose-Hatae, A., & Goetz, L. (1997). Promoting interactive partnerships in inclusive educational settings. *Journal of the Association for Persons with Severe Handicaps, 22,* 127–137.

Jones, K., & Bender, W. (1993). Utilization of paraprofessionals in special education: A review of the literature. *Remedial and Special Education, 14,* 7–14.

Kamps, D. M., Barbetta, P. M., Leonard, B. R., & Delquadri, J. (1994). Classwide peer tutoring: An integration strategy to improve reading skills and promote peer interactions among students with autism and general education peers. *Journal of Applied Behavior Analysis, 27,* 49–61.

Kauffman, J. M. (1993). How we might achieve the radical reform of special education. *Exceptional Children, 60,* 6–16.

Kauffman, J., & Hallahan, D. (Eds.). (2005). *The illusion of full inclusion: A comprehensive critique of a current special education bandwagon* (2nd ed.). Austin, TX: Pro-Ed.

Kavale, K. A., & Forness, S. R. (2000). History, rhetoric, and reality. *Remedial and Special Education, 21,* 279–296.

Kilburn, J., & Rosen-Lieberman, N. (1998). *An introduction to sensory processing.* Paper presented at the Autism Society of Michigan, Ann Arbor, MI.

Kishi, G. S., & Meyer, L. H. (1994). What children report and remember: A six-year follow-up of the effects of social contact between peers with and without severe disabilities. *Journal of the Association for Persons with Severe Handicaps, 19,* 277–289.

Klinger, J. K., Ahwee, S., Pilonieta, P., & Menendez, R. (2003). Barriers and facilitators in scaling up research-based practices. *Council for Exceptional Children, 69,* 411–429.

Koegel, L. K. (1995). Communication and language intervention. In Koegel, R. L., & Koegel, L. K. (Eds.), *Teaching children with autism: Strategies for initiating positive interactions and improving learning opportunities* (pp. 17–32). Baltimore: Brookes.

Koegel, R., & Koegel, L. (1995). *Teaching children with autism: Strategies for initiating positive interactions and improving learning options.* Baltimore: Brooks.

Koegel, R. L., Koegel, L. K., Frea, W. D. & Smith, A. E. (1995). Emerging intervention for children with autism: Longitudinal and lifestyles implications. In Koegel, R. L. & Koegel, L. K. (Eds.), *Teaching children with autism: Strategies for initiating positive interactions and improving learning opportunities* (pp 1–15). Baltimore: Brookes.

Koegel, L. K., Koegel, R. L., Harrower, J. K., & Carter, C. M. (1999). Pivotal response intervention. I: Overview of approach. *Journal of the Association for Persons With Severe Handicaps, 24,* 174–185.

Koegel, L. K., Koegel, R. L., Hurley, C., and Frea, W. D. (1992). Improving social skills and disruptive behavior in children with autism through self-management. *Journal of Applied Behavior Analysis, 25,* 341–353.

Koegel, R. L., Koegel, L. K., & Parks, D. R. (1995). "Teach the individual" model of generalization: Autonomy through self-management. In Koegel, R. L. & Koegel, L. K. (Eds.), *Teaching children with autism: Strategies for initiating positive interactions and improving learning opportunities* (pp. 67–77). Baltimore: Brookes.

Koegel, R. L., Rincover, A., & Egel, A. L. (1982). *Educating and understanding autistic children.* San Diego: College Hill.

Lancaster-Lebanon Intermediate Unit #13, 4 ECLPR 475 (SEA PA 2003).

Landa, R. (2000). Social language use in Asperger syndrome and high-functioning autism. In Klin, A., Volkmar, F. R., & Sparrow, S. S. (Eds.), *Asperger syndrome* (pp. 125–158). New York: Guilford Press.

Lewis, R. B., & Doorlag, D. H. (1999). *Teaching special students in general education classrooms.* East Saddle River, NJ: Merrill.

Lindsay, G. (2003). Inclusive education: A critical perspective. *British Journal of Special Education, 30,* 3–12.

Lipsky, D. K., & Gartner, A. (1989). *Beyond separate education: Quality education for all.* Baltimore: Brookes.

Livneh, H. (1982). On the origins of negative attitudes toward people with disabilities. *Rehabilitation Literature, 43,* 338–347.

Locke, W. R., & Fuchs, L. S. (1995). Effects of peer-mediated reading instruction on the on-task behavior and social interaction of children with behavior disorders. *Journal of Emotional and Behavioral Disorders, 3,* 92–99.

Lombardi, T. P., & Hunka, N. J. (2001). Preparing general education teachers for inclusive classrooms: Assessing the process. *Teacher Education and Special Education, 24,* 183–197.

Mandlowitz, M. (2002). The impact of the legal system on educational programming for young children with autism spectrum disorder. *Journal of Autism and Developmental Disorders, 32,* 495–509.

Mauk, J. E., Reber, M., & Batshaw, M. L. (1997). Autism and other pervasive developmental disorders. In Batshaw, M. L. (Ed.), *Children with disabilities* (4th ed.). Baltimore: Brooks.

McGee, G. G., Almeida, M. C., Sulzer-Azaraoff, B., & Feldman, R. S. (1992). Promoting reciprocal interactions via peer incidental teaching. *Journal of Applied Behavior Analysis, 23*, 117–126.

McGinnis E., & Goldstein, A. (2003). *Skillstreaming the Elementary School Child: New Strategies and perspectives for teaching prosocial skills* (Rev. ed.). Champaign, IL: Research Press.

McGregor, E., & Campbell, E. (2001). The attitudes of teachers in Scotland to the integration of children with autism in mainstream schools. *Autism, 5*, 189–207.

McLeskey, J., & Waldron, N. (2002). Professional development and inclusive schools: Reflections on effective practice. *The Teacher Educator, 37*, 159–172.

McNally, R., Cole, P., & Waugh, R. (2001). Regular teachers' attitudes to the need for additional classroom support for the inclusion of students with intellectual disability. *Journal of Intellectual & Developmental Disability, 26*, 257–273.

Meredith, B., & Underwood, J. (1995). Irreconcilable differences? Defining the rising conflict between regular and special education. *Journal of Law and Education, 24*, 195–226.

Mesibov, G. B., & Shea, V. (1996). Full inclusion and students with autism. *Journal of Autism and Developmental Disorders, 26*, 337–346.

Meyer, J. A., & Minshew, N. J. (2002). An update on neurocognitive profiles in Asperger syndrome and high-functioning autism. *Focus on Autism and Other Developmental Disabilities, 17*(3), 152–160.

Miller, L. (1990). The regular education initiative and school reform: Lessons from the mainstream. *Remedial and Special Education, 11*, 17–22.

Myles, B. S. & Simpson, R. L. (2002). Asperger syndrome: An overview of characteristics. *Focus on Autism and Other Developmental Disabilities, 17*(3), 132–137.

Myles, B. S., & Simpson, R. L. (2003). *Asperger syndrome: A guide for educators and parents* (2nd ed.). Austin, TX: Pro-Ed.

National Center on Educational Restructuring and Inclusion. (1995). National study on inclusion: Overview and summary report. *National Center on Educational Restructuring and Inclusion Bulletin, 2*, 3–10.

Nelson, C., & Huefner, D. S. (2003). Young children with autism: Judicial responses to the Lovaas and discrete trial training debates. *Journal of Early Intervention, 26*, 1–19.

Neptune Township Board of Education, 4 ECLPR 385 (SEA NJ 2002).

Odom, S. L. (2000). Preschool inclusion: What we know and where we go from here. *Topics in Early Childhood Special Education, 20*, 20–27.

Odom, S. L., Hoyson, M., Jamieson, B., & Strain, P. S. (1985). Increased handicapped preschoolers' peer social interactions: Cross-setting and component analysis. *Journal of Applied Behavior Analysis, 18*, 3–16.

Odom, S. L., & Watts, E. (1991). Reducing teacher prompts in peer-mediated interventions for young children with autism. *Journal of Special Education, 25*, 26–43.

Ogletree, B. T. (1998). The communicative context of autism. In Simspon, R. L., & Myles, B. S. (Eds.), *Educating children and youth with autism* (pp. 141–172). Austin, TX: Pro-Ed.

Peltier, G. L. (1997). The effect of inclusion on non-disabled children: A review of the research. *Contemporary Education, 68*, 234–238.

Pierce, K., & Schreibman, L. (1995). Increasing complex social behaviors in children with autism: Effects of peer-implemented pivotal response training. *Journal of Applied Behavior Analysis, 28,* 285–295.

Pierce, K., & Schreibman, L. (1997). Using peer trainers to promote social behavior in autism: Are they effective at enhancing multiple social modalities? *Focus on Autism and Other Developmental Disabilities, 12,* 207–218.

Pivik, J., McComas, J., & LaFlamme, M. (2002) Barriers and facilitators to inclusive education. *Council for Exceptional Children, 69,* 97–107.

Pleasant Valley School District, 4 ECLPR 347 (SEA CA 2001).

Pugach, M. C., & Johnson, L. J. (1995). *Collaborative practitioners collaborative schools.* Denver, CO: Love.

Pugach, M. C., & Johnson, L. J. (1996). Rethinking the relationship between consultation and collaborative problem-solving. In E. Meyen, G. Vergason, & R. Whelan (Eds.), *Strategies for teaching exceptional children in inclusive settings* (pp. 451–463). Denver, CO: Love.

Pugach, M. C., & Lilly, M. S. (1984). Reconceptualizing support services for classroom teachers: Implications for teacher education. *Journal of Teacher Education, 35,* 48–55.

Quill, K. A. (Ed.) (1990). *Teaching children with autism: Strategies to enhance communication and socialization.* Albany, NY: Delmar.

Quill, K. A. (2000). *Do-watch-listen-say: Social and communication intervention for children with autism.* Baltimore: Brookes.

Raab, M., & Dunst, C. (2004). Early intervention practitioner approaches to natural environment intervention. *Journal of Early Intervention, 27,* 87–94.

Ramsey Board of Education, 39 IDELR 59 (SEA NJ 2003).

Redlands Unified School District, 28 IDELR 1256 (SEA CA 1998).

Reeve, P. T., & Hallahan, D. P. (1996). Practical questions about collaboration between general and special educators. In E. Meyen, G. Vergason, & R. Whelan (Eds.), *Strategies for teaching exceptional children in inclusive settings* (pp. 401–433). Denver, CO: Love.

Reynolds, M. C., & Wang, M. C. (1983). Restructuring "special" school programs: A position paper. *Policy Studies Review, 2,* 189–212.

Reynolds, M. C., Wang, M. C., & Walberg, H. J. (1987). The necessary restructuring of special and general education. *Exceptional Children, 53,* 391–398.

Rimmerman, A., Hozmi, B., & Duvdevany, I. (2000). Contact and attitudes toward individuals with disabilities among students tutoring children with developmental disabilities. *Journal of Intellectual & Developmental Disability, 25,* 13–18.

Roncker v. Walter, 700 F.2D 1058 (6th Cir. 1983).

Rosenblatt, J., Bloom, P., Koegel, R. L. (1995). Overselective responding: Description, implications, and intervention. In Koegel, R. L. & Koegel, L. K. (Eds.), *Teaching children with autism: Strategies for initiating positive interactions and improving learning opportunities* (pp. 1–15). Baltimore: Brookes.

Rourke, B. P., & Tsatsanis, K. D. (2000). Non-verbal learning disabilities and Asperger syndrome. In Klin, A., Volkmar, F. R., & Sparrow, S. S. (Eds.), *Asperger syndrome* (pp. 231–253). New York: Guilford Press.

Sacramento City Unified School District v. Rachel H., 14 F.3D 1398 (9th Cir. 1994).

Sainato, D. M., Strain, P. S., Lefebvre, D., & Rapp, N. (1987). Facilitating transition times with handicapped preschool children: A comparison between peer-mediated and antecedent prompt procedures. *Journal of Applied Behavior Analysis, 20,* 285–291.

Sainato, D. M., Strain, P. S., Lefebvre, D., & Rapp, N. (1990). Effects of self-evaluation in the independent work skills of preschool children with disabilities. *Exceptional Children, 56,* 540–549.

Salend, S. J., & Duhaney, L.M.G. (1999). The impact of inclusion of student with and without disabilities and their educators. *Remedial and Special Education, 20,* 114–126.

Scruggs, T., & Mastropieri, M. (1996). Teacher perceptions of mainstreaming/inclusion, 1958–1995: A research synthesis. *Exceptional Children, 63,* 59–74.

Schuler, A.L. (1995). Thinking in autism: Difference in learning and development. In Quill, K. A. (Ed.), Teaching children with autism: Strategies to enhance communication and socialization (pp. 11–32.). Albany: Delmar.

Shade, R. A., & Stewart, R. (2001). General education and special education preservice teachers' attitudes toward inclusion. *Preventing School Failure, 46,* 37–41.

Shaw, M. E., & Wright, J. M. (1967). *Scales for the measurement of attitudes.* New York: McGraw-Hill.

Silberman, M., (1971). *Teachers' attitudes and actions toward their students.* In M. I. Silberman (Ed.), *The experience of schooling* (pp. 86–96). New York: Holt, Rinehart, and Winston.

Simpson, R. L., (2004). Inclusion of students with behavior disorders in general education settings: Research and measurement issues. *Behavior Disorders, 30,* 19–31.

Simpson, R. L., de Boer-Ott, S. R., & Myles, B. S. (2003). Inclusion of learners with autism spectrum disorders in general education settings. *Topics in Language Disorders, 23,* 116–133.

Simpson, R., de Boer-Ott, S., Griswold, D., Myles, B., Byrd, S., Ganz, J., Cook, K., Otten, K., Ben-Arieh, J., Kline, S., & Adams, L. (2005). Autism spectrum disorders: Interventions and treatments for children and youth. Thousand Oaks, CA: Corwin Press.

Simpson, R. L., & Fielder, C. R. (1999). Parent participation in individualized education program (IEP) conferences: A case for individualization. In M. J. Fine (Ed.), *The Second Handbook on Parent Education,* 145–171. San Diego, CA: Academic Press.

Simpson, R. L., & Myles, B. S. (1990). The general education collaboration model: A model for successful mainstreaming. *Focus on Exceptional Children, 23,* 1–10.

Simpson, R. L., & Myles, B. S. (1993). Successful integration of children and youth with autism in mainstreamed settings. *Focus on Autistic Behavior, 7,* 1–13.

Simpson, R. L., & Myles, B. S. (1996). *The general education collaboration model: A model for successful mainstreaming.* In E. Meyen, G. Vergason, & R. Whelan (Eds.), *Strategies for teaching exceptional children in inclusive settings* (pp. 435–450). Denver, CO: Love.

Simpson, R. L., & Myles, B. S. (1998). Understanding and responding to the needs of students with autism. In R. Simpson & B. Myles (Eds.), *Educating children and youth with autism: Strategies for effective practice* (pp. 1–20). Austin, TX: Pro-Ed.

Smith, I. M. (2000). Motor functioning in Asperger syndrome. In Klin, A., Volkmar, F. R., & Sparrow, S. S. (Eds.), *Asperger syndrome* (pp. 97–124). New York: Guilford Press.

Smith, A. E., & Camarata, S. (1999). Using teacher-implemented instruction to increase language intelligibility of children with autism. *Journal of Positive Behavior Interventions, 1,* 141–151.

Smith, T., Polloway, E., Patton, J., & Dowdy, C. (1995). *Teaching students with special needs in inclusive settings.* Boston: Allyn & Bacon.

Snyder, L., Garriott, P., & Aylor, M. W. (2001). Inclusion confusion: Putting the pieces together. *Teacher Education and Special Education, 24,* 198–207.

Soodak, L., Erwin, E., Winton, P., Brotherson, M., Turnbull, A., Hanson, M. (2002). Implementing inclusive early childhood education: A call for professional empowerment. *Topics in Early Childhood Special Education, 22,* 91–102.

Soodak, L.C., Podell, D.M., & Lehman, L.R. (1998). Teacher, student, and school attributes as predictors of teachers' responses to inclusion. *Journal of Special Education, 31,* 480–497.

Special Education Expenditure Project. (2004). SEEP report 7: Educating students with disabilities: Comparing methods for explaining expenditure variation. Retrieved on May 10, 2008 from http://csef.air.org/publications/seep/national/rpt7.pdf.

Stainback, W., & Stainback, S. (1984). A rationale for the merger of special and regular education. *Exceptional Children, 51,* 102–111.

Stanovich, P. J., & Jordan, A. (2002) Preparing general educators to teach in inclusive classrooms: Some food for thought. *The Teacher Educator, 37,* 173–185.

Staub, D., & Peck, C.A. (1994/1995). What are the outcomes for nondisabled students? *Educational Leadership*, Dec./Jan., 36–40.

Strain, P. S., Kohler, F. W., Storey, K., & Danko, C. D. (1994). Teaching preschoolers with autism to self-monitor their social interactions: An analysis of results in home and school settings. *Journal of Emotional and Behavioral Disorders, 2,* 78–88.

Sullivan, R. C. (1994). Autism: Definitions, past and present. *Journal of Vocational Rehabilitation 4,* 4–9.

Taylor, B. A., & Levin, L. (1998). Teaching a student with autism to make verbal initiations: Effects of a tactile prompt. *Journal of Applied Behavior Analysis, 31,* 651–654.

Treatment and Education of Autistic and Related Communication-Handicapped Children. (1996). *Inclusion for children with autism: The TEACCH position.* Retrieved 1998 from: http://www.unc.edu/depts/teacch/inclus.html

Tsai, L. Y. (1998). Pervasive developmental disorders. National Dissemination Center for Children with Disabilities, *FS20,* January, 1–15.

Turnbull, H. R., & Turnbull, A. P. (2000). *Free appropriate public education: The law and children with disabilities* (6th ed.). Denver, CO: Love.

U.S. Department of Education, Office of Special Education. (2004). *Individuals with Disabilities Education Improvement Act.* 20 U.S.C. § 1400 et seq. http://idea.ed.gov/explore/home

Van Meter, L., Fein, D., Morris, R., Waterhouse, L., & Allen, D. (1997). Delay versus deviance in autistic social behavior. *Journal of Autism and Developmental Disorders, 27,* 557–569.

Vaughn, S., Schumm, J. S., Jallad, B., Slusher, J., & Saumell, L. (1996). Teachers' views of inclusion. *Learning Disabilities Research and Practice, 11,* 96–106.

Villa, R. A., Thousand, J. S., & Chapple, J. W. (1996). Preparing teachers to support inclusion: Preservice and inservice programs. *Theory into Practice, 35,* 42–50.

Volkmar, F., Klin, A., & Cohen, D. (1997). Diagnosis and classification of autism and related conditions: Consensus and issues. In D. Cohen & F. Volkmar (Eds.), *Handbook of autism and pervasive developmental disorders* (2nd ed., pp. 5–40). New York: Wiley.

Webber, J., Simspon, R. L., & Bentley, J. (2000). *Parents and families of children with autism.* In M. J. Fine & R. L. Simpson (Eds.), Collaboration with parents and families of children with exceptionalities (pp. 303–324). Austin, TX: Pro-Ed.

Weiner, H. M. (2003). Effective inclusion: Professional development in the context of the classroom. *Teaching Exceptional Children, 35,* 12–18.

Werts, M. G., Wolery, M., Snyder, E. D., & Caldwell, N. K. (1996). Teachers' perceptions of supports critical to the success of inclusion programs. *Association for Persons with Severe Handicaps, 21,* 9–21.

Whelan, R. J. (1996). *Collaboration: From oversight to shared vision.* In E. Meyen, G. Vergason, & R. Whelan (Eds.), *Strategies for teaching exceptional children in inclusive settings* (pp. 391–400). Denver, CO: Love.

Willis, S., & Brophy, J. (1974). Origins of teachers' attitudes toward young children. *Journal of Educational Psychology, 66,* 520–529.

Winzer, M. A. (1998). The inclusion movement and teacher change: Where are the limits? *McGill Journal of Education, 33,* 229–251.

Wolfberg, P. W. (1999). *Play and imagination in children with autism.* New York: Teachers College Press.

Wolfe, P. S., Boone, R. S., Filbert, M., & Atanasoff, L. M. (2000). Training presevice teachers for inclusion and transition: How well are we doing? *Journal for Vocational Special Needs Education, 22,* 20–30.

Yell, M. L. (1998). The legal basis of inclusion. *Educational Leadership, 56,* 70–73.

Yell, M. L., & Drasgrow, E. (1999). A legal analysis of inclusion. *Preventing School Failure, 43,* 118–123.

Yell, M. L., & Drasgrow, E. (2000). Litigating a free appropriate public education: The Lovaas hearings and cases. *Journal of Special Education, 33,* 205–214.

Young, B., Simpson, R. L., Myles, B. S., & Kamps, D. (1997). An examination of paraprofessionals' involvement in supporting inclusion of students with autism. *Focus on Autism and Other Developmental Disabilities, 12,* 31–38.

Youngstown City School District, 4 ECLPR 532 (SEA OH 2003).

Zanolli, K., Daggett, J., & Adams, T. (1996). Teaching preschool-age autistic children to make spontaneous initiations to peers using priming. *Journal of Autism and Developmental Disorders, 26,* 407–422.

Zionts, P. (1997). *Inclusion strategies for students with learning and behavior problems.* Austin, TX: Pro-Ed.

Zirkel, P. A. (2002). The autism case law: Administrative and judicial rulings. *Focus on Autism and Other Developmental Disabilities, 17,* 84–93.

Index